Improvement Science as a Tool for School Enhancement:
Solutions for Better Educational Outcomes

"*Improvement Science as a Tool for School Enhancement: Solutions for Better Educational Outcomes* provides a wealth of case studies that teacher, school, and district leaders can use to address a wide range of systemic equity issues facing schools. Each case reveals important and useful insights about how improvement science processes move equity forward."

Dr. Sheldon Berman, Lead Superintendent for Social-Emotional Learning with AASA (American Association of School Administrators) and retired superintendent (Massachusetts, Kentucky, and Oregon)

"In my efforts to help improvement science land as a useful set of mindsets and skills for educators, the most consistent request I hear is for concrete examples of improvement projects in education. Imagine my delight to discover this book, filled with stories of improvement by teachers and school leaders. If you believe that disciplined inquiry by those closest to students can lead to more equitable outcomes, you will want to read this book."

Ben Daley, President, High Tech High Graduate School of Education

"*Improvement Science as a Tool for School Enhancement: Solutions for Better Educational Outcomes* is a timely and important book which draws on evidence from 17 school settings using equity focused improvement science efforts. It is written by school leaders for school practitioners who are committed to making positive changes for all students. It captures ways in which improvement science is enabling schools to address prevailing inequities and embrace meaningful change strategies. Edited by two gifted, passionate and committed social justice educators, this practical and accessible resource is the book to use to help schools and school systems identify and implement improvement projects."

David Imig, Professor of the Practice Emeritus, University of Maryland and Senior Fellow, Carnegie Foundation

"In *Improvement Science as a Tool for School Enhancement*, Peterson and Carlile provide an exemplary collection of cases, each of which uses improvement science tools to generate an equitable solution to a local, user-centered problem. The text and accompanying figures teach a wide continuum of educational professionals how to apply IS tools and strategies in their own laboratory of practice with culturally responsive results. It's an essential book to prepare innovative teachers and leaders, both pre-service and in-service."

Dr. Kristina A. Hesbol, Associate Professor of Educational Leadership and Policy Studies, Morgridge College of Education, University of Denver and Founding Director, Center for Innovative Rural Collaborative Leadership Education (CIRCLE)

"As a Gates Millennium Scholar, I became a teacher to give every student a sense of belonging and access to any career. This idealistic goal, held by most teachers, is often dropped when we don't have methods to deconstruct individual or systemic barriers. *Improvement Science as a Tool for School Enhancement: Solutions for Better Educational Outcomes* gives us the examples and framework to begin approaching our lofty goals with intentionality. As a teacher, I particularly appreciate that Peterson and Carlile highlight necessary steps in chapter 18 to engage in challenging work while sustaining the hopes and spirits of colleagues."

Enrique Mora, Gates Millennium Scholar
Middle School Teacher, Highline Public Schools

"*Improvement Science as a Tool for School Enhancement: Solutions for Better Educational Outcomes* focuses on the power of improvement science to accelerate meaningful change and increase equity in our communities. Peterson and Carlile provide numerous examples of how collecting data, applying research, and engaging students, families, and teachers in inquiry-based improvement in their communities can help students reach their dreams and become the leaders our global community needs. Inspiring and practical, this book will affirm educators everywhere."

Dr. Vicki Phillips, Chief Education Officer, National Geographic Society

"The pragmatism and power of utilizing Improvement Science in schools is on full display in *Improvement Science as a Tool for School Enhancement: Solutions for Better Educational Outcomes*. The use of practical examples implemented by teacher leaders and school administrators demonstrating real improvement, should provide a positive path forward for all educators."

Rob Saxton, Retired Oregon Schools Chief and District Superintendent

"Keeping equity at the center of every improvement effort, affirming the value of every child in our care, and supporting the teachers and leaders who work tirelessly to improve our schools is key to my work in rural and suburban schools. *Improvement Science as a Tool for School Enhancement: Solutions for Better Educational Outcomes* affirms our teachers and leaders while also providing guidance, tools, and processes as we collaborate to improve social-emotional health, the school experience, and academic outcomes for children of all backgrounds. Every chapter gives me hope that change can happen now."

Johnna Timmes, Executive Director of Early Learning,
Northwest Regional Education Service District

"Improvement Science as a Tool for School Enhancement: Solutions for Better Educational Outcomes, offers a needed contribution to the growing field of Improvement Science as a path to greater equity in school practices and outcomes. Sixteen case histories, authored largely by K-12 practitioners, show how teachers and leaders have effectively addressed persistent, real-world school challenges in very different settings by using Improvement Science as a method and equity as a values framework. In this book, students, teachers, parents, and leaders are agents of their own improvement work in elementary, middle, and secondary schools from Oregon to Texas to DC."

Steve Tozer, Professor Emeritus
University of Chicago Illinois, College of Education
Senior Fellow, Carnegie Foundation for Advancement of Teaching

"Improvement Science as a Tool for School Enhancement: Solutions for Better Educational Outcomes offers a deeper understanding of how to effectively utilize the tenets of improvement science across educational environments in creating a more just educational system. This book gives research-based tangible tools for educators to dismantle persistent barriers and reimagine how schools serve students."

Dr. Kevin Walker, Director of Elementary Education,
Salem-Keizer Public Schools

Improvement Science as a Tool for School Enhancement

THE IMPROVEMENT SCIENCE IN EDUCATION SERIES

Improvement Science originated in such fields as engineering and health care, but its principal foundation has been found to be an effective school improvement methodology in education. Although improvement science research is so quickly becoming a signature pedagogy and core subject area of inquiry in the field of educational leadership, the literature is still scant in its coverage of IS models. The Improvement Science in Education series is intended to be the most comprehensive collection of volumes to inform educators and researchers about problem analysis, utilization of research, development of solutions, and other practices that can be employed to enhance and strengthen efforts at organizational improvement. This series concentrates on the elements faculty, students, and administrators need to enhance the reliability and validity of improvement or quality enhancement efforts.

BOOKS IN THE SERIES

The Educational Leader's Guide to Improvement Science:
Data, Design and Cases for Reflection
by Robert Crow, Brandi Nicole Hinnant-Crawford, and Dean T. Spaulding (2019)

The Improvement Science Dissertation in Practice:
A Guide for Faculty, Committee Members, and their Students
by Jill Alexa Perry, Debby Zambo, and Robert Crow (2020)

Improvement Science in Education: A Primer
by Brandi Nicole Hinnant-Crawford (2020)

Teaching Improvement Science in Educational Leadership: A Pedagogical Guide
by Dean T. Spaulding, Robert Crow, and Brandi Nicole Hinnant-Crawford (2021)

Improvement Science: Promoting Equity in Schools
by Deborah S. Peterson and Susan P. Carlile (2021)

Reclaiming the Education Doctorate: The History, Impact, and Implementation of
the Carnegie Project on the Education Doctorate's (CPED) Framework
by Jill Alexa Perry (2022)

Improvement Science as a Tool for School Enhancement:
Solutions for Better Educational Outcomes
by Deborah S. Peterson and Susan P. Carlile (2022)

Improvement Science: Methods for Researchers and Program Evaluators
by Robert Crow, Brandi Nicole Hinnant-Crawford, and Dean T. Spaulding (2022)

Improving Together: Case Studies of Networked Improvement
Science Communities
by Robert Crow, Brandi Nicole Hinnant-Crawford, and Dean T. Spaulding (2023)

Improvement Science Across the Disciplines: Business, Health, and Social Sciences
by Robert Crow, Brandi Nicole Hinnant-Crawford, and Dean T. Spaulding (2025)

Editorial submissions

Authors interested in having their manuscripts considered for publication in the Improvement Science in Education Series are encouraged to send a prospectus, sample chapter, and CV to any one of the series editors:
Robert Crow (rcrow@email.wcu.edu),
Brandi Nicole Hinnant-Crawford (bnhinnantcrawford@email.wcu.edu),
or Dean T. Spaulding (ds6494@yahoo.com).

Improvement Science as a Tool for School Enhancement

Solutions for Better Educational Outcomes

EDITED BY Deborah S. Peterson
and Susan P. Carlile

Gorham, Maine

Published by Myers Education Press, LLC
P.O. Box 424
Gorham, ME 04038

Myers Education Press is an academic publisher specializing in books, e-books, and digital content in the field of education. All of our books are subjected to a rigorous peer review process and produced in compliance with the standards of the Council on Library and Information Resources.

Library of Congress Cataloging-in-Publication Data available from Library of Congress.

13-digit ISBN 978-1-9755-0479-3 (paperback)
13-digit ISBN 978-1-9755-0480-9 (library networkable e-edition)
13-digit ISBN 978-1-9755-0481-6 (consumer e-edition)

Printed in the United States of America.

All first editions printed on acid-free paper that meets the American National Standards Institute Z39-48 standard.

Books published by Myers Education Press may be purchased at special quantity discount rates for groups, workshops, training organizations, and classroom usage. Please call our customer service department at 1-800-232-0223 for details.

Cover design by Shelby Gates Designs.

Visit us on the web at **www.myersedpress.com** to browse our complete list of titles.

CONTENTS

List of Tables and Figures   xi

Acknowledgments   xv

Chapter 1. Introduction
• *Deborah S. Peterson, Susan P. Carlile,
and Gloria McDaniel-Hall*   1

Chapter 2. Teachers Can't Do It Alone: The Role
of Leadership in Implementing Equity-Driven
Social-Emotional Learning • *Amie B. Cieminski and
Thomas Lee Morgan*   9

Chapter 3. Improving School Culture Through the
Implementation of Social-Emotional Learning and
Restorative Practices • *Joanna Carrillo Rowley,
Michael Odell, and Teresa Kennedy*   23

Chapter 4. A Pandemic and a Wildfire Evacuation:
Serving Historically Underserved Students During
Disasters • *Ryan Carpenter, Benjamin Hargrave,
and Kathleen Oropallo*   47

Chapter 5. Combating Chronic Absenteeism:
Multitiered Systems of Supports at the Elementary Level
• *Greg Nelson*   67

Chapter 6. Increasing Attendance in Middle School
• *Emily Anderson*   81

Chapter 7. Disparities in Middle School Discipline:
English Learners, Students Receiving Special Education
Services, and Boys • *Cassandra Thonstad*   101

Chapter 8. Improving Our Response to Intervention
Program: Improvement Science • *Victoria Brown*   121

Chapter 9. Increasing Academic Success Through a
High School Advisory Program • *Bryce Bennett*   131

Chapter 10. Improving Ninth-Grade On-Track Rates
in an Urban Public High School • *Brian Rahaman*   151

Chapter 11. Addressing Equity Issues for Long-Term
Multilingual Learners: Using Improvement Science
Practices to Improve Understanding and Services
• *Bill Eagle and Susan Connolly*   169

Chapter 12. Improved Outcomes for All: Students
With Disabilities and Improvement Science
• *Kristine J. Melloy and Toby King*   185

Chapter 13. Equitable Special Education Evaluation
in the Time of COVID-19 • *Kileen Birmingham and
James Sanders*   203

Chapter 14. Student Engagement Through Shared
Power • *Jeffrey R. Waters*   221

Chapter 15. Increasing Equity Through Family
Engagement • *Gloria McDaniel-Hall, Ryan McCarty,
and Landon Brown*   239

Chapter 16. Family Engagement: Increasing Equity
Through the Reading Club Project • *Folusho B. Abayomi*   255

Chapter 17. Centering Equity and Starting Small to
Transform School Climate • *Michelle Li,
Kirsten Ebersole LaCroix, and Donna Braun*   271

Chapter 18. Sustaining One Another While Leading
Equity-Focused Improvement Science Efforts
• *Deborah S. Peterson*   291

About the Authors   295

Index   303

LIST OF FIGURES AND TABLES

Figures

Chapter 3

Figure 3.1. Plan Do Study Act Cycle 28
Figure 3.2. Discipline Fishbone Diagram 35
Figure 3.3. Primary Drivers for Improvement 35
Figure 3.4. Annual Attendance Percentage 39
Figure 3.5. Discipline Incidents by Grade Level 39
Figure 3.6. Count of Suspensions and Expulsions 40
Figure 3.7. Student Achievement Scores in Tested Subjects 41
Figure 3.8. Percentage of Students Who Believe Teachers
Care About Them 42
Figure 3.9. Percentage of Students Who Believe Administrators
Care About Them 42

Chapter 4

Figure 4.1. Engagement Continuum 55

Chapter 5

Figure 5.1. Theory of Improvement (Attendance) 73
Figure 5.2. Aim Statement and Driver Diagram (Attendance) 74

Chapter 6

Figure 6.1. Survey Data 88
Figure 6.2. Empathy Interview Responses 90
Figure 6.3. Fishbone 93
Figure 6.4. Driver Diagram 94
Figure 6.5. PDSA Cycle #1 95
Figure 6.6. PDSA Cycle #2 97

Chapter 9

Figure 9.1. Fishbone Diagram 138
Figure 9.2. Driver Diagram 139
Figure 9.3. PDSA Cycle #1 Overview 141
Figure 9.4. PDSA Cycle #2 Overview 143
Figure 9.5. PDSA Cycle #3 Overview 146

Chapter 10

Figure 10.1. The Diagnostic Process 157
Figure 10.2. Final Diagnosis and Adoption of the Change Idea 164

Chapter 11
Figure 11.1. Improvement Science Journey   173
Figure 11.2. Driver Diagram   177
Figure 11.3. Improvement Science Journey for Improving
       Outcomes for English Learners   181

Chapter 12
Figure 12.1. Students with Disabilities: Least Restrictive
       Environment >80% Trend by Race/Ethnicity in the
       School District of Sunshine River   199

Chapter 13
Figure 13.1. Fishbone Diagram   210
Figure 13.2. Driver Diagram   211

Chapter 14
Figure 14.1. Student Voice Fishbone Diagram   225
Figure 14.2. Student Council Model   225
Figure 14.3. School Climate Survey Statements   229
Figure 14.4. Selected School Climate Survey Results,
       Grade 6-8, 2014-2017   230
Figure 14.5. Theory of Action, Collaborative Improvement   231
Figure 14.6. Middle School Baseline Data, 2017-2018   233
Figure 14.7. Growth Perception Over Time, 2017-2019   234
Figure 14.8. Racial Equity Strategic Plan   235
Figure 14.9. Student Voice Statements Over Time, 2019-2021   236
Figure 14.10. Student Voice: Racist and Homophobic Language   236
Figure 14.11. Comprehensive Distance Learning Assessment,
       Fall 2020-2021   237

Chapter 15
Figure 15.1. Plan-Do-Study-Act Overview   243
Figure 15.2. Parent Focus Group Empathy Interview Protocol   245

Chapter 16
Figure 16.1. Grade One Reading Tracker Chart   263

Chapter 17
Figure 17.1. School Climate Transformation Network
       Driver Diagram   279
Figure 17.2. High Leverage Graph   282

Tables

Chapter 3
Table 3.1. Personnel Retention 41

Chapter 4
Table 4.1. Student Engagement 56
Table 4.2. Contact With Vulnerable Families During
   Wildfire Evacuation 57
Table 4.3. Percentage of Students Missing More Than
   20% of the Day 61

Chapter 5
Table 5.1. EES Equity Audit Data 70

Chapter 6
Table 6.1. Class and Social Data 83
Table 6.2. Discipline Data by Demographics 84
Table 6.3. District Data by Gender 85
Table 6.4. Demographics of Low-Attending Sixth Graders 87

Chapter 7
Table 7.1. Stakeholder List of Needs for Success 107
Table 7.2. Discipline Referrals: First 6 Weeks 109
Table 7.3. Demographics of Students Receiving Failing Grades 109
Table 7.4. Demographics of Discipline Trends 109
Table 7.5. Discipline Data by Demographics: End of Year 111
Table 7.6. Change in Referrals November to June 113
Table 7.7. Discipline Data Disaggregated 116

Chapter 10
Table 10.1. Graduation Requirements for Washington, D.C.,
   Public School Students 160

Chapter 11
Table 11.1. Washington State Report Card Diversity Report 170

Chapter 12
Table 12.1. Six Core Principles of Improvement Science and
   Examples of Their Application Related to Delivery of
   Special Education Services in an Inclusive School Settings 186

Table 12.2. Questions to Address Educational Needs
of Students With Disabilities 190
Table 12.3. Tools Used in the Improvement Science Process:
Tool, Purpose, and Resources 193
Table 12.4. Continuum of Supports for Students With and
Without Disabilities: Contextual Consideration 194

Chapter 15
Table 15.1. Seven Cs Code Descriptions and Example Quotes
From the Focus Group 247

Chapter 16
Table 16.1. Plan-Do-Study-Act (PDSA) Functions Utilized 262

Chapter 17
Table 17.1. Core Leadership Practices 272
Table 17.2. Center for Leadership and Educational Equity
(CLEE) Improvement for Equity Method Steps by Core
Leadership Practice 281
Table 17.3. Edward R. Martin Middle School Learning
Community Survey Means by Core Leadership Practice
Over 1 Year 286
Table 17.4. Key Learning in Leading Improvement for Equity
by Center for Leadership and Educational Equity (CLEE)
Core Leadership Practice 287

ACKNOWLEDGMENTS

We have been inspired to create this book, foremost, for those historically underserved in our schools: children of color, recent immigrants, those with special learning needs, and those who have been overlooked or ignored in our schools. We want to honor the teachers and leaders, students, families, and community members who persevere and inspire us. We would like to acknowledge the leadership of Portland State University's College of Education Deans Emeritus Randy Hitz and Dean Jose Coll, Educational Leadership and Policy Chair Candyce Reynolds, and School of Public Health Professor Sherril Gelmon, who have supported us in our exploration of applying improvement science to our focus on equity in our schools. We also want to thank the Carnegie Foundation and its support of our iLEAD work, Carnegie National Faculty Robert Crow and Senior Fellows David Imig, Paul LeMahieu, Louis Gomez, Mike Hansen, and Tony Bryk; iLEAD school district partners Tania McKey and Cassandra Thonstad; and our colleagues at Portland State University, Associate Professor Emeritus Pat Burk and Adjunct Professors Larry Becker and Cassandra Thonstad. This book is only possible with support and encouragement of Deborah's spouse Ned Perry, JD, and daughters Sylvia Peterson-Perry, MD, MPH, and Rebecca Peterson-Perry, MA, and Susan's spouse, Jim Carlile, MA, and her daughter, Paulette Campbell, MA, each of whom is a strong social justice advocate in their field. Our belief in the power of improvement science to radically enhance the experience of historically underserved students and families is based on the concepts of Paolo Freire and John Dewey, who continue to inspire us.

Introduction

DEBORAH S. PETERSON, SUSAN P. CARLILE,
AND GLORIA MCDANIEL-HALL

We need to improve our schools. The collective success of every family in our nation requires that we improve them now. We can't wait until a "rosier budget outlook" or until after "all staff are trained over the next 5 years" or until "our next textbook adoptions in 3 years." We need to improve now.

Over the past few years, what we learned is that when we have a national crisis, such as the recent global pandemic, we can change existing systems and improve every aspect of our schools—with no notice. When the dangers of the global pandemic became apparent, our schools adjusted how we taught, the materials we used to teach, how we delivered lunches to children, how we provided access to the internet to all students, and how and if we checked out laptops. We adapted our lessons for online learning and engaged students and families in new ways as every person in the United States faced the collective and compounding trauma of a national health crisis, increased racial violence, and national political strife. We had the will and the means to make changes to save people's lives. We need to ensure that we address educational disparities in our schools with the same urgency and the same commitment. Our nation's children are counting on us.

We believe that improvement science (IS) is a process that provides specific methods, processes, and frameworks for leaders to examine issues in their own school communities. IS emphasizes collaboration, inquiry cycles, and the use of formative data, and includes routines to help teachers and leaders define problems, implement changes, and determine whether these changes actually improve practice (Bryk et al., 2015; Crow et al., 2019; Peterson & Carlile, 2021). Methods such as IS that emphasize practitioner perspectives, including design-based research (a similar cyclical method that puts greater emphasis on building theory) have steadily grown in influence in recent decades (Hoffman et al., 2020; Reinking & Bradley, 2008). These approaches are an important counterpoint to so-called gold-standard random-ized controlled trials that intend to determine "what works." Critics argue that these large-scale experiments "tend to mislead rather than inform practice and are a major reason why efforts to reform high-poverty schools have had limited success" (Pogrow, 2017, p. 2). In contrast, IS provides insight into not only what works but also why, how, and under what circumstances it works (Donahue, 2015), such as how a well-intentioned new tool for teacher feedback can unin-tentionally monopolize principal time (Bryk et al., 2015). Finally, IS and other practitioner-focused research is more likely to foreground issues of equity and access in response to the needs of underserved communities (Hoffman et al., 2020).

We propose that each teacher, each school leader, and each district leader ask these questions, initially posed by Langley et al. (2009), which we have revised and enhanced to include our social justice orientation and equity goals:

1. What are we trying to accomplish, *and how do we ensure that this improvement benefits children of all racial, ethnic, socioeco-nomic, gender, and ability levels, especially those most under-served in our community?*
2. How will we know that a change is an improvement *for children of all racial, ethnic, socioeconomic, gender, and ability levels, es-pecially those most underserved in our community?*
3. What changes can we make that will result in improvement *for children of all racial, ethnic, socioeconomic, gender, and ability levels, especially those most underserved?*
4. How do we ensure we include the voices of those who are most impacted by the change such that the humanity of those in our schools is enhanced (Peterson, 2014)?

To reach these equity goals, we must deeply understand the context and the reason behind the problem. We must follow the principles successfully used in health care and business when they urge us to make improvement and adaption part of our everyday work, develop and use the capability of everyone in the school, and give the school the power to handle complex crisis environments (Rother, 2010). We must "get better" by attending to variability in performance, addressing the key issue of what works for whom and under what set of conditions, and advancing reliability at scale (Crow et al., 2019; Gwande, 2007). The chapter authors in this book tell us how and why these principles work in classroom practice and provide examples of specific tools that helped them learn from the problems encountered. IS tools, such as the Five Whys inquiry tool, and empathy interviews work synergistically to help teams make lasting improvements.

Jeff Water's team (Chapter 14) discovered that conducting a cycle of inquiry with students as a community event was a fundamentally democratic process. Students generated new questions, probed their own school system, asking why, for example, administrators who are the smallest stakeholders by volume have the most power and those with the least power (the students) have the least. McDaniel-Hall's team (Chapter 15) identified their initial problem by asking, "Why?" five times in order to identify root causes for their problem. This team also learned that empathy interviews can accelerate efforts to advance equity through parent engagement, thus prioritizing the voices of families and embedding their ideas in the solutions.

It is important to note that the practitioners in each of the chapters are "positive deviants," in that their laser-like focus on quality becomes the model for the rest of us. They are outliers, outperforming their peers in adverse conditions that include pandemics, wildfires, political unrest, and resulting riots. What contributes to their success? What about their systems looks just like ours? What is different? How are they using the IS tools? Is this an implementation issue? What about the solution that works well in these schools would work in our site? What would not? In short, what can we learn from these practitioners about making change, recognizing the unique conditions of our own environment?

During the global pandemic, schools quickly and agilely adjusted how they taught so students of all races, backgrounds, abilities, and needs learned. Certainly, we can also adjust our practices that harm the potential of so many of our nation's children: our children living in poverty, our Black children funneled into the school-to-prison pipeline, our Brown children who are not supported in achieving high school graduation, our girls who are pushed out of math and science courses, our boys who don't read or write at grade level, our children experiencing trauma, and our children with special needs.

We can use our experience, intelligence, knowledge of our context, and concrete tools to ensure that children of every race, ethnicity, gender, socioeconomic background, and ability thrive in our schools, a vision for a socially just society. Our commitment to social justice as a process and outcome is informed by Bell (2016), and we believe that using IS tools and processes is a concrete way to increase equity. We believe the teachers and school leaders who have chosen the teaching profession should be empowered to lead these improvements and encouraged to measure whether their change efforts result in improvements for children of all backgrounds. We exhort teachers and leaders to use regularly collected data to decide whether to adapt or adopt strategies that increase equity and abandon strategies that perpetuate inequities. We believe that teachers have considerable expertise, education, and deep knowledge of the specific context of their classroom and school and should be primary agents in improving our schools. And we should not work in isolation; rather, we should be soliciting and building on the ideas of students and families and collaborating with colleagues to improve our work. We know that collecting and analyzing data in short cycles of improvement makes a difference for the children in our classrooms today, not the children we might teach 3 to 5 years from now or the children we taught last year. We believe that sometimes it is best to abandon or adapt an idea that is not resulting in improvements in one particular context. We also believe that we should not point, shame, or blame the teachers and leaders working countless hours for our children when a change idea just does not work in one particular classroom or school. The context might call for a different improvement strategy.

As Rahaman notes in Chapter 10, "there are many books that describe the core principles and techniques of IS, including *The Improvement Guide* (Langley et al., 2009) and *Learning to Improve* (Bryk et al., 2016)." Although these books provide a foundational understanding of the field, this current volume makes an important contribution because it provides concrete examples of IS being applied in real school settings. In essence, these school-based examples of IS-in-action are case studies that can be used to foster learning and to spark ideas for improvement projects in your own school.

So why do we believe in IS as a method to increase equity in schools? Although we know we have much to learn, we also realize that the children in our schools deserve an equitable education now. We feel compelled to use IS to accelerate meaningful change, refining processes and tools to promote equity within the schools and communities we serve. IS has the power to change the traditional ways in which we identify, process, and solve problems in schools. However, in order to enact the changes that will be necessary, we must first define what equity in schools really looks like.

Although there are varied definitions of *equity* and practices that will lead to more equitable schools within the literature, there are common themes. Among these commonalities are the following:

- There must be a critical reexamination of current systems, policies, and practices using a lens that is committed to making the changes necessary to improve outcomes for all.
- There must be a focus on every person receiving what they need every day in order to develop their full academic and social selves and to thrive in the process.
- There should be no predictability of success based on social factors, that is, race, ethnicity, economic status, sexual orientation, physical disabilities, possible language concerns, or any other factors. Barriers to progress should be recognized and removed.
- Every person should be seen for who they are and for the gifts they have to give the world. These gifts must then be fostered and celebrated within the school community.

Finally, we must begin to emphasize abilities rather than deficits as solutions are proposed.

Reform-minded leaders often fall victim to a solutionist fallacy, assuming they know the solution before fully understanding the problem and its causes (Bryk et al., 2015). Instead, Landon, Gloria, and Ryan partnered to use IS to take a step back and focus on the user experience (in our case, the families) rather than assuming we understood their wants and needs (Crow et al., 2019; Peterson & Carlile, 2021). Such a process not only demonstrates respect for families; it also yields more effective solutions.

However, in order to truly and deeply understand the voices of those who have historically been underserved, ignored, or marginalized, it is clear that we need to actively *listen to* them (in order to more fully understand) rather than make plans *for them*—in the absence of those conversations and interactions.

We can't accomplish this task passively. Next steps will entail actively seeking input and actively using the information we gain. Our stakeholders will need to believe that we value their voices and that we are willing to be vulnerable, open-minded, and action-oriented.

Although this goal sounds admirable, and in some cases, we are making valiant attempts to improve in this area, can we really hear them or are we hearing what makes sense to us based on our own biases and social constructs? This question must be explored as part of the process.

To truly begin this process, we need an intentional focus, we need training, we will need ongoing feedback, and, most important, we need to understand that this process is ever-evolving and continual. We must improve our capacity to listen without ignoring our complicity in the systems that exclude those we are attempting to empower. We must enhance the humanity—not denigrate the potential—of every child, family, community member, teacher, and staff member as we work to improve (Peterson, 2014). As we wrote in 2019, we believe it is teachers' and leaders' *responsibility* to improve from within: "Although IS does respect the ability of teachers and leaders to understand the complexity of improvement in a particular context, it also places increasing **responsibility** (emphasis added) on teachers and school leaders for reform" (Peterson & Carlile, 2021, p. 175).

It is through our work with hundreds of current teachers and future school leaders who are increasing equity in schools through IS projects that we commit to those and additional concepts in IS: Context matters. Data matter. Research matters. Empowering and enhancing the humanity of those closest to the work matters. And examining who benefits from our improvement efforts matters. Every child deserves this focus. Addressing educational disparities in our schools with urgency, commitment, and a belief that every child, of every race, every ethnicity, gender, ability, and cultural identity deserves this focus. Our nation's children are counting on us.

References

Bell, L. A. (2016). Theoretical foundations for social justice education. In M. Adams & L. A. Bell (Eds.), *Teaching for diversity and social justice* (pp. 3–26). Routledge.

Bryk, A. S., Gomez, L. M., Grunow, A., & LeMahieu, P. G. (2015). *Learning to improve: How America's schools can get better at getting better.* Harvard Education Press.

Crow, R., Hinnant-Crawford, B.N., & Spaulding, E. (Eds). (2019). *The educational leaders's guide to improvement science: Data, design and cases for reflection.* Myers Education Press.

Donahue, C. (2015, March 15). *Learning our way into better education systems.* Carnegie Commons Blog. https://www.carnegiefoundation.org/blog/learning-our-way-into-better-education-systems/

Gwande, A. (2007). *Better: A surgeon's notes on performance.* Henry Holt and Company.

Hoffman, J. V., Hikida, M., & Sailors, M. (2020). Contesting science that silences: Amplifying equity, agency, and design research in literacy teacher preparation. *Reading Research Quarterly, 55*(51), S255–S266. https://doi.org/10.1002/rrq.353

Langley, G. J., Moen, R. D., Nolan, K. M., Nolan, T. W., Norman, C. L., & Provost, L. P. (2009). The improvement guide: A practical approach to enhancing organizational performance. John Wiley & Sons.

Peterson, D. S. (2014). A missing piece in the sustainability movement: The human spirit. *Sustainability: The Journal of Record, 7*(2), 74–77. https://doi.org/10.1089/SUS.2014.9810

Peterson, D. S., & Carlile, S. P. (2021). *Improvement science: Promoting equity in schools.* Myers Education Press.

Pogrow, S. (2017). The failure of U.S. education research establishment to identify effective practices: Beware of effective practices policies. *Education Policy Analysis Archives, 25*(5), 1–21. https://doi.org/10.14507/epaa.25.2517

Reinking, D., & Bradley, B. A. (2008). *On formative and design experiments: Approaches to language and literacy research* (Vol. 3). Teachers College Press.

Rother, M. (2010). *Toyota kata: Managing people for improvement, adaptiveness, and superior results*. Rother and Company.

CHAPTER TWO

Teachers Can't Do It Alone: The Role of Leadership in Implementing Equity-Driven Social-Emotional Learning

AMIE B. CIEMINSKI AND THOMAS LEE MORGAN

This chapter describes the implementation of a social-emotional curriculum initiative across a large urban school district. Terra Vista Independent School District (TVISD; pseudonym) serves more than 40,000 students across 60 schools. Of the student body, 93% identify as Latinx, 81% are classified as economically disadvantaged, and 25% are English learners. TVISD is a high-performing district with more than 90% of students graduating on time and 80% of students scoring satisfactorily on the state assessments without significant racial disparities. While nationally almost 80% of teachers are of European descent (Taie & Goldring, 2020), 84% of the 3,000 teachers and over 50% of school district leaders, principals, and board members in TVISD identify as Latinx. Leaders in TVISD, with community input, developed a 5-year strategic plan that addressed community priorities, including preparing globally competitive graduates, raising achievement and closing achievement gaps, and building positive relationships among students, staff, and community.

District leaders realized that they lacked a comprehensive strategy to help teachers and leaders create safe and connected learning environments. TVISD investigated how social-emotional learning (SEL) could be used as a driver for enhancing student outcomes and increasing school success. Schools employed a multiplicity of SEL programs; therefore, students demonstrated a wide range of social-emotional competence. Also, school district leaders did not have a common measure of the learning climate or students' social-emotional skills.

Improvement science is an iterative process about "making the many different parts that comprise an educational organization mesh better to produce quality outcomes more reliably, day in and day out, for every child and across the diverse contexts in which they are educated" (LeMahieu et al., 2017, p. 3). TVISD leaders resolved to implement a common SEL curriculum and to systematically gather the perceptions of staff, students, and families concerning their goal of developing a climate of respect and kindness with the potential to impact student success.

SEL

School personnel are crucial to developing students' overall growth, including social, emotional, and academic learning. With ever-increasing pressure and accountability to enhance academic performance, the social and emotional aspects of learning are often overlooked. A whole-child approach to learning rejects the narrow focus on improving one aspect of student performance, such as reading skills. It implements a sustainable, collaborative approach, ensuring that each student is healthy, safe, engaged, supported, and challenged. With a whole-child approach, gains in several indicators related to positive youth development leading toward sustainable long-term student success and school improvement are realized (Volk et al., 2016).

Given limited resources, educators should implement evidence-based approaches that produce multiple benefits (Durlak et al., 2011). Including SEL as an integral part of the educational program allows schools to better prepare students for college, career, and citizenship through a

> process through which all young people and adults acquire and apply the knowledge, skills, and attitudes to develop healthy identities, manage emotions and achieve personal and collective goals,

feel and show empathy for others, establish and maintain supportive relationships, and make responsible and caring decisions. (Skoog-Hoffman et al., 2020, p. 5)

Researchers have consistently found evidence that SEL is among the most successful youth development programs (Durlak et al., 2011; Payton et al., 2008). SEL is an evidence-based method that supports the whole child in a proactive and preventative manner. Developing students' social competencies has been linked to improving other indicators of student success and wellbeing, including achievement gains of 11 percentile points (Durlak et al., 2011). SEL has been found to increase student motivation in terms of engagement and academic commitment (Morgan & Cieminski, 2020) and is associated with increased prosocial and classroom behavior and decreased disruptive behavior (noncompliance, aggression, delinquent acts, bullying), student depression, anxiety, stress, and social withdrawal (Durlak et al., 2011). SEL has myriad benefits for all students and may especially benefit students who face additional stress due to trauma, adversity, and a lack of access to quality housing, food, health care, and safety (Aspen Institute, 2019).

Equity Focus

Given that the majority of students in TVISD come from historically underserved groups (students living in poverty, learning English, and identifying as Latinx, Black, Indigenous, and multiracial backgrounds), it was important to ensure that the implementation of SEL did not reinforce hegemonic norms of deficit thinking, devalue local customs, or further marginalize students and their families. Many SEL programs promote individualism that reflects Eurocentric, middle-class values rather than a culturally responsive approach that honors collectivist cultures with an interdependent model of self (Crowder, 2020; Jagers et al., 2018). Thus, TVISD represented a unique case to explore implementing an SEL curriculum in a predominantly Latinx community.

Creating and ensuring access to high-quality, safe, and equitable learning environments provides pathways towards more equitable futures for students of all backgrounds. Biag (2019) provided three actions that can help leaders approach improvement with an equity lens: practice critical reflection, promote inclusion, and focus on the whole child. The leaders in TVISD critically interrogated the organizational structure and culture (i.e., the way things are done around here) (Deal & Peterson, 2016) and realized that the variability in the system was leading to inequitable opportunities and outcomes. Leaders decided to guarantee all students access to the same evidence-based SEL curriculum.

Problem of Practice

As is the case with many large school districts, TVISD took an ad hoc approach to implementing SEL. Initiatives ranged from the highest level of evidence-based programming to homegrown SEL programs. While school district leaders felt that individual schools needed discretion in fitting social-emotional programming to their local context, a key concept of improvement science, they also felt strongly that students and teachers needed PK–12 common language and common skill development. This problem was evident at major transitions for students, including when students matriculated from elementary to secondary school or transferred schools at any point. As such, school personnel needed to engage students in unlearning maladaptive behaviors to learn the new expectations. Also, school district leaders understood the danger represented in the variability of students' social-emotional competence. Without a consistent measure of the students' SEL skills, leaders lacked the information to know how to intervene. Schools utilizing evidence-based programs generally had access to assessment data based on the goals of that program, but these results were not comparable across schools. Moreover, teaching social skills had been traditionally the responsibility of mental health providers. Although teachers felt that SEL was an important aspect of schooling, they perceived their primary role was to provide academic instruction.

TVISD leaders determined that implementing SEL could promote diversity and inclusion by giving all students skills to operate on a level playing field by making the hidden curriculum (i.e., success in school) explicit and consistent. Next, they felt that participation and inclusion would be promoted when they asked families, students, and staff about their experiences regarding school climate. Finally, they believed that this improvement that attended to the whole child would address more than academics and promote better long-term success for students.

Tools Used in the Improvement Science Process

Root-Cause Analysis

A root cause analysis indicated that the lack of a universal, proactive, and preventive approach to social, emotional, and academic development led to unintended adverse outcomes for students. While a safe and connected school climate can be challenging to measure, behavior incident data, bullying reports, and attendance data served as proxy data to verify that the approach lacked effectiveness. There was a need for a solution that could be implemented across all schools to align the district's SEL efforts, engage all educators in the process of social-emotional development, and assess effectiveness through common measures and metrics.

Program Review

When SEL is utilized as a universal strategy for instruction and promotion of self-awareness, self-management, social awareness, relationship skills, and responsible decision-making, students and staff benefit from a healthy school climate and culture (Collie et al., 2012). Within educational systems, students learn, practice, and apply SEL skills in the learning environment. As students and staff, SEL skills become heightened, nuanced, and integrated over time, enhanced social, emotional, and academic outcomes will result. Furthermore, implementing evidence-based SEL curricula and programs has demonstrated effectiveness at all levels of education and can be executed by teachers and staff as part of customary educational practice (Durlak et al., 2011; Payton et al., 2008).

After a thorough investigation of several programs, the district team selected The Kindness in the Classroom Curriculum© from the Random Act of Kindness (RAK) Foundation. All school personnel would be trained so that students could engage in a cohesive and graduated model of developing social-emotional competencies. Also, the district leaders determined that focusing on a districtwide culture of respect and kindness would support the improvement of relationships between various stakeholders. Additionally, the leaders planned to measure school culture and climate changes through behavior and academic data and surveys of students, staff, and families designed to provide a multi-informant measure of culture and climate.

Theory of Improvement

While the implementation of Terra Vista's strategic plan involved many different initiatives, the implementation of SEL programming to improve overall student outcomes is the focus of this chapter. The leaders interrogated the loosely coupled systemic structures that produced the volatility in the various learning environments across the school district. As such, strategically implementing a common SEL curriculum with common expectations for students and teachers helped focus the collective efforts of district leaders, school administrators, counselors, and classroom teachers toward increased efficiency.

Plan–Do–Study Cycles

The implementation team (the district SEL coordinator and school counselors) met monthly to discuss school site implementation throughout the first year. The team focused on providing just-in-time support, including consultation to colleagues to help solve problems of practice. The team also kept a record of issues with a plan to make more substantive improvements before the second implementation year. At the end of Year 1, the team determined that the areas needing the most change were access to lessons and coordinated kindness activities. Because teachers' awareness and skills in utilizing the resources varied, they planned to dedicate more time to helping teachers navigate the RAK resources. The team deepened their collective knowledge of the curriculum and aligned approaches to respond to local and national events. Events included a death by suicide of a TVISD student that impacted several campuses because of the network of family and friends and a planned national student walkout in protest of gun violence. As a district, leaders supported students' agency and activism with a districtwide "March for Kindness" in solidarity against gun violence and in support of kindness.

As teachers spent more time focusing on students' social-emotional development, they developed stronger relationships beyond perfunctory teacher–student transactional relationships. Teachers began to learn about the depth and impact of trauma on the lives of their students and felt unprepared to address the trauma appropriately. The implementation team determined that teachers needed knowledge about the effects of trauma on learning and its relationship to behavior, sensitivity to environmental triggers that might cause reactions rooted in trauma, awareness to anticipate difficult times, and the ability to provide additional support (Overstreet & Chafouleas, 2016).

They also realized the need to provide teachers with more tools and opportunities for self-care, especially as it related to secondary traumatic stress. Helping teachers develop a regimen of self-care was a strategic move to increase support for students. Infusing professional learning for teachers with trauma-informed practices and self-care techniques also helped develop adult competence and practice related to SEL.

The team identified technical changes that needed to be implemented, including project expectations, reflection journals for students, and secondary school-focused kindness posters. The team had set a goal of having each campus engage in two major kindness projects throughout the year, which proved difficult as teachers were learning the curriculum. Going forward, the expectation would be one major project, but individual school teams retained the flexibility to engage in more. Students would be provided a physical journal for reflective writing rather than using electronic devices. It was determined that the benefits of providing each student a journal outweighed the additional costs. The curriculum included posters, and during a technical support visit, it was discovered that all schools were using elementary-focused posters. Thus, over the summer, secondary-focused posters would be provided for each secondary school.

Lessons Learned

At the end of the first year, interviews were conducted with leaders from schools where implementation was perceived to be moving toward early sustainability. The team also interviewed school counselors in a focus group since they were program champions at the campus sites. Because on-site facilitation and local leadership have been instrumental in promoting fidelity to an intervention (Correnti & Rowan, 2007), listening to these leaders bolstered support for early adopters and informed implementation adjustments to garner more widespread implementation fidelity.

Counselors shared their learning, barriers to implementation, and adaptations, within their specific sites to support implementation. In the TVISD plan, school counselors, as the program champions, had the main responsibility to support quality implementation and build capacity specific to the innovation (Nordstrum et al., 2017). They participated in the train-the-trainers professional learning with the technical assistance provider before the school year started. They were responsible for the rollout of initial training at their campus sites, the day-to-day support for lesson implementation, and program sustainability. In supporting lesson delivery, counselors would model, provide side-by-side support, and observe.

The counselors would have "support days" to provide consultation, encouragement, and problem-solving. For the most part, counselors leveraged strong relationships with teachers as a key to support. However, one new counselor reported that it was challenging to implement "support days" because she did not have established relationships. Therefore, she was careful not to monitor compliance because that "could hurt relationships."

School counselors also coordinated two schoolwide kindness projects and spearheaded the evaluation data collection. They piloted Kindness Weeks and Kindness Clubs so that students could apply the skills they were learning through projects. Some counselors reported as many as 90 students participated in these clubs, noting that Kindness Club was a "place where kids want to belong."

Schools that had strong administrative support and fidelity of implementation experienced early success. At these campus sites, teachers and students were modeling prosocial behaviors. There was early evidence of students internalizing the kindness lessons and taking leadership to promote kindness. Upon returning to his home high school from Vista Alternative School, one high school student offered to lead the lessons saying, "What time do y'all do your Random Acts of Kindness? . . . Well, we need to start it. Let me show you how to get you started." Likewise, in one elementary school, two girls were hurting the reputation of the Kindness Club, and the counselor reported that other students said, "Nobody should be kicked out, but these girls need to behave in a way that reflects our values!"

The RAK curriculum had projects built into the lessons that served as a mechanism for students to practice their skills. Leaders across all schools emphasized the importance of these activities. For example, the principal of South High commented that "promoting any type of kindness to our students and then them taking it with them, home or outside of the school, is really essential." She also mentioned that both staff and students found value in the activities, such as writing thank-you cards to staff members. Similarly, a South counselor indicated that the lessons were positively transforming teacher–student relationships.

TVISD leaders acknowledged the need to strengthen adult SEL capacity. Within various schools, principals created structures to build efficacy across teams. At Woodlawn High, the core content departments used their common planning time for lesson and material preparation. The Vista Alternative School principal expressed that she paired teachers as a support strategy. At the end of the first year, the district SEL coordinator made plans to train school counselors on trauma-informed care, resiliency, and wellness so they could "sharpen their skills in that area and are able to help out the adults that are here and students." As one counselor stated, "I think it's really important to not forget to feed your teachers. Because your teachers won't have anything to give unless you do."

Leaders also set clear expectations and promoted mutual accountability, which included systems of monitoring. The principal at Ocean View Middle reflected on improving their process, saying,

> I think now, as we are planning a curriculum, we need to get in there and say, "Are your plans ready for RAK? . . . They have to be ready for me at 8 AM" so that they know what's there, and then they are accountable to each other.

Implementation was more successful when there was a balance of support and accountability. Some schools implemented more robust accountability, such as having students sign attendance rosters to indicate that teachers had provided the RAK lesson. Other leaders used a lighter and more flexible approach, saying, "Do it when they can and then let's see if that works."

Teachers were more engaged when school leaders helped them realize the connection between implementing RAK with their values and already established programs. The Baker Elementary principal expounded:

> I think you help them see that what they are doing for RAK is not simply an add-on to other things they have to do. . . . So they themselves start to see the proof, in what they are doing, that is worth the time you take to do it, and how you can integrate it into things that they are already doing. So, it is not something above and separate, and needless or worthless. It is very much a part of what we are trying to build on here.

Implementation involves complexity and requires change. Fixsen et al. (2005) explained that the change might be more dramatic for some individuals and, in this case, for individual schools. As individuals experience change, they go through predictable stages of concern regarding the innovation from unconcerned, concern for self, concern for task, and then concern about impact (Hall & Hord, 2015). For example, at initial implementation stages, if leaders did not attend to "self" concerns (e.g., "I am not sure I am ready for this. I am not a counselor") and task concerns (e.g., "How will I access the materials if the internet doesn't work?" "This seems to take too much time."), the implementation faltered. In TVISD, leaders responded to concerns by clarifying expectations, providing coaching, and removing barriers. One counselor explained, "The way my principal wanted it was, 'Let them do it when they can' because we did not want to pressure the teachers to add more to their plate." Another counselor illustrated the way their high school used a team approach:

> Each department worked together. They planned the lesson together. . . . So, there was a lot of support and [positive] peer pressure for them to get it done, present it, be part of this initiative, and not be in your negativity.

However, in attempting to address the teachers' management concerns in these instances, the school leaders and their solutions may have contributed to implementation drift.

Lessons Learned for Increasing Equity in Schools

Structural changes toward equity are difficult to detect after one year of implementation. Schools need a curriculum that propels them towards transformative SEL (Jagers et al., 2018) and is attuned to the school site needs across a large district to keep the implementation strong. Choosing RAK as a comprehensive curriculum was an equity lever for TVISD as it was implemented throughout the PK–12 system.

The strategy that increased equity in the districtwide implementation initiative was to utilize a loose–tight model (Spillane et al., 2011) that engendered participative decision-making that was dually responsive to the global (school district) and local (school site) needs. For initial professional learning, school counselors were provided with the framework for understanding the SEL curriculum and the district vision for implementing the curriculum consistently across the district. Yet counselors had the flexibility to conduct school-level professional learning in a manner that best fit the needs of their campus. Although schools were required to deliver the curriculum, the specifics of the operational aspects were left to individual school leaders.

Long-term sustainability is one of the challenges of implementing any program and has plagued the ability of SEL to be transformative in achieving deep, equitable change for students, especially students that have been traditionally marginalized within the educational system. The danger of the loose–tight model is providing adequate flexibility for a personalized approach and sufficient direction to promote fidelity to the evidence-based intervention to drive consistent outcomes. In the case of TVISD, the loose part of the model became initiative implementation drift, and thus, the initiative lost its power to impact change across the school district. Implementation at the various sites encompassed fidelity, supplementing established approaches, and intransigent, superficial compliance. Even in the dissipation of the districtwide impact, there were still school-level effects that promoted equitable outcomes by allowing students to develop social-emotional competence.

This case demonstrates the challenges of implementing SEL programs to scale. It is recommended that educational leaders learn from this case to develop an implementation plan that moves the initiative toward sustainability within the culture of the learning environment.

Discussion Questions

1. How does a PK–12 SEL curriculum support or hinder equitable outcomes for students?
2. What are the benefits and drawbacks of a loose–tight approach for program implementation?
3. What is the role of school and district leaders in supporting deep, equitable change through SEL?

References

Aspen Institute. (2019). *From a nation at risk to a nation at hope: Recommendations from the National Commission on Social, Emotional, & Academic Development.* https://files.eric.ed.gov/fulltext/ED606337.pdf

Biag, M. (2019). Navigating the improvement journey with an equity compass. In R. Crow, B. N. Hinnant-Crawford, & D. T. Spaulding (Eds.), *The educational leader's guide to improvement science* (pp. 91–123). Myers Education Press.

Collie, R. J., Shapka, J. D., & Perry, N. E. (2012). School climate and social-emotional learning: Predicting teacher stress, job satisfaction, and teaching efficacy. *Journal of Educational Psychology, 104*(4), 1189–1204. https://doi.org/10.1037/a0029356

Correnti, R., & Rowan, B. (2007). Opening up the black box: Literacy instruction in schools participating in three comprehensive school reform programs. *American Educational Research Journal, 44*(2), 298–338. https://doi.org/10.3102/0002831207302501

Crowder, M. (2020, May 19). *Key considerations for promoting culturally relevant SEL during COVID-19.* Pacific REL. https://ies.ed.gov/ncee/edlabs/regions/pacific/blogs/blog26_key-considerations-for-promoting-SEL-during-covid-19.asp

Deal, T. E., & Peterson, K. (2016). *Shaping school culture.* Jossey-Bass.

Durlak, J. A., Dymnicki, A. B., Taylor, R. D., Weissberg, R. P., & Schellinger, K. B. (2011). The impact of enhancing students' social and emotional learning: A meta-analysis of school-based universal interventions. *Child Development, 82*(1), 405–432. https://doi.org/10.1111/j.1467-8624.2010.01564.x

Fixsen, D., Naoom, S., Blase, K., Friedman, R., & Wallace, F. (2005). *Implementation research: A synthesis of the literature.* National Implementation Research Network. https://nirn.fpg.unc.edu/resources/implementation-research-synthesis-literature

Hall, G., & Hord, S. (2015). *Implementing change: Patterns, principles, and potholes.* Pearson Education.

Jagers, R. J., Rivas-Drake, D., & Borowski, T. (2018). *Equity and social-emotional learning: A cultural analysis* (CASEL Assessment Work Group Brief Series).

CASEL. https://measuringsel.casel.org/wp-content/uploads/2018/11/Frame
works-Equity.pdf

LeMahieu, P. G., Bryk, A. S., Grunow, A., & Gomez, L. (2017). Working to improve:
Seven approaches to improvement science in education. *Quality Assurance in
Education, 25*(1), 2–4. https://doi.org/10.1108/QAE-12-2016-0086

Morgan, T. L., & Cieminski, A. B. (2020). Exploring the mechanisms that influence
adolescent academic motivation. *Educational Studies.* https://doi.org/10.1080/0
3055698.2020.1729102

Nordstrum, L. E., LeMahieu, P. G., & Berrena, E. (2017). Implementation science.
Quality Assurance in Education, 25(1), 58–73. https://doi.org/10.1108/QAE-12-
2016-0080

Overstreet, C., & Chafouleas, S. (2016). Trauma-informed schools: Introduction to the
special issue. *School Mental Health, 8*(1), 1–6. https://doi.org/10.1007/s12310-
016-9784-1

Payton, J., Weissberg, R. P., Durlak, J. A., Dymnicki, A. B., Taylor, R. D., Schellinger,
K. B., & Pachan, M. (2008). *The positive impact of social and emotional learning for kindergarten to eighth-grade students: Findings from three scientific
reviews.* Collaborative for Academic, Social, and Emotional Learning. https://
files.eric.ed.gov/fulltext/ED505370.pdf

Skoog-Hoffman, A., Ackerman, C., Boyle, A., Schwartz, H., Williams, B., Jagers, R.,
Dusenbury, L., Greenberg, M., Mahoney, J., Schonert-Reichl, K., & Weissberg, R.
(2020). *Evidence-based social and emotional learning programs: CASEL criteria and updates.* CASEL. https://casel.org/wp-content/uploads/2021/01/11_
CASEL-Program-Criteria-Rationale.pdf

Spillane, J. P., Parise, L. M., & Schere, J. Z. (2011). Organizational routines as coupling
mechanisms: Policy, school administration, and the technical core. *American
Educational Research Journal, 48*(3), 586–619. https://doi.org/10.3102/000283
1210385102

Taie, S., & Goldring, R. (2020). *Characteristics of public and private elementary and
secondary school teachers in the United States: Results from the 2017–18 National
Teacher and Principal Survey. First look* (NCES 2020-142). U.S. Department of
Education, National Center for Education Statistics. https://nces.ed.gov/pub
search/pubsinfo.asp?pubid=2020142

Volk, D. T., Sanetti, L. M., & Chafouleas, S. M. (2016). The whole school, whole community, whole child model: An opportunity for school psychologists to show
leadership. *Communique, 44*(8), 1–18. https://www.nasponline.org/publications/
periodicals/communique/issues/volume-44-issue-8

Improving School Culture Through the Implementation of Social-Emotional Learning and Restorative Practices

JOANNA CARRILLO ROWLEY, MICHAEL ODELL, AND TERESA KENNEDY

Public School 155 is a middle school in a large urban school district in the Southwestern United States. The school was in danger of being closed due to its history of low performance. Simply closing the school was not a realistic option for the children and the community it served. Students primarily walk to school and receive academic and nonacademic services at the school. The campus is central to the local community as it provides other services and opportunities for neighborhood families. School improvement is a challenging endeavor. Improving schools in danger of being closed is even more challenging. The State Department of Education recognizes three turnaround models:

1. Restart—Close the low-performing school and open a new school under a charter operator, charter management organization, or education management organization.
2. Turnaround—Identify a new principal and engage in a comprehensive change in staff and instructional model.
3. Closure/Consolidation—Close a low-performing school and subsequently enroll students in higher rated school(s).

As a long-term struggling campus, the school faced the possibility of being closed by the state. There was considerable media attention in the local newspapers and on television. The community opposed the idea and asked that the neighborhood school be kept open. The State Department of Education worked with the school district to keep the school open under legislation designed to provide school districts a way to provide additional time for failing schools to meet accountability standards. The legislation was enacted in 2017 and provides incentives including additional resources for districts to contract and partner with an open-enrollment charter school, institutions of higher education, nonprofits, or government entities. A partnership was selected to manage the school and become an in-district charter school. Under the legislation, the campus would have the autonomy and flexibility with the budget, staffing, curriculum, and scheduling imposed on most traditional district schools. The partnership consisted of three non-profit entities, an educational professional organization, a social services agency, and a university affiliated program. Although the partners had experience in working with schools, none of the partners had managed a campus prior to selection.

The partnership uses a "design team," analogous to a "networked improvement community" (NIC) to drive improvement. In the case of Public School 155, the turnaround model was a hybrid of the "Restart and Turnaround" models described by the U.S. Department of Education. A new principal was installed, but all other school personnel were asked to stay. One of the greatest challenges of turnaround schools is staffing with qualified teachers. It made no practical sense to remove teachers without an opportunity to participate in the improvement process.

In addition to a new principal, the school would begin transitioning to become a STEM Academy and deliver rigorous innovative STEM education to sixth through eighth-grade students using a problem-/project-based model (PrBL/PBL). The partnership assumed management for the school in July 2018 and opened the school in August of the same year. Because the timeline provided minimal opportunities to provide professional development prior to the start of school, the 2018–2019 academic year became a data collection and planning year. Interventions were implemented as needed to support teachers and students; however, the STEM Academy Model was not formally implemented until the 2019–2020 academic year.

Opportunity Gaps

The campus had a history of instability prior to 2018. During that time, the school had endured failing accountability ratings and the highest discipline rates in the district that often resulted in negative press for the school, the district, and the community. This had a negative impact on student enrollment as parents chose to transfer their children to schools with better accountability ratings including traditional charter schools. There are multiple elementary schools that feed into the school, and all of the feeder schools met state accountability requirements. Data indicated that the highest performing students were transferring to other schools, and as a result, the student population enrolling included students disproportionately labeled as special education, 504 eligible, English-language learners, and other students who were more likely to not have passed the accountability tests in elementary school.

The school also had personnel retention problems. Data from the state showed that the school had the highest number of "novice" teachers on staff in the district as 39% of them had 5 years or less of experience. There was a lot of pressure on teachers to raise test scores, but the transience in leadership and the numerous needs of the student population caused many teachers to transfer or leave the district after one year. There is an assumption in school turnaround models that places heavy emphasis on replacing existing teachers. This implies that teachers are the primary drivers of student success. There is evidence in the literature that teachers can have a significant impact on students' achievement (Domitrovich et al., 2017); however, simply replacing teachers in hard-to-staff schools does not necessarily solve the problem. It was, therefore, determined that recruiting strong teachers would be problematic until other factors in the school were addressed.

Identifying sources in variation as part of the school improvement process is essential. Too often, it is assumed that if the scores are low, the issue is the teacher or the leadership. Improving student achievement and accountability scores requires examining the school as a system and finding the drivers that can have the most impact on improving student outcomes. Simply replacing personnel and focusing solely on improving academic achievement may not address the root causes leading to current outcomes. The design team used the first year of operation to access and collect data so that targeted interventions had realistic prospects to improve the school.

It was found that a significant opportunity gap existed that could account for lower student achievement in core courses. The opportunity gap was caused by policies and school structures that resulted in students losing learning opportunities. Instead of focusing solely on professional development in academic areas, the campus used decision-making processes regarding student exclusionary discipline to reform the campus culture. In any given week over the previous 5 years, data indicated as many as 120 children per week were assigned to a disciplinary action that caused them to miss formal instruction. That was almost 20% of the student population. It was concluded that there may be policy and structural issues within the school that were contributing a significant amount of variation in academic achievement. If students are not in class, they do not have the opportunity to receive quality instruction. This was not the only factor that could account for variation. There were several factors that potentially contributed to low achievement. These included

- novice teachers,
- curriculum,
- professional development,
- school climate,
- transfer out of higher performing students, and
- discipline policies.

Milner (2012) has described gaps in educational opportunity as the result of complex systems. He lists five components that contribute to opportunity gaps. These include poverty, a lack of social supports, limited early learning opportunities, unequal schooling, access to high-quality teachers, and access to a high-quality curriculum. There was evidence that all these factors were present at some level at the school. The school serves a population that is 95% economically disadvantaged, 53% English-language learners, and 24% special education. The school design team held meetings with teachers and students to identify structural issues that could be improved that could ultimately support higher student achievement. Improving school culture was identified as the primary driver for school improvement.

NIC

The partnership that manages the school is unique. As described earlier, it is not a charter management company. The partnership was a stroke of serendipity. Three organizations dedicated to working with schools to improve school culture and academics make up the partnership. The professional organization is a 501(c)3 organization dedicated to supporting schools that are STEM-focused. The organization provides professional development in PrBL/PBL and works with schools to implement K–12 STEM pathways. The organization focuses on a STEM model that is a vetted turnaround model for the state, and the organization specifically focuses on model fidelity.

The social services partner provides an integrated student support model to develop academic success by addressing academic and nonacademic barriers to success. They employ educational specialists and social workers to support students and families in and outside of school.

The university-affiliated partner is focused on preparing the nation's best teachers who will expand access to STEM education and STEM learning outcomes for *all* students. The organization also provides professional development and instructional assistance in mathematics and plays a lead role in collecting and analyzing data typically not provided by the school district.

In addition to the partners, teachers, parents, and community members, students also serve on the design team for the campus. The design team serves as the NIC tasked with identifying and implementing interventions for school improvement. Because school culture was the primary identified area for improvement, several data sources were addressed to fine-tune the intervention.

As a data driven organization, the school utilizes the Plan, Do, Study, Act (PDSA) process to evaluate school initiatives and foster school improvement. It should be noted that all data referenced in this chapter are from public sources, including the state accountability portal's school data that are available to the public on the district website, media reports, and public presentations at the school or district.

Plan-Do–Study–Act (PDSA) Cycle

A PDSA cycle was implemented. Figure 3.1 illustrates the PDSA cycle approach that was implemented by the campus design team.

The Planning Phase

During the planning phase, the design team analyzed data to determine an intervention that would improve school culture including

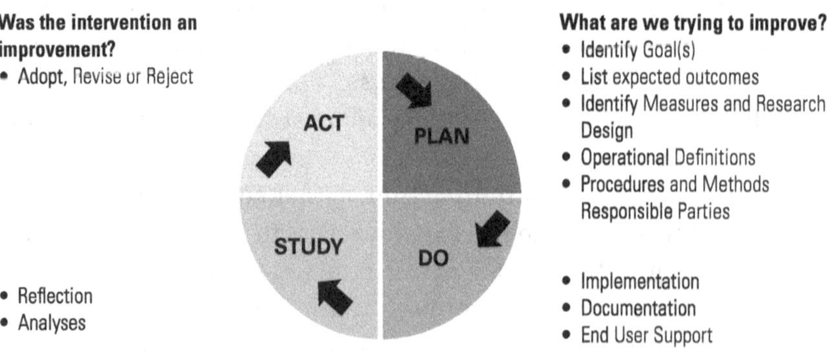

Figure 3.1. Plan Do Study Act Cycle

revising the discipline plan to increase students' attendance in class for instruction and support teachers in building positive relationships with students. To identify structural barriers, discipline policies and discipline data were analyzed. Feedback from assistant principals, counselors, social workers, teachers, and students was gathered and analyzed. It was found that the student discipline policies were not only contributing to the negative school culture but also contributing to a lack of student opportunities to learn. To oversimplify, students needed to be in class, but the code of conduct was rigid and punitive, resulting in students being out of class for minor offenses. As a result, the student code of conduct was revised to be realistic and fair.

For example, many students were in violation of dress code requirements that were not realistic for students and families to meet due to financial implications. The master schedule was also found to contribute to student discipline referrals for tardiness and altercations in the hallways. It was recommended that the school implement a block schedule and restructure the bell schedule to limit large numbers of students in the hallways at one time by staggering grade-level bells. These two interventions resulted in immediate reductions in discipline referrals. However, those two interventions alone could not change the larger school culture issues that were impacting teacher retention and student achievement. Therefore, the overarching intervention was to develop a focused student support system by increasing social-emotional learning (SEL) opportunities for students and teachers and the implementation of restorative practices (RPs) to provide equity and social justice on campus.

A school culture design team was created to directly involve stakeholders (administration, teachers, community members, SEL coordinators, and students) to develop protocols and standards that would be easily followed and not be misconstrued. Involvement from different stakeholders, such as administrators, staff, instructional coaches, counselors, teachers, and students, allowed for multiple voices from different perspectives.

As part of the planning phase, a literature review was conducted. The literature review focused on improving school culture by reimagining the school's approach to discipline. The following questions helped guide the literature review. The questions include the following:

1. How, if at all, will SEL/RP opportunities contribute to the decrease of disciplinary rates?
2. How, if at all, will SEL/RP opportunities contribute to student attendance rates and academic growth?
3. How do teachers iteratively interact with SEL practices and RP opportunities?
4. How, if at all, will SEL implementation impact personnel retention on campus?

Literature Review. Discipline is a significant issue in addressing student academic achievement and behavioral outcomes. Students around the nation face exclusionary discipline—in-school suspension (ISS), out-of-school suspension (OSS), expulsion, and police referrals. The rate of exclusionary discipline is alarming, especially for students of underrepresented groups, students who are economically disadvantaged, and students labeled as special education. This was of particular concern because this is the population that the school serves. Although research shows that White children receive exclusionary discipline consequences, minority students receive them at a higher rate (Riddle & Sinclair, 2019). Researchers such as Blood and Thorsborne (2013) and Durlak et al. (2011), find that exclusionary discipline at the school level leaves lasting impacts.

There is speculation that exclusionary discipline from an individualistic and outcome-based perspective uncovers problems that are far more issues than individual student-centered issues. Exclusionary discipline centers the problem on the social and physical environment or on educators' bias(es) directed toward students of low socioeconomic status. Hewitt et al. (2010) note, "Exclusion from the classroom, for even a few days, disrupts a child's education and may escalate misbehavior by removing the child from a structured environment and giving him/her increased time and opportunity to get into trouble" (p. 78). Although it is vital to understand the extent of exclusionary discipline, establishing interventions within the campus structure are needed to transform the campus policy, procedure, and practice that produce the exclusionary discipline outcomes. Removing students from a classroom setting for disciplinary problems denies children opportunities to learn and thus predicts future issues such as adult unemployment (Hewitt et al., 2010).

Many students lack social-emotional competencies and become less connected to school as they progress from elementary to middle and then to high school, and this lack of connection negatively affects their academic performance, behavior, and health (Durlak et al., 2011). As practices such as SEL strategies and RPs begin to emerge, the results of lowered exclusionary discipline rates begin to evolve.

As schools face an all-time-high exclusionary rate, the use of specific interventions, such as SEL and RPs, campus-wide training, and the possible changes in campus policies, procedures, and practice, can help reduce the number of exclusionary discipline rates avoiding the future impactful events to students as adults (Durlak et al., 2011).

A study by Valdebenito et al. (2018) indicated that school exclusion, better known as suspension, is the removal of a student from the classroom by school authority where they would be receiving direct instruction from the teacher of record. They also found that exclusionary discipline in the school's host state has a higher rate than those of other U.S. states. Findings reported ISS rates of 9.24% (2014–2015), OSS rates of 4.33% (2014–2015), and expulsion rates of 3.39% (2014–2015). Texas, by far, outweighed the other regions listed by more than 50% in all areas.

As Baker et al. (2014) describe, almost a third of all students may experience an out-of-school suspension or expulsion at some point in their school career. Students receiving exclusionary discipline consequences are experiencing more simplistic disruptive behaviors like defiance and noncompliance more often than more serious offenses.

Building Relationships. Developing a sense of community by building relationships with students and learning more about each students' background is essential in building a sense of culture and nurturing since their personal situation(s) could be causing the disturbance. Using a support system could take the place of a discipline consequence. Are the administrators in such deep turmoil that they have no sense of the true nature of the behavior? Is their protocol to use exclusionary means to "get rid of the problem," or is there an implicit bias? Schools facing high rates of exclusionary discipline rates must research the underlying causes. "Significant interaction term suggests that schools need to consider the combination of structure and support. . . . Schools in which the students experience neither a strong sense of support by teachers nor high expectations of academic achievement appear to be most vulnerable" (Cornell et al., 2011, p. 929). In a hierarchical regression analysis, the research results of Cornell et al. (2011) showed characteristics of structure and support in interaction with each other, as correlated with schoolwide suspension rates for Black and White students and with the gap between Black and White suspension rates.

Building relationships is not easy. Some teachers find it very difficult. They may be strong in academic pedagogy but lack the skills needed in building relationships. Blood and Thorsborne (2013) believe that teachers need to facilitate and nurture a healthy classroom environment, one conducive to learning and includes reaching students at a personal level and allowing students to learn from their mistakes. Implementing practices to help build a positive school community by the faculty and staff not only help create a positive school culture but also eliminate the discipline procedures that are punitive in nature and create a student-centered learning climate (Bryk et al., 2010).

SEL. The US Department of Education (DOE), in conjunction with the Every Student Succeeds Act, created guidelines for schools to consider SEL practices to help harness student behavior in order to curtail exclusionary discipline. SEL processes, practices, and procedures are fundamental in avoiding lifelong effects impacting our school-to-prison pipeline and produce a more inclusive disciplinary reform strategy (Fergus & Gregory, 2017). This reform would "help develop self-discipline, and social emotional efficacy and enable students to improve and correct inappropriate and unskillful behaviors" (Fergus & Gregory, 2017, p. 112).

RPs. Developing a safe and caring environment for students, in support of their academic efforts, is a goal for many schools (Vaandeering, 2014). In recent studies, RPs are being used across the nation to transform schools from implementing a punitive approach to a more supportive, caring, and relationship-building approach. Unlike traditional school discipline, restorative approaches have helped ameliorate a school culture into a safer and caring one. Schools need to rethink the punitive approach to discipline practices; as Clawson et al. (2016) note, "as a result, policymakers are seeking alternatives to current discipline practices that (a) reduce the reliance on school exclusion and (b) reduce the overrepresentation of ethnic minorities in the discipline system" (p. 326).

RPs in schools allow students to focus on building relationships that allow for strong connections and responsibilities to self and others (Clawson et al., 2016). RPs generally follow a problem-solving approach that allows all those affected to work collaboratively to have a voice. This allows students to express their emotions and reactions, ultimately avoiding possible exclusionary discipline consequences (Clawson et al., 2016). Although the use of restorative practices has emerged as of late, more research must be conducted to confirm the results of the use of restorative practice.

An approach to restorative practice can be conducted through restorative circles and conferences with SEL opportunities. When a discipline-oriented incident occurs, the person with the infraction should be given an opportunity to reflect on their actions. Although more research on the circle approach is needed, Clawson et al. (2016) state that these types of reflections enhance "students' self-awareness, self-management, social awareness, relationship skills, and responsible decision-making. . . . In restorative justice, those affected by an infraction come together to identify how people were affected by the incident. Together, they decide how to repair the harm" (p. 327).

In Clawson et al. (2016), regression models for the number of defiance referrals found that "degree of restorative practice implementation was linked to the quality of teacher-student relationships, which confirms the well-established relationship between fidelity of implementation and student outcomes" (p. 343). The use of RPs must be enveloped into the school system "as a long-term and continual process, rather than simply a tool kit" (Hahn et al., 2020, p. 38). The overarching goal of an RP approach is to build healthy relationships and repair the relationships that have caused harm, whether in the community or in the school building. Sometimes what happens in the community resounds in the school building (Silverman & Mee, 2018).

Upon completion of the planning phase, the School Culture Design Team set about to implement SEL and Restorative Practices as an intervention. Due to timing constraints, there was overlap in the Study and Do phases of the PDSA cycle.

The Do Phase

During the do phase, an assistant principal (AP) was assigned to support the school culture design team. The campus sought to make changes to the entire school system and to enhance the SEL opportunities. Figure 3.2 highlights a fishbone diagram developed with the design team when examining discipline outcomes.

After identifying possible causes, a driver diagram was created to illustrate primary and secondary drivers, change ideas, and measures to address the aim of improving school culture by decreasing exclusionary discipline actions and improving student access to classroom learning opportunities. Figure 3.3 illustrates the driver diagram that was generated during the SEL professional learning community (PLC).

Based on the fishbone and driver diagrams, the recommended intervention consisted of the following components:

- the SEL coordinator
- the SEL curriculum
- embedded professional development
- mindfulness suite
- RPs
- the expansion of SEL personnel

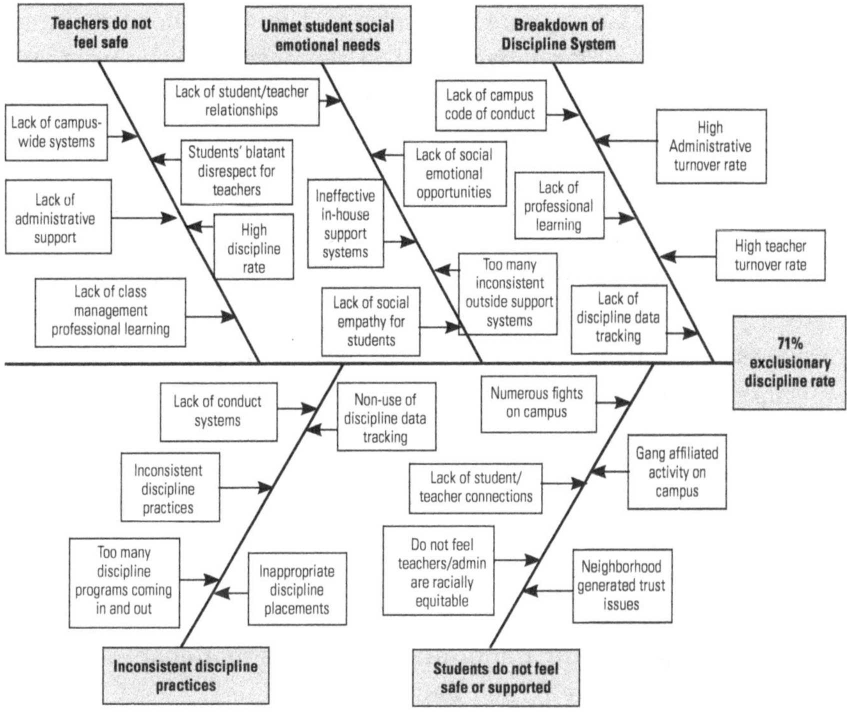

Figure 3.2. Discipline Fishbone Diagram

AIM	Primary Drivers	Secondary Drivers	Change Ideas	Measures
	Targets SEL/RP Practice	Relevant SEL/RP programming with teacher/administrators	Revise SEL/RP teacher/ administrator driven practices	Professional Development Administrator/ Teacher Attendance
Decrease Exclusionary Discipline Campus-wide	Campus Support	Relevant SEL/RP model programming campus-wide	Implement campus induction SEL/RP program	Anonymous Surveys (ESF, UTeach, AISD TELL)
	Address Discipline Concerns	Increase SEL/RP opportunities	Prioritize SEL/RP opportunities/practice	5LAB - Discipline Data (ISS, OSS, total), Attendance Data
	Address discipline practices	Increase teacher/administrator input on decisions	Develop SEL/RP shared model	Administrator/teacher Interviews
	Address teacher working conditions	Increase teacher support	Develop onboarding and embedded PD	Teacher retention data

Figure 3.3. Primary Drivers for Improvement

A teacher was reassigned to serve as the SEL coordinator to oversee the daily work related to SEL. This coordinator helps create opportunities for both students and staff that help set the foundation for connectedness and compassion at the campus and better prepare students for interacting with others and their community.

The coordinator oversees the creation of SEL lesson plans for teachers to be added to their daily lessons. The lessons are based on the Collaborative for Academic, Social, and Emotional Learning (CASEL) curriculum and include lessons on self-awareness, social awareness, responsible decision-making, self-management, and relationship skills. This model helps make evidence-based SEL an integral part of the campus system and provides an opportunity to close the achievement gap.

The SEL coordinator has also created a "mindfulness suite" that is available to both teachers and students. This suite is a classroom that is available to both students and teachers, allowing both to utilize the space throughout the school day to recharge and self-regulate their thoughts using mindfulness activities that enable them to de-escalate and return to their daily routine.

To provide training and support to teachers, a second planning period was built into the master schedule to support the implementation of PLCs and provide professional development embedded into the school day for maximum participation. The planning period is used to support academic and SEL professional development, as well as time for teachers to examine student data.

Campus-based SEL/RP training opportunities were developed using the CASEL (2018) and Circle Forward (Boyes-Watson et al., 2015) restorative models to allow both the adults and the students to understand the practices being instilled at the campus level. Expert trainers could train at the most basic level to a more advanced level, adjusting as needed to provide extensive support. In other words, training could be produced at a large-group level or with small groups or even a one-to-one basis depending on need. Training was produced at a larger level to ensure all participants understood the basic knowledge and skills needed to use SEL and RP appropriately. Once the basics were taught, continuous training was embedded to ensure practices, strategies and opportunities for support were maintained and implemented accordingly. Practices involving both adults and students in SEL allowed them to understand and manage their emotions inside of the classroom and out. Practices were embedded into teacher lesson plans to facilitate transforming training into weekly practice. The practices enabled students to show empathy toward others and establish positive relationships, which, in turn, helped them make responsible decisions that would not impact others negatively.

The implementation of restorative practices was led by the social services partner and the school coordinator. Providing RP opportunities with both adults and students help build the understanding of the basic values of self and others (Public School 155, 2020). These opportunities define protocols that bring together those who have caused harm or have been directly harmed, with a nonbiased advocate leading the helm. The opportunities, as shown in Figure 3.2, allow those involved to reach an agreement resulting in a positive outcome. RP opportunities also drive the reaction from a punitive approach to a more supportive approach. As shown in Figure 3.2, these practices are taught in hopes that they are not only used within their school community but can also be transitioned into life experiences.

SEL/RP coaches teach teachers the strategies that can easily be embedded into their everyday lessons. These strategies are taught, modeled, and coached to ensure the teachers understand the practice. The teachers can then turn the strategy around to be used in the classroom with students. Teachers can then embed the strategies in their lessons or can use the strategies when situational opportunities arise. Students, in turn, can use the strategies in everyday life with their friends, family, and community.

While the implementation process occurs, there are four main short-term outcomes in which the initiative reviews: (1) increased number of students and staff who understand the code of conduct, SEL practices, and RP opportunities; (2) increased number of students and staff participating in SEL/RP opportunities; (3) increased use of SEL practices and RP opportunities by both students and staff; and (4) increased support for student leadership opportunities in SEL/RP. As the initiative continues, there are four main medium areas to analyze in reaching the goal of reducing exclusionary discipline consequences: (1) a decrease in the number of student fights, (2) a decrease in the number of students walking out of class, (3) an increase in positive relationships between students and teachers, and (4) an increase in understanding of the code of conduct and the adoption of SEL practices and RP opportunities.

Other participating staff included two designated campus counselors, whose primary role is to implement a comprehensive developmental guidance and counseling program. They help promote student success through a focus on academic achievement, prevention and intervention activities, advocacy, and social/emotional and career development to meet the needs of the students and the community. There was a need to expand the number of SEL personnel on campus and the partnership invested in an additional six CIS caseworkers and two grant-funded caseworkers to meet the nonacademic needs of our students. The average caseload of the SEL team is 200-plus students.

The Study Phase

During the study phase of the cycle, data were reviewed to examine the impact of the intervention on school culture and indirectly on student achievement. This included retention rates among school personnel and student enrollment overall as well as daily attendance percentages. Discipline referrals were analyzed and compared to previous years.

The students' attendance rates have consistently been low. In 2017–2018, the campus saw its all-time low of 91.07%, seeing a fluctuation between 91% and 93% in the last 5 years. In 2019–2020, the campus reached its all-time high of 95.3% (see Figure 3.4).

The campus also had the highest discipline counts in the district for the last 3 consecutive years before 2018–2019, with an all-time high in 2016–2017, with 2,586 total discipline referrals. However, the 2019–2020 academic year closed with only 518 discipline referrals with the use of SEL and RP opportunities (see Figure 3.5).

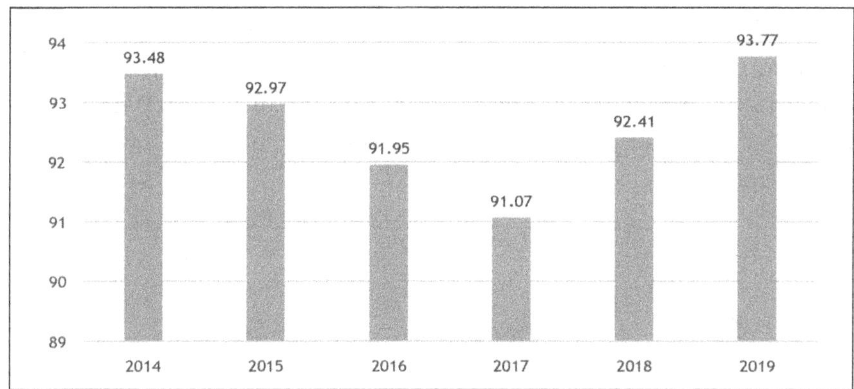

Source: School District Database

Figure 3.4. Annual Attendance Percentage

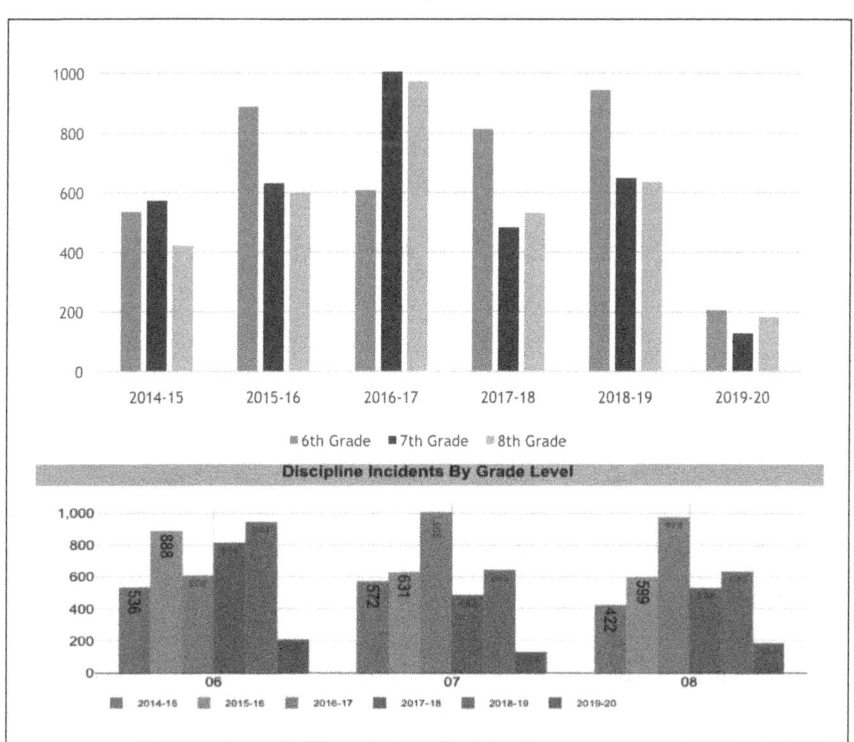

Source: School District Database
Note: this table depicts the discipline rate at school from 2014 – 2019-2020.

Figure 3.5. Discipline Incidents by Grade Level

OSS and ISS choices held the highest form of consequences on the campus, which was populated by 20% of the students on campus. In 2017, the campus had an all-time high of 761 offenses of OSS and ISS combined. In 2020, the campus had an all-time low with 172 combined (see Figure 3.6).

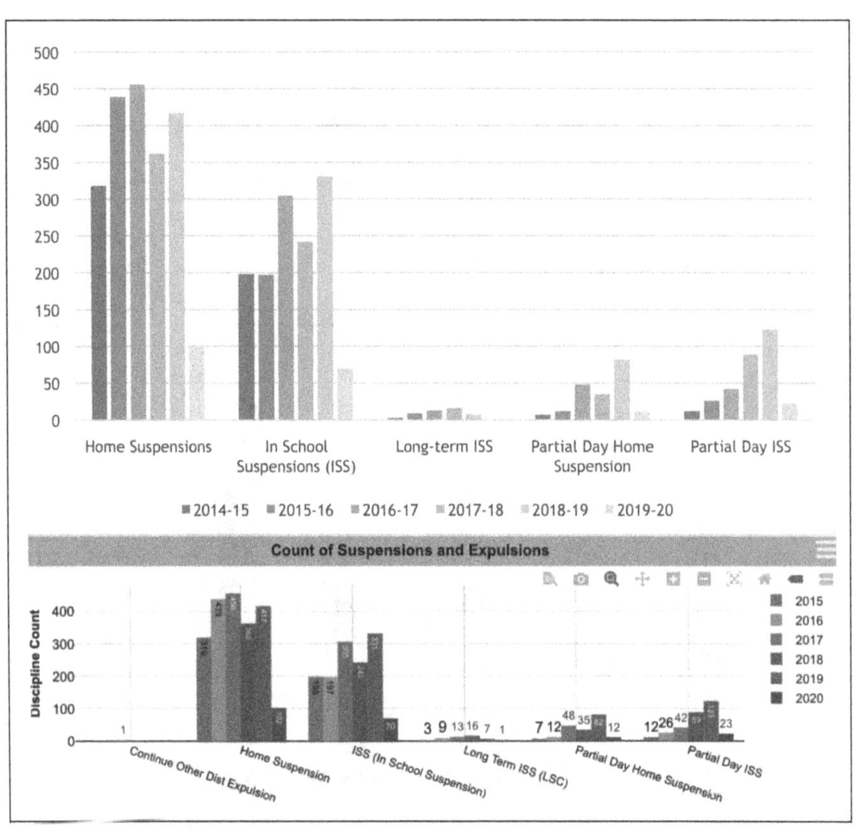

Source: School District Database

Figure 3.6. Count of Suspensions and Expulsions

The campus has experienced significant opportunity gaps that could account for lower student achievement in core courses. In 2019, the campus did not meet accountability standards based on the criteria of the state accountability system. Figure 3.7 shows significant low scores on the 2019 state assessments. As implementation of PBL/PrBL, SEL, and RP practice began, benchmark scores in December 2019 began to see a significant increase on the approaches and meets categories (see Figure 3.7.) Although the state cancelled the 2020 state assessments due to the COVID Pandemic, the campus had calculated a projected passing rate based on their December 2019 benchmark test scores.

		State Assessment Spring 2019		Benchmark Fall 2019		Benchmark Spring 2020	
Grade	Subject	% Appr	% Meet	% Appr	% Meet	% Appr	% Meet
6	Math	42	8	32	5	66	25
7	Math	15	2	23	3	63	15
8	Math	38	7	24	7	33	4
8	Algebra	97	50	75	19	88	18
6	ELA	28	5	21	10	50	18
7	ELA	39	13	14	3	46	14
7	Writing	32	9	n/a	n/a	63	28
8	ELA	57	18	24	3	48	24
8	Science	53	25	37	7	57	31
8	Social Studies	37	10	34	2	77	39

Source: 2019 State Education Agency Database

Figure 3.7. Student Achievement Scores in Tested Subjects

The campus has consistently seen a high turnaround in campus staff, with 2018–2019 employing a completely new mathematics staff. In 2018, 36 new teachers had to be hired. In 2020, there were only 11 teacher vacancies, with the math department still seeing the highest turnover rate (see Table 3.1).

Table 3.1. Personnel Retention

Year	2018–19	2019–20	2020–21
Teachers	33%	52%	80%
Administration	25%	100%	100%
Counselors	100%	100%	100%

Source: School District Human Resources

As a partner of the campus, the university-affiliated partner conducted internal polling of students and staff for program evaluaton purposes. These surveys ask questions derived from the SEL/RP model. The results help the campus organize future planning of interventions needed using PDSA cycles. From 2018 to 2019, student results show they feel that teachers (see Figure 3.8) and administrators (see Figure 3.9) care about them.

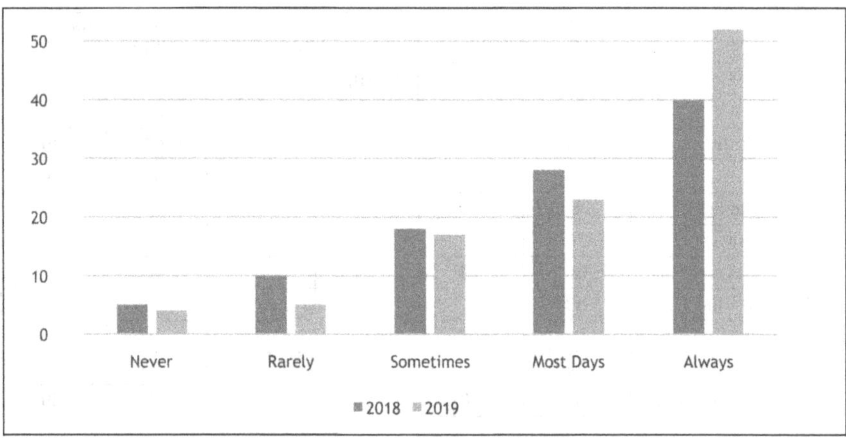

Source: University-affiliated Annual Survey of Students

Figure 3.8. Percentage of Students Who Believe Teachers Care About Them

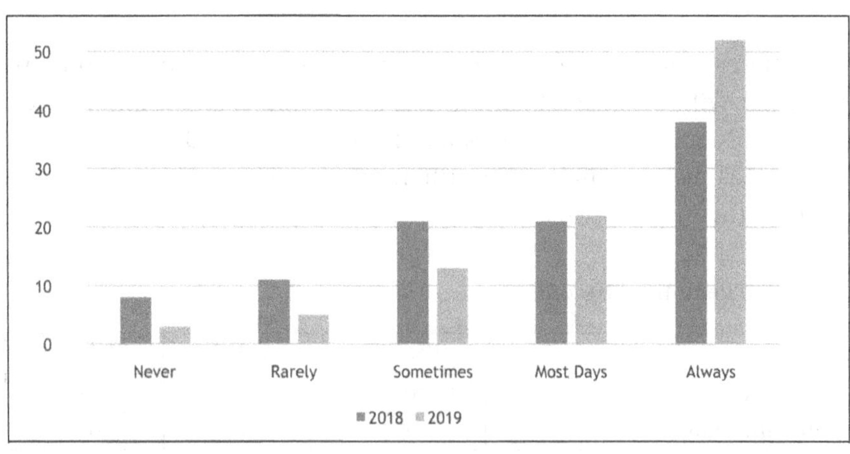

Source: University-affiliated Annual Survey of Students

Figure 3.9. Percentage of Students Who Believe Administrators Care About Them

Conclusion and Discussion

Initial results show that both SEL strategies and RPs are having a significant impact resulting in positive nonacademic outcomes as well as positive academic outcomes. These data also demonstrate that a significant impact on school culture and student behaviors can result in a relatively short time. Exclusionary discipline rates have declined with the implementation of both SL and RP approaches. There is still more work to be done. One of our goals for the 2021–2022 academic year is to achieve 100% implementation of RP by all teachers. Some teachers are still uncomfortable with the approach. That said, the significant climb in attendance, the drop in discipline referrals, and the gains in academics are compelling local evidence that the approaches are working. The design team is also documenting promising and best practices that can be shared with other schools experiencing similar challenge. As described, personnel retention has improved dramatically and that has also provided public relations opportunities that are helping to repair the reputation of the school. In 2020, the campus received the honor of having the district Middle School Teacher of the Year and the Teacher of the Year. The teacher was selected by an external panel. In addition, in 2021, the campus received three district nominations: Principal of the Year, Assistant Principal of the Year, and Administrative Assistant of the Year. Improvements are becoming recognized at the local and district levels.

Discussion Questions

1. What preparations are needed by partners who are selected to transform a turnaround school with a focus on equity?
2. What are the challenges and opportunities of replacing teachers to address a turnaround model of improvement that focuses on equity?
3. What changes would you like to see in the culture of your school, particularly related to equity and school discipline policies?

References

Baker, T. L., Chung, C., Hughes, R. L., Sheya, A., Skiba, R. J., & Trachok, M. (2014). Parsing disciplinary disproportionality: Contributions of infraction, student, and school characteristics to out-of-school suspension and expulsion. *American Educational Research Journal, 51*(4), 640–670. https://journals-sagepub-com.ezproxy.uttyler.edu/doi/pdf/10.3102/0002831214541670

Blood, P., & Thorsborne, M. (2013). *Implementing restorative practices in schools: A practical guide to transforming school communities.* Jessica Kingsley Publishers.

Boyes-Watson, C., Pranis, K., & Riestenberg, N. (2015). *Circle forward: Building a restorative school community.* Living Justice Press

Bryk, A. S., Sebring, P. B., Allensworth, E., Easton, J. Q., & Luppescu, S. (2010). *Organizing schools for improvement: Lessons from Chicago.* University of Chicago Press. https://doi.org/10.7208/chicago/9780226078014.001.0001

Collaborative for Academic, Social, and Emotional Learning. (2018). *Core SEL competencies.* https://CASEL.org/core-competencies/

Clawson, K., Davis, A., Gerewitz, J., & Gregory, A. (2016). The promise of restorative practices to transform teacher–student relationships and achieve equity in school discipline. *Journal of Educational and Psychological Consultation, 26*(4), 325–353. https://doi.org/10.1080/10474412.2014.929950

Cornell, D., Fan, X., & Gregory. A (2011). The relationship of school structure and support to suspension rates for Black and White high school students. *American Educational Research Journal, 48*(4), 904–934. https://doi.org/10.3102/002831 21139853

Domitrovich, C., Durlak, J., Greenberg, M., & Weissberg, R. (2017). Social and emotional learning as a public health approach to education. *The Future of Children, 27*(1), 13–32. https://doi.org/10.1353/foc.2017.0001

Durlak, J. A., Dymnicki, A. B., Schellinger, K., Taylor, R. D., & Weissberg, R. P. (2011). The impact of enhancing students' social and emotional learning: A meta-analysis of school-based universal interventions. *Child Development, 82*(1), 405–432. https://doi.org/10.1111/j.1467-8624.2010.01564.x

Fergus, E., & Gregory, A. (2017). Social and emotional learning and equity in school discipline. *The Future of Children, 27*(1), 117–136. https://doi.org/10.1353/foc.2017.0006

Hahn, M., Recchia, H., Velez, G., & Wainryb, C. (2020, October). Rethinking responses to youth rebellion: Recent growth and development of restorative practices in schools. *Current Opinion in Psychology, 35,* 36–40. https://doi.org/10.1016/j.copsyc.2020.02.011

Hewitt, D. T., Kim, C. Y., & Losen, D. J. (2010). *The school-to prison pipeline: Structuring legal reform.* New York University Press.

Milner, H. R. (2012). Beyond a test score. *Journal of Black Studies, 43*(6), 693–718. https://doi.org/10.1177/0021934712442539

Public School 155. (2020). *Forecast5analytics: decision solution supports for K–12.* https://www.forecast5analytics.com/

Riddle, T., & Sinclair, S. (2019). Racial disparities in school-based disciplinary actions are associated with county-level rates of racial bias. *Proceedings of the National Academy of Sciences of the United States of America, 116*(17), 8255–8260. https://doi.org/10.1073/pnas.1808307116

Silverman, J., & Mee, M. (2018). Using restorative practices to prepare teachers to meet the needs of young adolescents. *Education Sciences, 8*(3), 131. https://doi.org/10.3390/educsci8030131

U.S. Department of Education. (2009). *The American Recovery and Reinvestment Act of 2009: Saving and creating jobs and reforming education.* https://www.govinfo.gov/content/pkg/BILLS-111hr1enr/pdf/BILLS-111hr1enr.pdf

Valdebenito, S., Eisner, M., Farrington, D. P., Ttofi, M. M., & Sutherland, A. (2018). School-based interventions for reducing disciplinary school exclusion. *Campbell Systematic Reviews, 14.* https://www-proquest-com.ezproxy.uttyler.edu/docview/d2058234786?accountid=7123

Vaandeering, D. (2014). Implementing restorative justice practice in schools: What pedagogy reveals. *Journal of Peace Education, 11*(1), 64–80. https://doi.org/10.1080/17400201.2013.794335

Valdebenito, S. Eisner, M., Farrington, D., Ttofi, M., & Sutherland, A. (2018). School-based interventions for reducing disciplinary school exclusion: A systematic review. *Campbell Systematic Reviews, 14*(1), i–216. https://doi.org/10.4073/csr.2018.1

A Pandemic and a Wildfire Evacuation: Serving Historically Underserved Students During Disasters

RYAN CARPENTER, BENJAMIN HARGRAVE,
AND KATHLEEN OROPALLO

Like many schools nationwide, children in our district experience adverse childhood experiences (ACEs) proportional to the national averages. Nationwide, approximately 38% of our students have experienced some type of traumatic event (Mendelson et al., 2015). ACEs are proportionate across racial and geographic groups (Whiteside-Mansell et al., 2019); children living in rural areas are at greater risk for adverse experiences, and children living in poverty within rural communities face unique challenges (Whiteside-Mansell et al., 2019). Events such as the pandemic and a local wildfire compounded and increased the effects of trauma with students already struggling with ACEs. The pandemic is also creating trauma through the sustained uncertainty and ongoing risk from ambiguous loss (Woods, 2020).

When a student is triggered, their responses to trauma manifest in behaviors that adults describe as "disengaged," "dysregulated," and "lacking perseverance"; the behaviors impede student learning. Without proper training and understanding, phrases such as "this is a *will* problem and not a skill problem" can often be heard by educators engaging with students whose behaviors impede learning. Unqualified diagnoses and misinterpretations of behaviors can lead to escalated behaviors and inconsistent support for the very students who need it the most. Professional development that increases knowledge in trauma-informed and restorative practices and helps staff identify barriers to student learning while practicing additional engagement strategies enhances student outcomes and reduces already existing educational disparities.

Context of the Estacada School District

This case study describes the improvement work of the Estacada School District (ESD) as the leaders used improvement science (IS) processes to develop collective efficacy with faculty and staff during the dual crises of the pandemic and a wildfire evacuation.

ESD is a rural public school district in the Portland metropolitan area of Oregon. ESD serves students in kindergarten through Grade 12 with two K–5 elementary schools, one Grades 6–8 middle school, and one Grades 9–12 high school (Carpenter & Peterson, 2019). The student population consists of more than 1,800 students and is 80% White, 17% Hispanic/Latino, 1% African American, 1% Asian, and 1% American Indian. Fifty percent of students qualify for free and reduced-price lunch, 10% were classified as English-language learners, while 16% receive special education services.

Estacada Middle School (EMS) enrolls 420 students supported by 37 employees, 20 of whom are certified classroom teachers. At 25%, EMS has the highest percentage of students in any ESD school receiving special education services. Principal Benjamin Hargrave has served as the leader of EMS for 4 years, and under his leadership, EMS embarked on a transformational leadership effort focused on a system-wide implementation of a DuFour model professional learning communities (PLCs) for all grade- and content-level teaching teams in the school (DuFour et al., 2016), eventually using the PLCs to conduct IS efforts.

Several school structures exist in the ESD to encourage and support teachers in their development of curriculum and project design, including 8 days of professional development training and 2 hours every Friday to conduct PLCs. During this time, teachers regularly collaborate on student learning data and design intervention strategies together to improve student engagement and close learning gaps. EMS also uses Plan–Do–Study–Act (PDSA) continuous improvement cycles to create systems to efficiently and effectively address root cause problems and measure improvements. For the last 2 years, the ESD has partnered with Studer Education, a national consulting firm, to develop an evidence-based leadership framework (Studer, 2003) to further support the development of organizational excellence matching the culture of the ESD.

The Problem of Practice: Addressing Equity Concerns During Rapid Change and Uncertainty

Problems of practice are directly observable, actionable, and connect to a broader strategy of improvement (Elmore et al., 2004). ESD began the 2020 school year under complex learning conditions, amid a pandemic, a local wildfire, and rapidly shifting COVID-19 guidelines from state and federal agencies. The system had responded to the pandemic by successfully shifting to distance learning in the spring, but now their community had also faced a wildfire that displaced 100% of families and staff living within our boundaries. Recovery efforts once again placed basic needs ahead of all else. The district remained committed to serving students, families, and employees and kept a relentless focus on continually striving to provide the highest quality of education despite these conditions.

EMS did not want to lose sight of these district priorities and its larger aim of establishing high-quality learning experiences and opportunities for students. Additional subpar external conditions were impacting the inconsistent status of students' learning conditions due to the wildfire's disruption in power, a lack of access to the internet, and the displacement of students, families, and staff affected by the fire. Early in the process, EMS needed to identify who was affected and what barriers these external conditions had created for students, many already at risk in the system. EMS began to develop collective efficacy with faculty and staff which helped to focus on two actions to address the barriers brought on by the pandemic and fire:

- targeted wellness checks system for vulnerable students and
- ensuring engaging, high levels of academic learning.

Why IS Strategies Worked During the Crises

IS seeks to answer the question, "What works, for whom, and under what conditions?" In our case, addressing this question required that we adopt an improvement mindset and engage in inquiries related to our classrooms and schools. Six principles have been identified that are helpful to guide IS work in education (Bryk et al., 2015). These are (1) make the work problem-specific and user-centered, (2) focus on variation in performance, (3) see the system that produces the current outcomes, (4) you cannot improve at scale what you cannot measure, (5) use disciplined inquiry to drive improvement, and (6) accelerate learning through networked communities. IS provides educators with methods and tools to engage in inquiry around improving teaching and learning, collaborating to share promising practices, and learning from variation and scale practices that lead to improvement (Bryk et al., 2015).

IS replaces top-down reform initiatives that strip educators of their professionalism with a localized strategy for improvement and situates control over the educator's practice closest to the practitioner. Barriers are identified, problems of practice are developed, and change ideas are implemented on a localized scale, using quick, iterative PDSA cycles. Data for improvement are collected to determine whether the change idea should be abandoned, adapted, or adopted. The goal is to improve but to use early failures as a way to learn quickly. Once we have evidence that a practice works in one context, it can be shared through collaborative learning communities to be tested in other contexts. In this way, those closest to the problem are instrumental in the problem-solving process, and improvement can occur rapidly, in a specific context, and then expanded at scale. In our case, our PDSA cycles had to be conducted within 24-hour cycles.

We learned what was working in one school and adapted that strategy to implement in another school, *or* we abandoned a strategy and tried another strategy during our 24-hour PDSA cycles.

The Need to Promote Collaboration and Build Collective Efficacy

Change often comes from a desire to improve. Isolation has been identified as a significant barrier to the implementation of effective improvement efforts (Eisener, 1992). Donohoo et al. (2018) write, "When teams of educators believe they have the ability to make a difference, exciting things can happen in a school" (p. 78). Collective efficacy yields significantly higher levels of academic achievement because educators share a common belief in their combined ability to influence student outcomes (Bandura, 1993). Promoting collaboration can be a powerful process on the road to improvement, but when collaboration evolves into collective efficacy, the impact can achieve far greater results because individuals share a collective commitment to each other and the work. Hattie's (2008) meta-analysis also supports the impact of collective teacher efficacy. Ranked high on his list of factors that contribute to student achievement, he found that collective efficacy had more than double the effect of prior achievement on learning and triple that of the effect of the home environment and family involvement (Hattie, 2008). Although we have not conducted rigorous correlation studies, teachers' feedback indicates that IS processes and tools contributed to their sense of their collective efficacy during our wildfire and pandemic crises.

Our Focus on Transformative Socio-Emotional Learning (SEL), Equity, and Restorative Practices

Although much is written about SEL and about equity, a new body of research examines critical linkages through the work of transformative SEL. Transformative SEL's aim is to establish educational equity by creating equitable learning environments that produce equitable outcomes for children and young adults (Jagers et al., 2019).

Educational equity occurs when every student of every race, gender, ethnicity, language, disability, family, or income background has what they need when they need it (Council of Chief State School Officers, 2017). The transformative SEL research posits that collective teacher efficacy, educators' collective ability to promote student learning, and the lessons we have learned from civic efficacy are essential to inequity transformation to foster SEL growth with students in schools (Jagers et al., 2019). Transformative SEL is described thus:

> Transformative SEL connotes a process whereby students and teachers build strong, respectful relationships founded on an appreciation of similarities and differences, learn to critically examine root causes of inequity, and develop collaborative solutions to community and societal problems. (Jagers et al., 2019, p. 131)

To establish equitable learning environments, practitioners must also consider examining bias, committing to eliminating past practices that produced inequities, and creating new inclusive learning environments to support each child (Smith et al., 2017). The Transformative SEL Report recommends that schools focus on the following intentions when supporting students from diverse cultural backgrounds:

- cultivating a caring and supportive environment,
- explicit instruction of SEL competencies (CASEL.org),
- multiple supports for individual students, and
- instructional strategies that use collaborative and inquiry-based learning opportunities (Jagers et al., 2019)

The Collaborative for Academic Social and Emotional Learning (CASEL) developed Equity Elaborations that align with its five competencies: self-awareness, self-management, social awareness, relationship skills, and reasonable decision-making (Jagers et al., 2019). The Equity Elaborations were designed to emphasize communal values, positive ethnic-racial identity, and key components of self-awareness. The addition of the Equity Elaborations to its five SEL competencies helped provide pathways for constructive, collective efficacy and buffer children and youth from the "negative impacts of internalized, interpersonal, and institutional oppression" (Jagers et al., 2019, p. 168). This is particularly relevant to schools' focus on decreasing inequities and supporting students' SEL development.

Creating inclusive environments also means supporting students who are currently or who have experienced trauma and ACEs. Historically underserved students who are living in poverty experience living conditions that result in toxic stress (Centers for Disease Control and Prevention, n.d.). For students who have faced ACEs, many also have a mistrust of adults (Jagers et al., 2019). As a result of this mistrust, educators need professional training with trauma-informed practices to understand student reticence and behaviors that often manifest in children with adverse childhood experiences. Trauma-informed practices involve first creating a sense of safety in the learning environment, as well as promoting trust between the student and adult.

Managing Change Through Agile Leadership

Although it would not know the later impact of its ability to lead during the wildfire and pandemic crises, the leadership development that ESD began in 2018 as a means of operationalizing its strategic plan and aligning goals, values, and processes contributed to its ability to lead through the crises. Two years prior to the crises, Superintendent Ryan Carpenter engaged senior and site-based administrators in Studer Education's Evidence Based Leadership[SM] (EBL) framework and the Nine Principles for Organizational Excellence® (Studer & Pilcher, 2015), which prepared the district to face its numerous simultaneous challenges. The EBL helped ESD align its goals, behaviors, and processes that operationalized the priorities of its strategic plan. To do so, senior leaders learned critical behaviors such as leader rounding, the rollout of data results, aligned action plans, and building a culture around improvement by engaging in regular expressions of gratitude and recognition. These practices helped them implement and test change ideas through continuous improvement cycles, feedback loops driven by leader rounding and survey administration to monitor progress, and nine leadership processes that drive results (Studer & Pilcher, 2015). The early commitment to organizational excellence created critical dispositions that contributed to agility across the system and allowed them to adapt quickly through daily PDSA cycles to manage their response to the simultaneous crises of the pandemic and wildfire.

Identifying Vulnerable Students During Virtual Schooling

EMS knew it needed to identify vulnerable students and to adjust its practices to meet students' needs. The leaders determined they would begin with online attendance as a measure, believing that if students were not attending, they might be vulnerable. The school recognized that the traditional methods of attendance did not fit in a virtual learning paradigm. EMS made the decision to define attendance by two-way communication. The intent was to ensure that students responded to the teacher's cues, questions, and feedback. However, "two-way communication" turned out to be a low standard for identifying effective teacher instruction, student learning, and high outcomes for student success.

Using "rounding," a simple, yet powerful, check-in tool borrowed from the health care field that builds relationships and allows educators to monitor and validate their theories of change (Studer & Pilcher, 2015). Rounding gives improvement stakeholders a way to generate a feedback loop around the changes they seek (Studer, 2003) and provides data regarding whether the change ideas were leading to the outcomes they were trying to achieve. Rounding revealed a common theme: Staff were more concerned about student engagement than attendance, and as a result, EMS adjusted its criteria to include more indicators for identifying vulnerable students and recognized that they needed to clearly define engagement.

EMS's improvement team developed an engagement continuum to provide more guidance to teachers and staff for identifying student engagement. The continuum measured the degree of engagement by examining *how* students participated in the learning. Using data from the continuum helped teachers redesign lessons, helped administrators provide specific feedback to families when contacting them, and allowed the administration to determine which teachers were in need of support with virtual instruction. The engagement continuum described four levels of engagement (see Figure 4.1).

Not attending	Participating	Completing	Engaging
The student is missing, or the student has only sent "I'm here" with no other communication or efforts.	The student is present in zoom sessions or attempts a task within 48 hours AND the participation shows limited-partial-to-full effort in schoolwork but is incomplete.	The student completes the standard or accommodated schoolwork in its entirety to the best of her/his academic ability (although, it may not be measured proficient).	The student responds to feedback while completing the schoolwork or after it is turned in. The student shows evidence of perseverance and is progressing toward or is at proficiency.

Note: This engagement continuum describes four levels of engagement used to identify vulnerable students in need of mediation or intervention.

Figure 4.1. Engagement Continuum

All EMS staff were then asked to complete the engagement continuum. The engagement continuum results showed that overall student engagement was low, and many students were not attending. The results also validated earlier inquiry from the student attendance reports and the feedback leaders obtained from teachers during rounding.

The use of the continuum to identify students and families in need of support provided EMS with the data it needed to begin to cascade the work across all faculty and staff. Grade-level teams were formed and worked together to consolidate the data from the engagement continuum survey to identify vulnerable students by grade level. Next, counselors, administrators, and teachers identified specific students to reach out to and to make personal phone calls to throughout the academic week. Staff began with a small number of students with whom to make a connection. Over the next several weeks, the grade-level team monitored the improvement, maintenance, or regression of each student's engagement. Table 4.1 illustrates EMS's improvement over 3 weeks by grade level using a simple dashboard.

Table 4.1. Student Engagement

Targeted engagement continuum indicators	6th Grade			7th Grade			8th Grade		
	# Students not attending	# Students Participating and not completing	# Students fully engaged	# Students not attending	# Students Participating and not completing	# Students fully engaged	# Students not attending	# Students Participating and not completing	# Students fully engaged
Week 6	20	9	N/A	13	13	N/A	20	22	N/A
Week 7	18	8	20	19	6	22	17	9	25
Week 8	14	4	28	18	11	23	12	14	34

Note: The table shows the last three weeks of the school year after having developed the grade-level rubrics.

The trends in each column elicited reflection from the staff to determine what next steps must be taken to increase engagement in virtual learning.

Early Learning, Engagement, and Care Connections

It was important to harvest and celebrate the early success as the school demonstrated increased engagement with its vulnerable population. After additional reflection, the team learned through the phone calls and personal contacts that many families needed access to materials and resources such as personal devices and access to the internet that were necessary for the students to be successful in a virtual school environment. Learning from this first PDSA cycle prompted the grade-level team, the team leads, and counselors to implement "care and connection" visits to the home of every student who had not been attending any classes for 2 consecutive weeks. However, during the wildfire, care-and-connection visits to student homes were suspended as the entire city had been evacuated. Instead, Principal Hargrave provided each staff member a list of 10 families whom they were asked to personally call on the phone, with students and families in the moderate- to high-risk groups called first (see Table 4.2).

Table 4.2. Contact With Vulnerable Families During Wildfire Evacuation

Students/families in high risk	Student /families moderate risk	Total number of families reached
Includes families who • lost homes, property, animals • were unable to secure shelter during the evacuation	Includes families who evacuated and • stayed in a camping trailer/tent • sheltered at an unknown property • abandoned animals • no access to internet or power	120 families contacted with personalized phone messages 200 calls leading to email follow-ups or messages
		320 Families

Principal Hargrave also provided staff with specific questions and call conversation protocols to facilitate the conversation between the families and the staff. The focus of these calls was to ask households specifically about student safety and to determine what resources were needed to reengage with learning so that the school might provide these supports when evacuated students and families returned to Estacada after the wildfire. Within 2 days, EMS successfully contacted 320 families. When EMS had completed conversations with each family, staff members published notes for the counseling and administrative teams to review. These notes helped EMS determine which families were the most vulnerable and most in need and, thus, a priority to visit once the city lifted the wildfire evacuation orders.

Principal Hargrave's staff and teachers were able to make data- and trauma-informed instructional choices about pacing and rigor after having these conversations. Teachers and staff felt much more confident that they had developed a strategy for outreach and could make differentiated decisions regarding instruction and emotional support for their students in the aftermath of the fire and even while the pandemic still strained the system.

The process of implementing "compassion calls" highlighted the strengths of the school's background in trauma-informed instruction. Once students were allowed back to our virtual school, many families and students received individualized attention. The "by-student, by-need" approach led to a reduction of stress and anxiety about school. However, we also learned that some staff did not attempt to make the compassion calls because of their lack of confidence, discomfort, or lack of knowledge of how best to communicate with families, which led to some families not receiving resources or receiving inaccurate information.

PDSA Cycles to Support Teacher Instructional Decisions

As we began to address student and family support, we also had to work simultaneously on supporting our teachers and instructional staff as they navigated the virtual environment. Instructionally, many teachers struggled to settle into the virtual setting. In addition to the regular professional demands of the teaching position, all teachers were introduced to a new learning management system and a virtual platform used to virtually connect to students and provide instruction. In order to ensure that there was no learning loss and each student had access to high-quality learning opportunities, the PLCs began implementing two strategic actions: (1) Each team committed to actions that supported a culture of collective efficacy, a shared set of beliefs and values about the quality and conditions for optimum learning, and their role in supporting this environment. (2) Teachers committed to shared ownership of their data used to support decisions for increasing student success. As part of each PLC improvement effort, teachers participated in PDSA cycles to test their ideas and strategic actions. In addition, teachers were asked to document their teacher action plans and identify strategic actions for engagement practices and instructional practices designed to support student success. PLCs were asked to review their shared values and student data weekly to validate, monitor, and adjust their actions.

As teachers participated in these cycles of improvement, they were able to identify what worked and make adjustments for strategies and ideas that did not. Engaging teachers in first-time PDSA cycles revealed how collective inquiry leads to collective responsibility and an alignment toward a common purpose. At first, PLC teams' strategic actions were too broad. When team members began to implement the action, they learned that their strategic action was not as specific as it should have been. They also learned that the action was not being implemented across the PLC team, therefore, not leading to the results they had intended. Teachers made growth in clearly articulating their strategic actions and their progress monitoring measures.

Despite being in a pandemic and surviving a wildfire, EMS's language arts (LA) PLC decided to focus on "writing with elaboration including citing textual evidence." Each teacher used the previous week's formative assessment to inform their virtual small-group teaching. To measure progress, each teacher was to tally the number of students attending in small-group instruction. After the first 30 days of implementing the strategic action, the team reviewed the data and discussed the outcomes. The team learned that they needed to be more purposeful when deciding which students to include in small-group teaching. One teacher was using small-group time to build relationships because the students had not demonstrated any output for providing textual evidence. Another teacher was using small-group time to teach conventions of quotations when citing textual evidence. And a third teacher was walking students through a reflection about their misconceptions regarding elaborating. All three teachers realized their misalignment and decided to be more specific: Small-group time will be focused on earning a measurement of 2 on the standard as students' textual evidence did not fully describe nor support the argument of the text.

The team also learned that they did not know whether their strategic action improved proficiency indicators. To resolve this issue, Principal Hargrave leveraged the district's resources and the "ELS Dashboard" to provided weekly updates about the increase or regression of student achievement. Teachers then saw in real time whether their actions led to improved outcomes for students. The ELA team, at the end of the 90-day cycle, reviewed the achievement of students within the specific writing standard. The data revealed that despite all teachers engaging in the same improvement strategy, students did not make progress. The team celebrated their collective efforts to implement a consistent plan and then abandoned the strategic action. In their particular context, the strategy proved to not work during distance learning, given the students' and teachers' strengths and weaknesses. Next, the team decided to adopt a new strategic action in order to achieve the school's goal.

Using Improvement Cycles and Aligned Actions to Combat Chronic Absenteeism

Grade-level PLC teams decided to focus on chronic absenteeism, which had begun to increase in the second month of school, as well as on how to improve the academic outcomes of students. Through the relationships we established with families, we learned how the rigors of the virtual instructional model impacted student mental health and wellness and their engagement in the learning model. We also learned that misconceptions and misinformation were being given from students to families. The grade-level teams and the PLCs worked collaboratively to ensure that the instructional, cognitive, and workload demands being put on students were appropriate for age, development, and context. The teams also developed a communication plan, through Facebook Live events, as well as within their instructional days, to clearly communicate the expectations to families and students.

After we tried a new change idea and adjusting our instructional model, and based on what we learned from communicating with families and the collaborative approach between the grade-level teams and the PLC teams, we made adjustments to our instructional model. After this adjustment in November, we experienced a decrease in student chronic absenteeism (see Table 4.3). With increased engagement in school, there were more opportunities for our PLC teams to execute their strategic actions and improve student outcomes.

Table 4.3. Percentage of Students Missing More Than 20% of the Day

Grade	Sept	Oct	Nov	Dec	Jan
6th	19%	33%	41%	29%	
7th	34%	47%	54%	36%	
8th	29%	60%	67%	40%	

Overcoming Sustained Uncertainty Through Connection and Care

ESD's relentless focus on providing high-quality learning opportunities in a remote environment amid the ongoing pandemic and wildfire evacuation made it clear we needed to operate with empathy, care, and connection. Employees, students, and families were experiencing ambiguous loss during a time of lasting uncertainty. Ambiguous loss is any loss that is unclear or lacks a resolution. This loss can be physical or psychological and often is discussed around unresolved death or tragic circumstances (Jagers et al., 2019)). The wildfire further exasperated the loss, but with a natural disaster, there is some resolution that eventually occurs. One year after its onset, the COVID-19 pandemic had not yet had any resolution; with that lack of resolution comes fatigue and stress, especially in communities of color and those living in poverty (Wedell-Wedellsborg, 2020). These circumstances reminded both district and school leadership that employees, families, and students needed to feel safe and connected during the disruption.

As ESD's leadership addressed the impact of the pandemic, they found ways to support employees as they remained committed to ensuring all students had access to high-quality learning. EMS's staff made strategic and heroic efforts to engage students in virtual learning; they put their students in the best position to improve academic outcomes. Boundaries between professional and private life became hard to balance since no teacher wanted any student to feel uncertainty or be unable to access learning support. Most teachers made themselves available to support students at all hours of the day. It was not just teachers who were exhausted. Students were also stretched in new ways and needed time to react and settle into the new learning routines of virtual school, especially because the fall started with students being taught new technology skills, being asked to manage time independently (without a bell), and were, for many for the first time, the initiators and participants in their learning rather than participants in their learning. Families managed full-time work with full-time classroom management. Many parents and guardians reported emotional outbursts from their students at home. Families also expressed burnout as well as confusion: "How is my student not making gains and being marked absent? They are in the front of the computer for five hours each day." For a school community, high-quality learning with high expectations for success also carried an unintended consequence: fatigue.

To address fatigue, EMS focused on climate, care, and connection. Structurally, EMS adjusted the virtual bell schedule to allow for a 10-minute break between academic classes. These extended separations between classes reduced the pressure students and staff reported because of the fast pace without the breaks. The time also provided an opportunity for students and staff to prepare for the upcoming class. A structural change, like the adjustment of the bell schedule, improved the overall confidence in the school and showed staff and students alike that their voices were being listened to and that action was being taken because of their concerns. Adjusting the bell schedule caused students to indicate this was a very positive adjustment (22%) or a positive adjustment (39%).

Additionally, the follow-through of a traditional Spirit Week served as a positive, fun break from the rigors of maneuvering distance learning. The school utilized the grade-level-team systems, when reaching out to vulnerable families, to make personalized invitations to participate in Spirit Week. More than 73% of students indicated that Spirit Week was fun and that they were likely or very likely to participate again in a Spirit Week.

Conclusion

Without a culture of EBL, critical fundamentals such as focusing on measuring what matters, hardwiring behaviors and aligning actions to ESD's core values would not have been possible this early in the improvement process. Those early fundamentals were essential when facing two high-stakes crises such as the Riverside wildfire and a global pandemic at the same time. The improvement process also brought forth trauma-informed educator development needs that were tested by these events. Leadership and staff were able to be mindful of equitable support to students and families. Through a vision of care and connection and trauma-informed teaching practices, EMS developed an emotional bank account with both the employee workforce and the school stakeholders. Principal Hargrave's frequent collection of employee voices through rounding developed the resiliency of the teachers, promoted more effective classroom practices to better meet the needs of each student, and effectively identified which students needed specific supports. EMS continues to improve its results for all students, as well as building an inclusive culture for children of all backgrounds, while hardwiring IS tools to allow staff and students to thrive.

Discussion Questions

1. How might we redesign how we prepare and support school leaders so they more effectively support their communities experiencing trauma-inducing events?
2. How might the six principles of improvement science guide your work to address collective efficacy in your site during events such as a pandemic, a wildfire evacuation, or other natural disaster? (Bryk et al., 2015, note these principles: [a] make the work problem-specific and user-centered, [b] focus on variation in performance, [c] see the system that produces the current outcomes, [d] you cannot improve at scale what you cannot measure, [e] use disciplined inquiry to drive improvement, and [f] accelerate learning through networked communities.)

References

Bandura, A. (1993). Perceived self-efficacy in cognitive development and functioning. *Educational Psychologist, 28*(2), 117–148. https://doi.org/10.1207/s15326985 ep3802_3

Bryk, A. S., Gomez, L. M., Grunow, A., & LeMahieu, P. G. (2015). *Learning to improve: How America's schools can get better at getting better.* Harvard Education Press.

Carpenter, R., & Peterson, D. S. (2019). Using improvement science in professional learning communities: From theory to practice. In R. Crowe, B. N. Hinnant-Crawford, & D. Spaulding (Eds.), *Teaching improvement science in educational leadership: A pedagogical guide* (pp. 275 - 293). Myers Education Press.

Centers for Disease Control and Prevention. (n.d.). *Preventing adverse childhood experiences* | https://www.cdc.gov/violenceprevention/aces/prevention.html

Donohoo, J., Hattie, J., & Eells, R. (2018). Educational leadership: Leading the energized school abstract. http://www.ascd.org/publications/educational-leadership/mar18/vol75/num06/abstract.aspx#The_Power_of_Collective_Efficacy

DuFour, R., DuFour, R., Eaker, R., Many, T., & Mattos, M. (2016). *Learning by doing: A handbook for professional learning communities at work* (3rd ed.). Solution Tree Press.

Eisner, E. W. (1992). Educational reform and the ecology of schooling. *Teachers College Record, 93*(4), 610–627.

Elmore, R. F. (2004). School reform from the inside out: Policy, practice, and performance. Harvard Education Press.

Hattie, J. (2008). *Visible learning.* Routledge.

Jagers, R. J., Rivas-Drake, D., & Williams, B. (2019). Transformative social and emotional learning (SEL): Toward SEL in service of educational equity and excellence. *Educational Psychologist, 54*(3), 162–184. https://doi.org/10.1080/00461 520.2019.1623032

Mendelson, T., Tandon, S. D., O'Brennan, L., Leaf, P. J., & Ialongo, N. S. (2015). Brief report: Moving prevention into schools: The impact of a trauma-informed school-based intervention. *Journal of Adolescence, 43*, 142–147. https://doi.org/10.1016/j.adolescence.2015.05.017

Smith, D., Frey, N., Pumpian, I., & Fisher, D. (2017). Building equity: Policies and practices to empower all learners. ASCD.

Studer, Q. (2003). *Hardwiring excellence.* Fire Starter Publishing.

Studer, Q., & Pilcher, J. (2015). *Maximize performance: Creating a culture for educational excellence.* Fire Starter Publishing

Wedell-Wedellsborg, T. (2020). *What's your problem? To solve your toughest problems, change the problems you solve.* Harvard Business Review Press.

Whiteside-Mansell, L., McKelvey, L., Saccente, J., & Selig, J. (2019). Adverse childhood experiences of urban and rural preschool children in poverty. *International Journal of Environmental Research and Public Health, 16*(14), 2623. https://doi. org/

Woods, S. (2020, May 8). *COVID-19 and ambiguous loss: Stress in the face of a pandemic can take the shape of frozen grief.* Psychology Today. https://www.psychologytoday.com/us/blog/in-sickness-and-in-health/202005/covid-19-and-ambiguous-loss

Combating Chronic Absenteeism: Multitiered Systems of Supports at the Elementary Level

GREG NELSON

Nestled in the Willamette Valley, just minutes away from Portland, Oregon, sits the ever-growing, sprawling community of Eventide. What started in the 1870s as a small rural district serving K–8 students and then a K–12 district in the mid-20th century, Eventide School District (ESD) has since evolved into one of the state's largest districts, serving more than 40,000 students in 50 schools. I have the amazing opportunity to teach and serve students in the same district I received my own K–12 education, which allows for continuous reflection and appreciation for how far ESD has come while noting how much work is yet to be done. Current demographics show that most K–12 students are students of color, and more than 90 languages are spoken by our families in their homes. Evergreen Elementary School (EES) is the district's second-largest elementary school, enrolling 700 students; more than 32 languages are spoken by students in the school.

Background

At EES, staff continue to seek new information and training to prepare our staff to serve our diverse students to the highest standards.

EES was one of the first schools to receive a student success coach, the position I hold, as part of the district's pilot Culture of Care program. Much of the professional development and goals for the school the past 3 years have focused on the district's vision of social-emotional learning (SEL) and how that translates to student learning and effective teaching practices. Our strategies have included trauma-informed teaching, transitioning from punitive discipline to restorative practices, and incorporating brain science into our work with students and staff. As the student success coach, I have facilitated much of professional development, including current schoolwide interventions and multitiered systems of support.

For this improvement project, we focused on chronic absenteeism and truancy. Chronic absenteeism predicts high school graduation, which impacts the quality of students' financial and health conditions after leaving school (U.S. Department of Education, n.d.). Historically underserved students, including those navigating homelessness, living in poverty, students of color, English-language learners, and those with physical or mental disabilities are more likely to experience chronic absenteeism.

Our Improvement Team

Our improvement team included eight members, each of whom was strategically chosen. When I approached each prospective member, I included anecdotal or quantitative data that highlighted the reasoning behind the team's selection. I sought current administration and counselors who have an aerial view of the school's needs, current and previous efforts of intervention, multitiered systems of support, and overall climate in the school. After diving into school, district, and state data trends and noticing higher rates of absences among students with disabilities, I invited our resource room teacher to the team. Finally, school data showed that 2018–2019 kindergarteners and fourth graders had the two highest rates of absences, which indicated to me that a representative from first-grade and fifth-grade teachers needed to be on the team.

We were excited to start on important work. As a team, we decided to meet two Wednesdays a month, and counselors indicated flexibility to meet more if needed. We had our first official meeting where we examined background data collected from the district's audit, identified the problem of practice, and worked through our fishbone activity, followed by our driver diagram.

Need for Improvement

Equity Audit

Our first step was to conduct an equity audit. Without having a wealth of knowledge or experience in conducting an equity audit outside of an assignment in a previous university course, I casually perused my way through the seven-page, 102 itemized data collection inquiry found in Frattura and Capper's (2007) book *Leading for Social Justice: Transforming Schools for all Learners*. While reading the components of this equity audit, I soon realized there was going to be nothing casual about this assignment. I contacted the ETSD administrator for equity to share Frattura and Capper's template and hear his thoughts. Although he wasn't familiar with this specific audit and seemed a bit intimidated by the format and how in depth it was, he was also encouraging. "Be a risk-taker, be thorough, search for these hard truths," he advised. I reflected on what I tell my students, the teachers I coach every day, and the phenomenal administrators I've had in the past: *Be a risk-taker! Have a growth mindset! If it ain't hard, you ain't working! There is no easy day.*

Working through the audit template, I couldn't find an area of equity that it didn't address. It prompted and promoted me to look at all areas of educational disparities, whether it be students enrolled in Talented and Gifted (TAG) services, students receiving special education services, students of color, emerging bilinguals, and English-language learner (ELL) students, as well as students who are navigating poverty, homelessness, or foster care. The audit was a match for our state's Student Success Act and equity focus.

Using the Frattura and Capper (2007) equity audit template was also a good chance to network and connect with people with diverse roles and backgrounds throughout the district. The end result was an equity audit that was a team effort—an activity that I think benefited and resonated with everyone with whom I was in contact. I reached out to and leaned on our ELL team to complete the "English Language Learners (ELL) and Bilingual" portion of the equity audit. Our special education team (learning specialist, speech-language path, and school psychologist) completed the section on students receiving special services. Our principal and assistant principal worked with me to compile information from our district website, internal data system, and state report cards. Our district administrator of equity shared the ESD journey for equity in gender, sexual orientation, and gender identity. The ESD administrator for accountability and instruction helped me navigate online resources and internal files, providing half a dozen data spreadsheets encompassing statewide discipline data, general achievement K–12 analysis, attendance data, results of a student survey, and the ESD's certified staff by gender, race, and ethnicity data. The data for EES are included in Table 5.1.

Table 5.1. EES Equity Audit Data

Criteria Statement/Question	**EES**
Students of color	400/480 (80%)
Students receiving SPED services	40/480 (8.3%)
Students receiving ELL services	162/480 (25%)
Of students who receive special education services, what percentage are also students of color?	**32/162 (20%)**
Of students who receive special education services, what percentage receive EL services?	**23/162 (14%)**

Note: EES = Evergreen Elementary School; SPED = special education; ELL = English language learner; EL = English learner.

Additional analysis of the data reveals that 36% of EES's students are Asian, but only 2% receive ELL services. In addition, 50% of students receiving ELL services are also dual identified as in need of special education, indicating overidentification of students of color as both ELL and special education students. Recently, the state department of education audited the ESD for overidentifying students of color for special education students.

Our team asked several questions and reflected on what is not working with our current students. Are we able to assess ability and knowledge in a student's native language in all areas of their education? Are our attendance policies and disciplinary procedures aligned with our students' cultural identities?

Empathy Interviews

We decided to conduct empathy interviews with community members from a wide variety of racial, ethnic, linguistic, and socioeconomic backgrounds to shed light on why students don't attend school. Questions included

1. Tell me a bit about your childhood experience with school.
2. Based on their response:
   a. Positive—probe or dive deep about what made them enjoy school or reasons they attended school regularly.
   b. Negative—what could have been better? What structures/ supports would have helped the situation?
3. Did you attend regularly? If so, why?
4. What are your thoughts about attendance currently at EES? In your own classroom?
5. What factors do you think prevent students from coming to school, specifically chronic absenteeism?

Common themes were cultural considerations, families needing more support from social workers for health care, needing help with preventative measures, not knowing the impact of absenteeism on school success, a lack of connection to school, and a lack of warm, connected relationships with the school.

Theory of Improvement

During the infancy of our school improvement work, a team of general education teachers, special education representatives, administration, counselors, and I spent a good deal of time looking at large picture trends of our district's attendance data. I had structured the work sessions to highlight and annotate their thoughts about the information, specifically asking if they noticed patterns, trends, and discrepancies that connected with our previous work around academic achievement gaps and behavioral data regarding students of color or other historically underserved students, such as those receiving ELL services, special education support, and/or students of color and those living in poverty.

Fishbone Activity

Next, I led a fishbone activity, which resulted in six areas my team hypothesized had an impact on attendance and getting to school on time: family culture and responsibilities, connection and sense of belonging to the school, social, academics, physical and mental health, and a lack of resources (see Figure 5.1).

Aim Statement and Driver Diagram

Next, our team discussed primary drivers within our control that could potentially make an impact on whether students were coming to school on a regular basis: family culture and responsibilities, connection and sense of belonging to the school, and a lack of resources. Furthermore, we identified secondary drivers that we felt influenced attendance within this domain, such as outside cultural responsibilities, navigating the political landscape, outside travel and vacation, and language barriers (see Figure 5.2).

Some questions or wonderings arose during this discussion around equity, feasibility, what might work (Nauer, 2016; Surgrue et al., 2016), and our change ideas. We decided to start with student awareness around the importance of attendance, even at an elementary level. We decided that the first change idea would be to implement classroom lessons and activities promoting awareness around school attendance: bulletin boards around the school, signage, and phone calls home to families when their student was absent or late. Our team thought the pacing and overall scope of this project would be sustainable; we took a schoolwide issue and implemented small changes. As a leader, for me, it confirmed that it indeed takes a village to improve our schools; this would not be a practical process if I were to complete it on my own, nor would I have the perspectives of my teammates whose cultural backgrounds differ from my own. Moving forward, we identified what worked and what didn't about our change idea; we either continued with our next steps or identified what didn't work, making adjustments or abandoning our change idea.

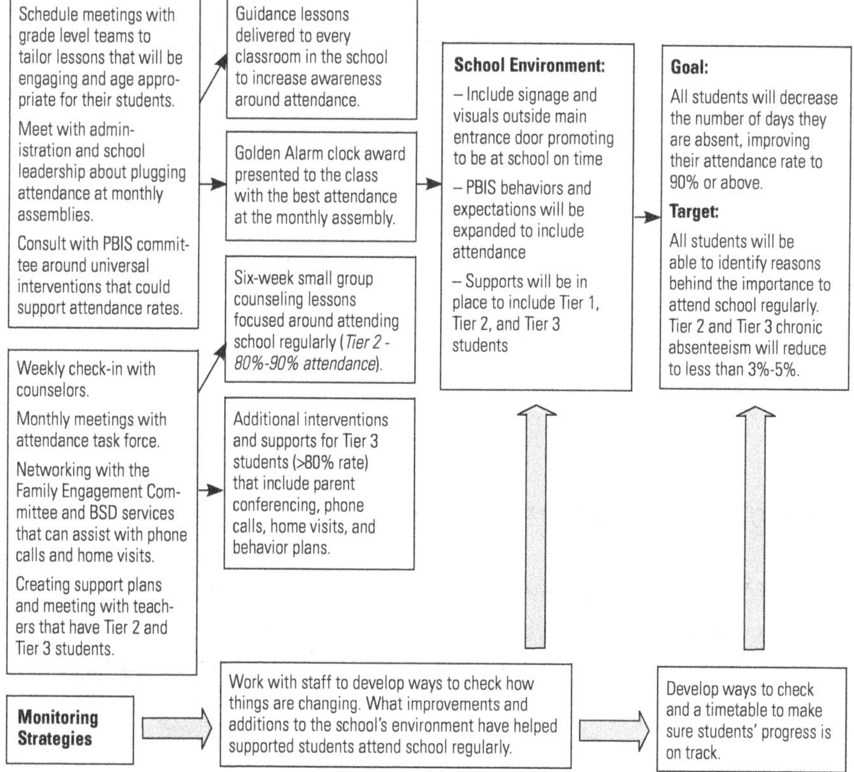

Figure 5.1. Theory of Improvement (Attendance)

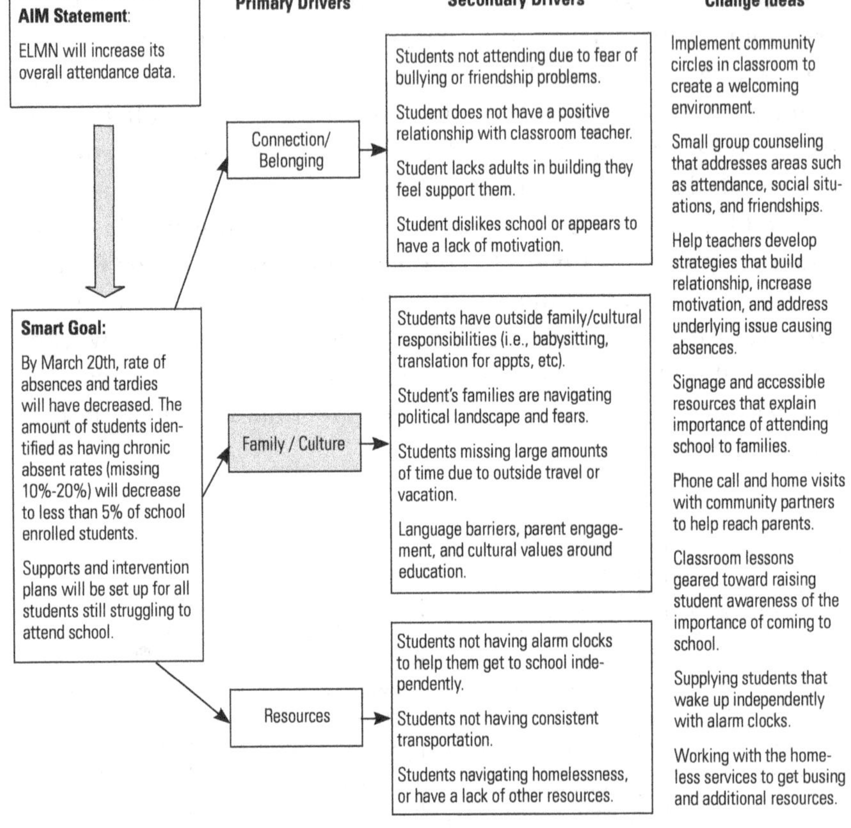

Figure 5.2. Aim Statement and Driver Diagram (Attendance)

Testing the Change

Plan–Do–Study–Act (PDSA) Cycle 1

In PDSA Cycle 1, the team decided that we would lead classroom guidance lessons around attendance awareness and the importance of coming to school each and every day. These lessons would be led by the counselors and me and would be differentiated for the different grade levels we were presenting to. The goal of this change was to implement and establish a common message for all students around attendance with the goal being to decrease the number of absences and tardies when compared to our baseline data. We were hoping for a decrease of total absence numbers by 10%.

To record our results, we had requested support from our head secretary and our attendance and enrollment secretary. We had asked that they use our district data reporting system to print attendance reports for each week during the 3-week PDSA cycle for my team and me to analyze. Next, classroom teachers were asked to highlight students that fall within the definition of chronic absenteeism and document any trends or new patterns following the classroom lessons. Teachers would need to connect with the school improvement team to outline their own procedures on how they communicate with families if there were any attendance issues.

Our baseline data reflected that over that period, EES had a total of 490 absences and 400 tardies. After conducting attendance lessons in every classroom at our school over a 2-week period, total absences dropped to 448, a decrease rate of 8.66%. We decided to continue our work on increasing student attendance and being at school on time by test another change idea by working with families and the community.

PDSA Cycle 2

Our principal had asked that we continue with our efforts around supporting students and eliminating barriers, but asked if the team could look at these other areas, as well. Thus, the change idea for PDSA Cycle 2 was to create an automatic system that called families when their child was absent and/or tardy. Our team also wondered: (a) How many families would we reach if we had posters regarding the importance of attendance at school entrances and drop-off points? (b) How could we navigate and eliminate language barriers with our automated messages and newsletter? (c) Would these change ideas result in increased on-time attendance over the next 3-week PDSA cycle, and throughout the rest of the school year? and (d) Could we track online school newsletters' views?

The change ideas in PDSA Cycle 2 improved on-time attendance more than we had expected. While Change Idea 1 resulted in an 8.66% reduction in absences, it resulted in tardies decreasing from 408 (baseline) to 303, a 25% decrease. Based on these improvements, we decided to adopt and continue this change idea for the remainder of the year. Continued signage, awareness, and highlighting the importance of attendance is continuing to work. These strategies took a little extra required work from the team, but we knew we had to drill down in the data to discover who else needed our support and what additional change ideas might work.

PDSA Cycle 3

When the team started the planning process for PDSA Cycle 3, we decided to dive into structuring small-group (Tier 2) and individual (Tier 3) counseling sessions to address students with attendance issues. Our goal would encompass students who were already identified as vulnerable or chronically absent. Our next change idea was for our two counselors to create attendance groups composed of students already currently on their caseload who were chronically absent. For two of the students who had the most severe attendance issues, we changed how we delivered the instruction, and rather than having a group time set, we met with the two students individually.

The data from PDSA Cycle 3 revealed that small-group counseling did not work, and for that reason, we decided to abandon attendance groups. The team decided to brainstorm and adapt new policies around embracing families in a culturally responsive way and providing culturally responsive support that families indicated they would need. We had much more success as a school implementing universal interventions (classroom lessons, signage, positive behavioral intervention, and strategies awards), but this strategy did not reflect the culture or needs of all our families. However, moving forward, to a future PDSA cycle, we decided to connect with students and families in culturally responsive ways through our district social workers.

Lessons Learned

Toward the end of the year, fear about COVID-19 impacted our attendance. Communities experiencing trauma must adjust their strategies to meet the needs of the community and their context, a key component of improvement science. Although our improvement efforts in PDSA Cycle 3 did not reach all students with severe attendance problems, we recognized that the compounded impact of mental health, physical health needs, homelessness, and food insecurity impacted our most vulnerable students.

We learned that equity-focused leadership needed to be the foundation of our work, and with that, a team was created that was diverse and represented the population that we served. On the team were several staff members of color, some of whom had persevered through their own hardships growing up and battled with their own absenteeism as schoolchildren. We included counselors, special education, and English teachers who already had strong relationships with some of our most impacted students and their families. It was these connections that proved invaluable.

What we also had learned through this process was that teacher-leader facilitation of improvement efforts, instead of the traditional, administrator-led workshop efforts, increased our ability to seek improvement, test change ideas, and succeed—or fail—and learn from our efforts. We were peers at the table, all bringing our own personal experiences, research, and perspectives. Was it important to have our administrators there? Absolutely, they cross-checked, let us bounce ideas around, and brought an aerial view of school, district, and state dynamics, and helped us lead equity discussions during our improvement efforts.

Moving forward, we need to increase communication among community partners and the school, specifically around the importance of attending school. Community partners such as Head Start, the YMCA, the Police Activity League, and after-school care programs could start to look at their own trends, or how they can scaffold support for families to minimize school absences. The team also processed the idea of getting information to families earlier, before absenteeism habits start to form. When auditing our own school's data, the past 2 years, kindergarten students had a higher number of absences than many of the other grades.

A large unknown regarding attendance is what impact the COVID-19 pandemic of 2020 will have on students over time. We worry that the trauma caused by COVID-19 will exacerbate the complexity of chronic absenteeism, but we believe that using improvement science processes will help us engage in improvement cycles that will address the issue.

Discussion Questions

1. With chronic absenteeism being a nationwide problem, how do we structure our schools to eliminate barriers and scaffold supports for individual students and communities?
2. When identifying some of the barriers for on-time attendance (lack of school relationships, cultural norms of the school or family, out-of-school responsibilities, ability level, physical/mental health, access to resources), how could you use improvement science tools and processes to improve support for students and families?
3. Due to the COVID-19 pandemic or any community trauma, how might large urban schools and districts or smaller rural schools and districts approach the challenges using improvement science tools and processes?

References

Frattura, E. M., & Capper, C. (2007). *Leading for social justice: Transforming schools for all learners*. Corwin.

Nauer, K. (2016). Battling chronic absenteeism. *Phi Delta Kappan, 98*(2), 28–34. https://doi.org/10.1177/0031721716671903

Surgrue, E. P., Zuel, T., & LaLiberte, T. The ecological context of chronic school absenteeism in the elementary grades. *Children & Schools, 38*(3), 137–145. https://doi.org/10.1093/CS/CDW020

U.S. Department of Education. (n.d.). *Chronic absenteeism in the nation's schools: A hidden educational crisis.* https://www2.ed.gov/datastory/chronicabsenteeism. html

CHAPTER SIX

Increasing Attendance in Middle School

EMILY ANDERSON

Staytonville Middle School (SMS) is located in the heart of a suburban school district of 5,000 students located in Staytonville, Washington (pseudonyms used throughout). The district is composed of seven schools: four elementary, two middle, and one high school. During the time of this project, SMS was in a year of transition as two middle schools in this district were merging into one building in the fall of 2020 with a projected student body of 1,300 students. SMS enrolls 750 students in Grades 6 through 8. SMS's principal, who had previously led only SMS, began leading both SMS and Lelow Ridge Middle School this past year. Both middle schools have an associate principal, and the district has added the position of dean of students in both schools to help support students and staff during the transition.

Much of the work at the middle level is a continuation from the previous year when SMS adopted a new science and language arts curricula. A majority of professional development was, and continues to be, centered on implementing the curriculum with grade-level, content-specific team meetings. This year there was a focus on the adoption and implementation of a new social studies curriculum, with added support for our grade-level social studies teams. In addition, the middle schools are in Year 2 of becoming an AVID school; initiatives have been added around interactive notes and student binder organization. An additional schoolwide focus is Accountable Talk (The Teacher Toolkit, n.d.). Professional development was delivered in August, planning time had been set aside for implementation ideas, and the instructional coach and dean of students delivered content-specific lessons using the strategies and structures presented in the August in-service week.

The goal for this improvement project was to increase the number of regular attenders. Last year at SMS, 14% of the student body was considered nonattenders, which means roughly 105 students attended school less than 90% of the time, missing more than 18 days of the school year. Because attendance rates in Grade 6 are one of the strongest predictors of high school graduation, attendance became the focus area for this improvement effort, with the intended outcome of improving schoolwide systems and support structures.

Meet the Team

The attendance team includes school employees who would focus on determining which students were in which phase of truancy. This team had taken a new form with each new associate principal, with a significant turnover rate in the past 5 years. In an effort to establish a sustainable system that addressed the root of the issue of attendance and to collectively determine next steps to create positive change, school leadership created a new team with more available resources. Each member of this team played a valuable role in supporting students academically, behaviorally, and/or emotionally. The team was composed of

- an associate principal who was in Year 3 at SMS;
- two counselors who know a majority of the student body and have insight into family and home dynamics;
- the dean of students, a position that is new this year and works directly with student discipline. The new dean had previously served as the math instructional coach and is familiar with the multitiered instruction (MTI) and response-to-intervention (RTI) processes and intervention options to support academic needs;
- a Language Arts/Social Studies instructional coach who is currently in Year 3 of the position and a veteran teacher familiar with MTI/RTI process and intervention options to support academic needs; and
- the attendance secretary who knows family and student backgrounds.

Need for Improvement

Equity Audits

To gather the appropriate equity data, three sections were used from the Frattura and Capper (2007) equity audit: (1) general and social class data, (2) discipline data, and (3) gender data and analysis. The team chose social class data in an effort to get a fuller picture of the school and the staff associated with student services (see Table 6.1).

Table 6.1. Class and Social Data

Criteria	Data	Number of Students/ Percentage of Population
Number of students in the district:	5,300 students	N/A
Number of staff in your school (certified and noncertified):	80 staff members	N/A
Number of students in your school:	750 students	N/A
Number of students who transferred or moved into the school the last academic year:	Total: 25 Race: 3 Hispanic, 1 Asian, 21 White Disability: 4 Male: 8 Female: 17 Free/reduced-priced lunch: 4	1/30 = 3.3%
Number of students who transferred out of the school in the last academic year:	Total: 32 Race: 6 Hispanic, 1 Pacific Islander, 2 Multiracial, 1 Asian, 22 White Receiving special education services: 11 Male: 12 Female: 20 Free/reduced-price lunch: 10	10/32 = 32% Students of color 11/32 = 34% Receiving SPED services 20/32 = 62% female 10/32 = 32% FRL
Fraction and percentage of staff in your school who are associated with student services:	SPED 4 SPED IAs: 15 Counselors: 2 Psychologists: 2 Nurses: 2 Bilingual specialists: 2 Reading specialists: 2 TAG specialists: 1	4/80 = 5% 15/80 = 19% 2/80 = 2.5% 2/80 = 2.5% 2/80 = 2.5% 2/80 = 2.5% 2/80 = 2.5% 1/80 = 1.25%

Note: N/A = Not Applicable; SPED = special education; FRL = free/reduced-price lunch; IA = Instructional Assitant; TAG = talented and gifted.

We also analyzed discipline data to see if there were a link between repeated discipline issues and attendance (see Table 6.2).

The team was also interested in seeing if the disproportionate levels of males with discipline incidents would reflect in the attendance data. Knowing the high number of male discipline referrals in the building, the team also wanted to analyze data by gender for teachers and administrators, discipline by gender, and achievement rates by gender throughout the district (see Table 6.3).

Table 6.2. Discipline Data by Demographics

Criteria	Data (all ratios written as female:male)	
Students who were suspended in the past year:	**In-School Suspension** Male: 25 Female: 0 Race: 3 Hispanic, 1 Asian, 21 White Receiving SPED services: 8 ELL: 2	**Out-of-School Suspension** Male: 18 Female: 2 Race: 3 Hispanic, 1 Asian, 14 White Receiving SPED Services: 6 ELL:1
Students who were expelled in the past year:	N/A	
Students who were placed in an Alternative Interim Placement in the past year:	2 students: male, 1 Hispanic, 1 White	
Low attendance and/or truancy:	Total: 134 Male: 79 Female: 55 Race: 4 Asian, 15 Hispanic, 9 Multi-racial, 106 White Disability: 15 ELL: 9	134/750 = 18% of students out of the population of SMS were below a 90% attendance rate. 92% is the cutoff to determine a "school attender." Male 59%, female 41% Students of color 21%
Incidents disaggregated by a. Economically Disadvantaged b. SPED c. TAG d. ELL (Active, Monitored, Post Monitored)	208 196 93 39	208/554 = 38% 196/554 = 36% 93/554 = 17% 39/554 = 7%
Incidents disaggregated by ethnicity: a. White b. Hispanic c. Asian d. Multiracial e. American Indian/Alaskan Native	465 53 22 12 2	465/554 = 84% 53/554 = 9.5% 22/554 = 4% 12/554 = 2% 2/554 = 0.5%

Note: SMS = Stayton Middle School; SPED = special education; ELL = English-language learner; TAG = talented and gifted.

Table 6.3. District Data by Gender

Criteria	Data (all ratios written as female:male)		Percentages female:male
Females to males on the teaching staff	Elementary schools Middle school High school Overall	99:13 49:14 42:35 190:59	88%:12% 78%:22% 55%:45% 76%:24%
Females to males teaching science and math classes at the middle/high school level	Middle level High school Overall	113:8 12:7 25:15	62%:38% 63%:37% 63%:37%
Females to males teaching English (and related courses) at the middle/high school level	Middle level High school Overall	17:1 4:6 21:7	94%:6% 40%:60% 75%:25%
Females to males teaching history (and related courses) at the middle/high school level	Middle level High school Overall	14:1 3:8 17:9	93%:7% 27%:73% 65%:35%
Females to males teaching the highest level of math students at your school	1:1		50%:50%
Females to males teaching advanced placement course at the high school	8:11		42%:58%
Females to males on the administrative team at SMS	1:1		50%:50%
Females to males administrative team at the elementary, middle, and high school	Elementary schools: 2:2 Middle schools: 2:1 High school: 1:3		50%:50% 67%:33% 25%:75%
Females to males on school board:	2:3		40%:60%
SBAC achievement (% of students earning 3 or higher) by ethnicity:	**Math:** 33% Native American, 68.5% Asian, 20% Black, 45% Hispanic,73% Multiracial, 33% Pacific Islander, 72% White ***All Students: 68%*** **ELA:** 33% Native American, 79% Asian, 60% Black, 59% Hispanic, 76% Multiracial, 83% Pacific Islander, 81% White ***All Students: 78%***		
SBAC achievement (% of students earning 3 or higher) for students with testing accommodations:	**Math:** 14.81% **ELA:** 30%		
SBAC achievement (% of students earning a 3 or higher) by gender:	**Math:** Female 69%, Male 68% **ELA:** Female 81%, Male 75%		
Female to male enrollment in PE elective courses:	49:203		20%:80%
Females to males receiving referrals:	50:504		9%:91%

Note: SMS = Stayton Middle School; ELA = English language arts;
Smarter Balance Assessment Consortium = ; PE = physical education

We noticed significant equity issues, including the low number of male teachers and teachers of color and the fact that more than one in 10 students is Latinx, yet there are no Latinx teachers employed at SMS. Representation matters. In terms of attendance, the *lowest* attendance rates were among males, students receiving free/reduced-price lunch services, and students who identify as ELL. Despite low attendance rates, males received a disproportionate ratio of disciplinary actions, as did students receiving free/reduced-price lunch services and students who identify as ELL. This led the team to wonder what the connection between discipline and attendance might be. This also led the team to the potential problem of practice, which is that 14% of the student population, 100 students, were identified as nonattenders last year. This means they attended school less than 90% of the 175 school days. The team wondered how many students who were on the attendance watch were identified as ELL, receiving free/reduced-price lunch services, or had one or more discipline referrals this school year. These categories of information were added to the weekly attendance report from the district office.

The data were then shared at the next 1-hour attendance team meeting. Synthesizing the information was critical. After synthesizing the data and looking at trends, and prior to creating the fishbone diagram and completing the empathy audits, the team cross-referenced the current year's attendance data (year to date for all students) with some of the trends mentioned earlier: male students with discipline incidents this year, students receiving free/reduced-priced lunch services, students identified as ELL, and students receiving special education services. Cross-referencing those data points highlighted trends that helped the team narrow the area of focus to make a greater impact on the highest number of students. Next the team developed empathy interview questions.

Previous attendance teams at SMS focused on trying to reach the students who were farthest from the 90% threshold of being considered attenders. However, looking at the previous year's state report cards, it is obvious that this strategy had not been effective in increasing the attendance rate as a school; in fact, regular attendance actually decreased over the last few years (89%, 87%, and 86%

attenders over the last three school years, respectively). In an effort to make the greatest impact, the team thought it could be beneficial to focus on the 5% of students who fall just below the 90% mark. The team chose sixth graders with the hope that the interventions put in place would have a lasting effect on their middle school years and hopefully carry over into high school and beyond.

Student information is shown in Table 6.4. These 13 students were all the sixth graders who fell within the range of attending school 84.48% to 90.91% of the year.

Table 6.4. Demographics of Low-Attending Sixth Graders

Grade	Gender	Race/ Ethnicity	% Attendance (by days/ ADA)	TAG	504	ELL	SPED	FRM	Discipline Incidents (19–20)	Discipline Incidents (18–19)	Discipline Incidents (All Years)
6	M	White	84.85								2
6	F	White	84.85				SPED	Y			
6	F	White	84.85				SPED	Y			
6	M	White	84.85					Y			
6	M	White	86.36				SPED				6
6	M	White	86.36	Y							
6	F	White	86.36								
6	F	White	87.88							2	2
6	M	White	87.88								
6	M	White	87.88								
6	M	White	89.39								2
6	F	White	90.91								1
6	F	White	89.39					Y			3

Note: days/ADA = average daily attendance; TAG = talented and gifted;
ELL = English-language learner; SPED = special education;
FRL = free and reduced lunch membership

Survey Data

Each low-attending student took a survey to identify why students come to school and how strong their relationships are. Students at SMS come to school because they believe education is important and they want to see their friends. These students feel socially connected with adults and peers, but almost 30% of students do not feel academically successful at school. When students are absent, they feel that their teachers, friends, and parents notice that they're not attending. Oftentimes, the absence is due to sickness or an appointment, which are external factors not within the control of the student or school, and 92% of students feel that they can get caught up after an absence by accessing Canvas—the schoolwide online learning management system.

Qualitative Data. To attempt to find themes in the qualitative data, responses to Questions 1, 2, and 4 were color coded. The answers to Question 3 were harder to categorize as they were often whimsical in nature, but it did lend to creativity and the start of a conversation around realistic supports and interventions for individual students. The themes noticed were social, teachers and classes, learning, sick/tired, and school systems. Extremely common throughout all categories were indicators that students come to school to see their friends and the more social opportunities provided, the more the attendance numbers would increase. The second-most prevalent theme was around teachers and classes. Students want classes they choose and with teachers with whom they connect. They also hope to learn in the classroom rather than learning at home while doing homework (see Figure 6.1).

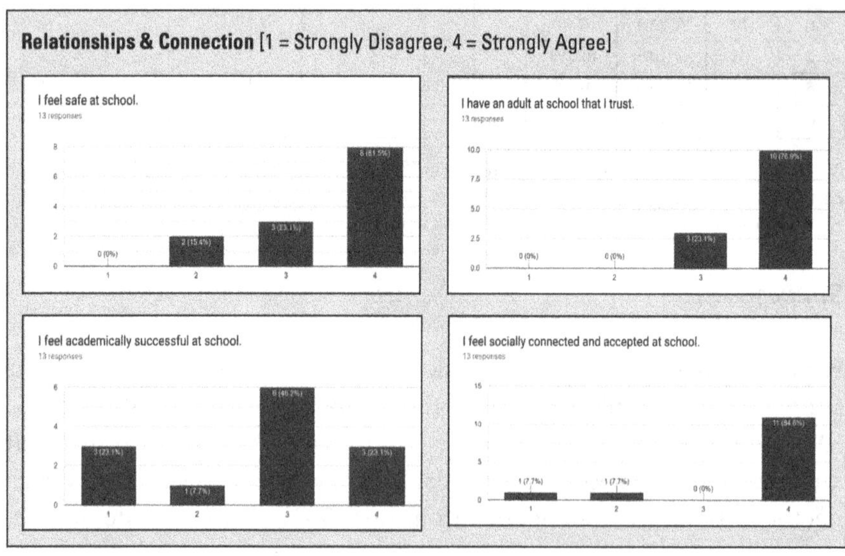

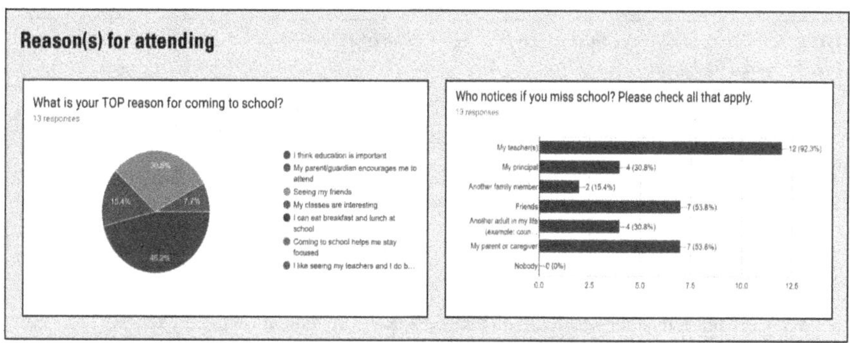

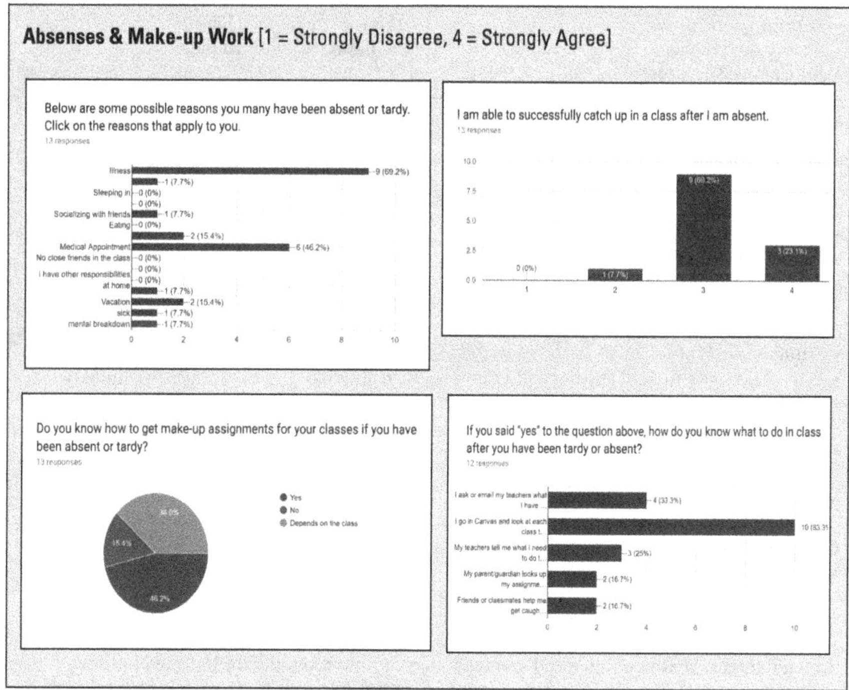

Figure 6.1. Survey Data

Empathy Interviews

School counselors also met one-on-one with students to conduct empathy interviews (see Figure 6.2).

Q1: *What are some things that make you want to be at school? (social, teachers & classes, future plans, learning)*

- Friends
- Coming to school makes me feel like I can get better at things
- Education & learning new stuff
- Want to go to college to study interior design
- Education comes first
- Seeing friends - school is fun
- Really fun people
- I enjoy my math teacher - picks up on jokes and brings humor into teaching
- Friends
- Learning new things
- Seeing my teachers
- Education is important
- Friends make me happy
- Like math and like my science teacher
- Want to get into a good college
- Striving for a doctorate, but might be happy with a master's
- Friends
- Enjoy my first period (Engineering)
- Friends and classes
- Gives me something to do during the day
- Need an education to play sports
- Like to see my teachers
- Want to go to Stanford
- Want to get a good job
- Hanging out with friends

Q2: *What are some things that make you not want to be at school? (social, teachers & classes, sick/tired, stress of learning)*

- Worry - stressed out when I don't know how to do things
- School is exhausting
- People are often sick and I'm a germaphobe
- I get sick a lot and visit the doctor
- Worry about getting picked up by my dad every Friday
- Student incidents
- Fear of messing up and getting bad grades
- Tired in the morning, but there's nothing specific about school
- Certain teachers
- Too much HW which leads to stress
- Tired from reading late or watching TV
- Bored sometimes
- The day feels long and certain classes feel longer
- Mad that we have HW
- I have nervous breakdowns
- Soooo long - physically and emotionally wiped out
- Too much HW and no time to relax
- Feeling like I've missed school and now have to play catch up
- Fear of getting bullied
- No friends
- Learning
- Not in the mood or just don't feel well

Q3: *If you could throw magic dust all over the school, what would you change that would make you want to come to school every day?*

- Knowing everything at home is okay
- Teachers would do my HW instead of me
- Magic fingers that read my mind and type for me
- If someone threw candy at the end of every class (mixture of nerds and macaroons)
- Kindness - I wish people would be nice to each other
- Our Chromebooks would have more abilities
- Educational games to play on Chromebooks
- More school work and less HW
- Vitamin water in the water fountains
- Classes I like the most to be my first classes
- FACS and Dance 1st period because electives drive the excitement to get to school
- Monday would be added to the weekend
- Fizzy drinks allowed in school
- Students could have their phones out during free time
- Team Sports every class period
- Longer passing times
- No one would be rude or mean to one another
- No rumor spreading
- Teachers won't yell or get upset
- Everyone will be respectful yet still have fun!
- Engineering and STEM every day
- Skate park for recess
- Water fountains are gatorade
- Pizza for lunch every day!

Q4: *Since we don't have magic dust, what would be a reasonable support that we could put in place to help you want to be here every day? (social, teachers & classes, school systems)*	
• Unsure • No HW • Hanging out with friends more • Nicer teachers • Easier assignments • Later start time • Core classes that I like, first • Wall of interests with name and grade so students can make connections	• More teachers at lunch to help with conflict • Longer passing time • An art class, or social class where you get to talk and work with other people • A room to go to when I'm stressed • A punching bag to release anger • Get parents involved when there are bullying issues

Figure 6.2. Empathy Interview Reponses

After reviewing the empathy data, the team was surprised and excited to see that students feel connected and that the primary reason for absences involved outside factors, such as being sick or having an appointment. The answers to the question, "Who notices when you miss school? Check all that apply" were data points that really caught the attention of the team. Out of the 13 students interviewed, 92% of them said that a teacher noticed when they were absent. However, only 53% of students reported that a parent or caregiver noticed when they missed school. After further review and conversation, the team felt this was where they could make some positive change. How might an increase in family involvement and education affect attendance rates?

Supporting Literature

Three research studies helped drive and support the attendance work at SMS. The first study took place in the Philadelphia school district, partnering with Regional Educational Laboratory (REL). This study looked specifically at whether education and engagement, through personalized postcards, would reduce student absenteeism. Including 51,000 students, roughly 40% of the school district population, the study showed that over a 43-day period, they were able to increase student attendance by 2.4% by sending only one round of mailed postcards to families. This research provided information to the team regarding a potential personalized intervention that would not only communicate concerns with families but also engage them in understanding the importance and long-term effects of absenteeism.

Research provided by the Baltimore Education Research Consortium (2011), regarding early-warning indicators for high school graduation, provided key research around sixth-grade warning indicators. The study found that chronic absences, course failures, discipline, and student retainment were the four factors most closely linked to dropout in high school. Chronic absenteeism was the number one predictor of high school graduation, where the probability of graduating fell from 70% for students with 10 or fewer days absent in sixth grade to 28% for students identified as chronically absent. This research helped support the decision to focus on a sixth-grade cohort of students to test the determined improvement science change ideas. Effective intervention needs to be implemented early and monitored effectively throughout middle school.

The third study by Rogers et al. (2017) focused on a cohort of students in Chicago Public Schools from Grades 5 to 9. Focusing on performance in the ninth-grade year, the longitudinal study worked backward to identify which middle school factors were most closely related to performance in high school. The study found that if students are attending school less than 85% of the time in middle school, they are at high risk of failing in high school. Furthermore, if they are attending less than 80% of the time, they are almost certain to be off track to graduate at the end of their ninth-grade year. This study helped support the percent range used to determine who would receive a postcard and how it would be communicated.

Theory of Improvement

For the purpose of this improvement science project, the attendance team focused on sixth-grade attendance, primarily those students who are close to the state 90% attenders benchmark. First, the team constructed a fishbone diagram to include all potential barriers when it comes to students attending school (see Figure 6.3).

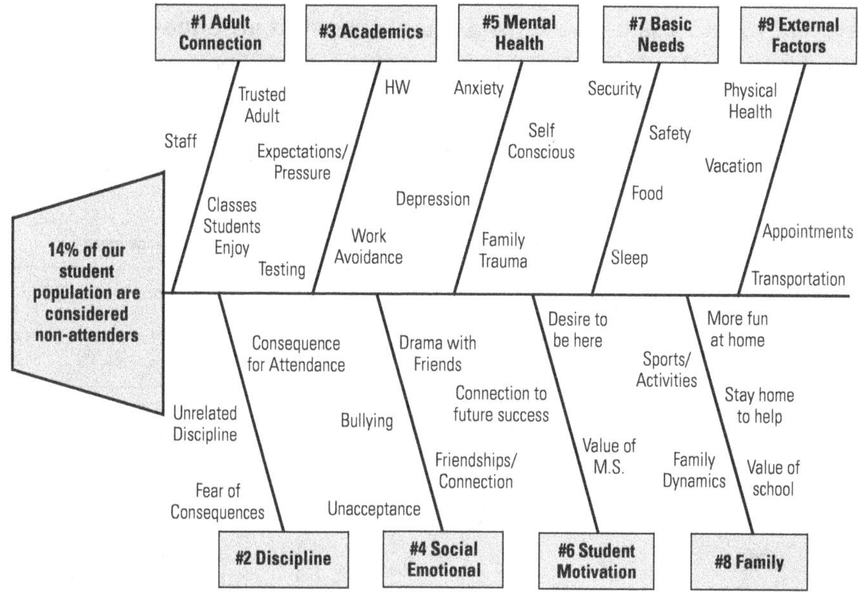

Figure 6.3. Fishbone

The barriers were then put in order based on which barriers, given the current school systems, the team had the most influence to control or change. During initial discussions about this project, the team anticipated focusing on one of the first three categories: (1) adult connections, (2) discipline, and/or (3) academics. However, after examining data from the student survey and empathy interviews, and considering the research, it became clear that connection with families is an area in which there is more control and opportunity to change than originally thought. During those discussions, the team realized that SMS doesn't currently have a system that supports communication with families regarding the importance of attendance.

Once we identified a barrier on which to focus, the team brainstormed ideas for addressing that barrier. The first two ideas—(1) personalized postcards for students who fall between 80% and 89% attendance and (2) an information letter, Attendance Matters, sent home with trimester report cards—will be tracked using the Plan–Do–Study–Act (PDSA) cycles. The third idea—changing the auto-response system to address both excused and unexcused absences—would be implemented by the end of the school year and will be in place to start another PDSA cycle in the 2020–2021 school year. The driver diagram (see Figure 6.4) shows the primary and secondary drivers and change ideas.

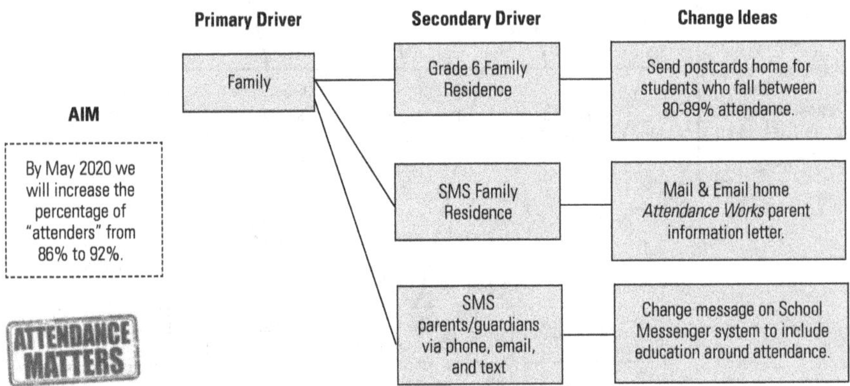

Figure 6.4. Driver Diagram

Testing the Change Idea

PDSA Cycle 1

The PDSA Cycle 1 is displayed in Figure 6.5, including our change idea, the goal of the change, what we learned, and what our next actions would be.

Postcards were sent on February 14, 2020. Data were tracked for attendance on February 14, 2020, then rechecked and recorded on February 21, 2020, and then again on February 28, 2020, during a 2-week PDSA cycle.

PDSA Cycle 2

After an attendance meeting on March 4, 2020, the team opted to host check-in interviews with students who were still showing a decrease in attendance since receiving the personalized attendance postcard. Of the five students who decreased in attendance, two of the

<table>
<tr><td colspan="4">PDSA (1) Name: Postcards
Attendance Team members: AP, counselors (2), Dean of Students, Instructional Coach, Attendance Secretary</td></tr>
<tr><td></td><td>Test cycle: 1</td><td>Start date: 2/14/20</td><td>End date: 2/28/2020</td></tr>
<tr><td>PLAN</td><td colspan="3">What change is being tested?
Informative postcards are being mailed to grade 6 students who have 9 or more absences, more than half way through the school year.</td></tr>
<tr><td></td><td colspan="3">What is the goal of the change?
Grade 6 was chosen as a test group for this change idea. The goal is to increase attendance and/or get more parent support with attendance because there has been some education around the importance of attendance and its early predictor warning signs.</td></tr>
<tr><td></td><td colspan="3">Details of implementation plan (who, what, where)
Who: Attendance Team   What: Postcards were sent to 23 families.
Where: family residence (both parents if living is separate residence)</td></tr>
<tr><td></td><td colspan="3">What is your first question?
Will direct communication home with families of 6th grade students with 9 or more absences, increase the individual student's attendance percentage? The communication includes the number of days absent as well as facts around attendance and its direct link to high school success and graduation.
What is your prediction?
A few families will reach out to get more information about attendance or to explain why their student has been absent.
What are the measure(s)?
Percent of attendance (days present/total days of school)
Details about data collection (Who is responsible for data collection? When? How?)
Who: Attendance Secretary & Dean of Students
When: Data will be recorded weekly
How: Attendance report generated from the District Office every Monday</td></tr>
<tr><td>DO</td><td colspan="3">Was implementation of the change carried out as intended? (x) Yes ☐ No
Describe modifications: No modifications on the first round.</td></tr>
<tr><td>STUDY</td><td colspan="3">What were the results? Did the results match the prediction?
Of the 23 students we sent postcards to, 17 of the students' attendance increased. The range of percent increase was 0.1-0.63. There has been one school contact from a family regarding attendance since the postcard was sent. We were hoping for more family engagement or inquiry.</td></tr>
<tr><td></td><td colspan="3">What did you learn?
Two weeks is probably too small of a cycle window to see real impact when it comes to moving a percentage. At the time of this cycle, students had been in school for 103 days. That means each day is worth less than 1% of a student's overall attendance percentage. To see real change, it will take more time.</td></tr>
<tr><td>ACT</td><td colspan="3">What will you do?   (X) Adapt   (X) Adopt ☐ Abandon
What is the rationale for that decision?
This specific form of communication and education for families has potential to be beneficial as it did peak interest from one family. The team needs more time and potentially a follow up plan with families when improvement isn't seen in that first week.</td></tr>
<tr><td></td><td colspan="3">What will you do next?
For students that didn't show an increase in this first PDSA, we will contact home via phone or email and express a similar message. The team will continue to send a postcard to other students who reach the 9+ absences mark and track their data as well, and then also monitor with a phone call or email follow up.</td></tr>
</table>

Figure 6.5. PDSA Cycle #1

five students were not available for a check-in due to being absent; three students reported absences due to illness or injury. The team then opted to implement a positive behavioral intervention and strategies system, positive referrals, to support the 74% of our focus students who demonstrated an increase in attendance over the 2-week PDSA Cycle 1. Positive referrals were handed out to all 17 students on March 6, 2020, or March 10, 2020. Attendance would then have been tracked on March 13, 2020, to look for trends and determine next steps. We started our PDSA cycle the week of global awareness of the pandemic, and within 2 weeks, our schools shut down (see Figure 6.6).

What We Learned

Out of the 23 sixth-grade students who we closely tracked during this case study, 17 showed improvement in their attendance in a very short time. Of the students who did not demonstrate improvement, three of them were out for a week or more with a virus, absent for doctor appointments, or out of the country with family. The team considered these types of absences to be out of their control as they are driven by external factors. The other three students who did not demonstrate improvement were absent when the dean or counselors attempted to check in. As the attendance team progressed through the school year, the postcards were used more frequently with more families in the sixth grade to communicate and educate families about their student's absences.

There were certainly challenges with the implementation of this attendance intervention, which mostly revolved around time and access to students. Our recommendation is to start sending postcards in mid-November and base it solely on the number of days a student has been absent. By the middle of November, if a student has been absent for 5 or more days, they should receive a postcard. We also recognized we should focus on students who are missed school intermittently rather than on those who have consecutive days' absences due to a onetime illness.

	Test cycle: 2	**Start date: 3/6/20**	**End date: 3/20/2020**
PLAN	**What change is being tested?** If an increase in attendance from the postcards sent during the first PDSA cycle is not seen, the team will check in with each student and determine if more communication needs to be sent home. For all students who have shown an increase, the team will reward the behavior with a Positive Referral (PBIS).		
	What is the goal of the change? Grade 6 was chosen as a test group for this change idea. The goal is to increase attendance and/or get more parent support with attendance because there has been some education around the importance of attendance and its early predictor warning signs. Checking in with students who are still decreasing in attendance, will give the team further information about why a student is absent, in an effort to understand if families need more communication (email or phone call). Positively rewarding students for an increase in attendance, supports the positive behavior and let's students know that the school sees their efforts and their attendance matters.		
	Details of implementation plan (who, what, where) *Who:* Dean of Students *What:* Student check-in, communication home if needed, or Positive Referral *Where:* Email, phone call, school		
	What is your first question? Will a follow up conversation with students who aren't making positive progress in their attendance, give further insight into why they aren't attending and whether families need further communication specific to their student's absences? **What is your prediction?** Families will respond to email and potentially not answer the phone call. **What are the measure(s)?** Percent of attendance (days present/total days of school) **Details about data collection (Who is responsible for data collection? When? How?)** *Who:* Attendance Secretary & Dean of Students *When:* Data will be recorded weekly *How:* Attendance report generated from the District Office	**What is your second question?** Will positive reinforcement with increased attendance, promote and perpetuate the cycle of improvement? **What is your prediction?** The team predicts that the PBIS strategy will reinforce the positive behavior and support a continued positive change. **What are the measure(s)?** Percent of attendance (days present/total days of school) **Details about data collection (Who is responsible for data collection? When? How?)** *Who:* Attendance Secretary & Dean of Students *When:* Data will be recorded weekly *How:* Attendance report generated from the District Office	
DO	**Was implementation of the change carried out as intended? ( ) Yes (x) No** **Describe modifications:** The team found that students who still had a decrease in attendance after the postcard were out of school due to injury or illness. The team instead opted not to communicate again with families whose students had seen a decrease in attendance - not during this PDSA cycle. However, positive referrals were handed out to all students who showed an increase (any increase) in attendance over the two-week cycle.		
STUDY	**What were the results? Did the results match the prediction?** Results could not be collected due to school closure.		
	What did you learn?		
ACT	**What will you do?** ☐Adapt (x) Adopt ☐Abandon **What is the rationale for that decision?**		
	What will you do next?		

*The Study and Act sections of PDSA cycle 2, were unable to be completed due to school closures. All positive referrals were distributed to students prior to the school closure and move to distance learning.

Figure 6.6. PDSA Cycle #2

The second challenge regarded access to students to get follow-up information regarding absences and access for families when it comes to getting information about their student's absences. For students whose attendance declined during PDSA Cycle 2, it became a challenge to catch them at school. If they were at school, it was challenging to check in because that would require them to miss more instructional time. However, the information collected during those check-ins was primarily to know what each individual student needed and to test what changes could be made to the system to reach more students. In terms of access for families, we learned through this improvement process that families don't realize how much school their student is missing. If a family consistently calls and excuses their student, then they never receive the robocall information that tells them how many overall days their student has been absent. In a district where most families call and excuse their student, that could lead to most families being unaware of the overall number of absences their student has accrued. Even for families who have the information and total number of absences, they might not know the impact of the absences on their student's education.

Our overall goal was to increase the percentage of attenders from 86% to 92%, to align with the school improvement plan at SMS. This project took a three-pronged approach for creating schoolwide change, with each prong addressing a different system or avenue to educate families. Putting a team together that is innovative yet understands and is willing to use data that will examine research on what has worked elsewhere, test small-scale changes in context, and then adapt, adopt, or abandon a change idea is key to the success of a project of this magnitude and importance.

Discussion Questions

1. If social opportunities are a driving force in getting kids to school, how can we incorporate these types of opportunities into the school setting to increase engagement and attendance without losing instructional time?

2. What is the impact of a student's home culture on attendance? How can we honor home cultures and increase attendance?
3. What are classroom activities that are culturally responsive and motivate students to want to attend class?
4. What are some potential empathy interview questions you could ask students about what motivates them to attend school?

References

Baltimore Education Research Consortium. (2011, February). *Destination graduation: Sixth grade early warning indicators for Baltimore City Schools.* http://www.baltimore-berc.org/pdfs/SixthGradeEWIFullReport.pdf

Frattura, E. M., & Capper, C. (2007). *Leading for social justice: Transforming schools for all learners.* Corwin.

Rogers, T., Duncan, T., Wolford, T., Ternovski, J., Subramanyam, S., & Reitano, A. (2017, February). *A randomized experiment using absenteeism information to "nudge" attendance.* National Center for Education Evaluation and Regional Assistance. https://www.attendanceworks.org/wp-content/uploads/2017/09/Todd-postcard-Nudge-research-publis-REL_2017252.pdf

The Teacher Toolkit. (n.d.). *Accountable discussions.* https://www.theteachertoolkit.com/index.php/tool/accountable-discussions

Disparities in Middle School Discipline: English Learners, Students Receiving Special Education Services, and Boys

CASSANDRA THONSTAD

In this chapter, the author focuses on the process of implementing improvement science (IS) as a means to reduce gender disparities in student disciplinary referrals. Students at Rural Middle School (RMS), a high-poverty Grades 6–8 school with more than 500 students, have not received the supports to perform at rates similar to the more affluent middle school within the district, as measured by grades, normed formative assessments, and on state tests. The problem of practice explored in this case study is common to many educational institutions: Male students disproportionately receive referrals and lose instructional time due to in-school and out-of-school suspensions. Although the RMS administration, like many schools in the United States, understands the importance of collecting data that include nonbinary students, at the time of this particular improvement work, the state had not yet allowed the option of indicating one's gender as nonbinary.

We applied IS principles, starting with understanding the system as it currently exists, conducting "deep dives" into current discipline data, conducting empathy interviews, and brainstorming many potential change ideas. As a result of this improvement effort, the overall referral count has dropped dramatically, and students are staying in their classrooms able to learn. The team continues to review data and dig into new trends each grading period to serve the ever-changing needs of the students and to improve outcomes for students of all backgrounds.

The Setting

Rural School District (RSD) is a smaller district serving approximately 5,000 K–12 students in 10 schools: six elementary schools, two middle schools, one high school, and one alternative high school. RSD is situated in a rural community of 22,500 people, with strong industries of wine production and agriculture and is well known for recreational opportunities in and around the area, making tourism a large contributor to the local economy. Two of the elementary schools qualify as Title I schools, and both feed into RMS.

RMS is a Grades 6–8 school and has approximately 500 students who identify as Asian (1%), Black/African American (2%), Hispanic (26%), multiracial (5%), and White (66%). Approximately 15% of the students receive special education services, and 49% applied and qualified as economically disadvantaged. There are 11 languages spoken by the students, and 21% qualify as Ever English learners.

In comparison, the district's other middle school, Close Middle School, is also a Grades 6–8 school that has approximately 600 students whose students identify as Asian (2%), Black/African American (1%), Hispanic (17%), multiracial (4%), and White (76%). Approximately 15% of the students receive special education services, and 39% applied and qualified as economically disadvantaged. There are six languages spoken by the students and 15% qualify as Ever English learners.

RMS is more racially diverse than Close Middle School and has a higher percentage of students receiving special education (SPED) services, English-language learner (ELL) services, and qualifying for free and reduced-price lunch. Perhaps as a reflection of biases against students and families of color, RMS has a reputation for a more challenging environment with student discipline issues and a perceived lack of both family and community support.

Need for Improvement

In the fall of 2017, two new administrators began their tenure at RMS. Both were veteran educators who had served in other roles in the district for over a decade prior to assuming their new positions. The principal had more than 35 years of experience, and the assistant principal had 12; they were replacing two administrators who were moved to other buildings in the same year. These two new leaders were assigned to RMS because the school was not meeting expectations and significant changes needed to be made. These two administrators were ready for the task.

One of the first tasks for the assistant principal was to determine how to welcome back a student who had been expelled the previous year. With little knowledge and understanding of past practices within the building, the assistant principal organized a restorative circle using restorative justice prior to the start of the school year. Staff members present at the time expressed an interest in the process and shared these were not disciplinary procedures they had heard of or seen before. This shift in how we used an antiracist, culturally responsive equity lens to respond to discipline referrals was only the beginning.

As the assistant principal reviewed data from the previous year, she conducted an equity audit and discovered where the school was regarding who was receiving referrals and who experienced resulting disparities for academic achievement: Students of color were disproportionately receiving referrals, and male students were disproportionately being removed from classrooms for detentions, in-school suspensions, and out-of-school suspensions at alarming rates. The need for improvement was clear. Discipline procedures and practices in the building were systems that desperately needed to be changed. As Thonstad (2019) notes, "in understanding a problem deeply, it is important to recognize that your system is set up to get exactly the results it is getting" (p. 271).

The First Year

Seeing the System as a New Building Leader

The assistant principal was deeply familiar with the use of IS and how it could be used to change systems at scale to improve student outcomes. While some administrators may prefer to lead by directive and some teachers may prefer to just be told what to do, IS methods do not reflect this belief. Leaders and teachers thrive when they are involved, included, and their expertise respected. Peterson and Carlile (2019) note: "Although IS does respect the ability of teachers and leaders to understand the complexity of improvement in a particular context, it also places increasing responsibility on teachers and school leaders for reform" (p. 175). Their call to take responsibility for our educational disparities and to take action was heard by the new administrators.

Collecting and Analyzing Data

In the first year, the assistant principal started with asking teachers at an August in-service meeting to predict what the data would show and reviewing the data. The assistant principal asked all staff to make predictions about the following:

- Who receives the most referrals:
  - Female or male?
  - 6th or 7th or 8th graders?
  - Hispanic or White?
- When are more referrals written?
  - What time of the day?
  - Which day of the week?
  - Which week of the year?

After asking each staff member to individually predict these trends, she started with the first question. When every single hand went up to indicate that the staff believed male students received more referrals than did female students, her comment was "If we can predict it, we can be proactive about it." If staff knew that male students were struggling with behavioral expectations, that was a clear area where work could be done to better support the students. The staff spent time over the next hour reviewing the school board policies around student discipline and equity.

The school board policy for discipline stated that discipline in the district is based on a philosophy designed to produce behavioral changes that will enable students to develop the self-discipline necessary to remain in school and to function successfully in their educational and social environments. This was the groundwork for the steps that were to follow.

Creating an Improvement Team

A newly created improvement team that would focus on discipline included the assistant principal, three licensed staff, one classified staff, an administrative intern, and the district community liaison. The assistant principal shared the results of the data collection and analysis with the newly created discipline team. In this first meeting, the staff moved through a brainstorming protocol around two key pieces: the purpose of discipline and the ideal outcomes of disciplinary procedures. The following are some of the intentions set by the team when thinking about the purpose of discipline:

- To give feedback
- To help students engage successfully
- Equity in expectations and consequences
- To teach
- To offer/learn new options for handling challenges
- To strengthen relationships among students, staff, and families
- Order and safety
- To allow students to work together with staff and students in a respectful manner
- To guide behavior of staff and students
- Schoolwide discipline to encourage structure, fairness, common behaviors

- All shareholders feel safe in all ways
- To help students to solve the what and why of behavior
- To be aware of shortcomings
- Consistency in staff expectations
- Create change where needed
- To change behavior to help the flow of the classroom
- Plan so stakeholders know expectations
- To remind students of expectations when needed
- A new behavior skill is stated, developed, and honed
- The opportunity for a conversation
- The opportunity for a solution
- Demonstrate that students are loved and cared for
- To teach students appropriate social interaction strategies
- To create an environment conducive to learning

The discipline team also spent time sharing what they thought each stakeholder would need to succeed. This list was brainstormed without including other stakeholders, a temporary breach in IS protocols. When the lack of student and family voice was identified, students and family voices were also included (see Table 7.1).

Change Ideas

Our next step was to have the team review the data and existing policies and procedures around discipline and suggest change ideas. Change ideas included increasing our communication, having a clear set of procedures, students engaging in problem-solving before an office referral, and teachers connecting with families before an office referral was written. Ideally, we would test one change idea and then adopt, adapt, or abandon the strategy based on whether our strategy resulted in improvement. However, we made a different choice.

The team created a new discipline flow chart that indicated expectations based on student conduct. The goal was to make procedures clear, increase communication, and ensure that each staff member knew their role in support student behavior. It also emphasized the importance of in-classroom supports through which teachers and support staff were building relationships with students daily.

Table 7.1. Stakeholder List of Needs for Success

What do we need to succeed?	

Students
• Staff touching base with families early on in the year, making connections that are positive to ensure negative phone calls/emails resonate more!!!
• Clear expectations
• Clear systems of support
• Reminders throughout the year about expectations, especially at key times (spring, right before/after breaks)
• Advocates—who is my person?
  – Advisor? Core teacher?
• Empathy
• Self-advocacy skills
• Peer-conflict resolution skills
	Staff
	• Clear expectations—flow chart/rubric on relationships/discipline
	• Effective vs. noneffective; counseling time-outs
	• Safety in asking for assistance
	• Clear system for what is classroom- vs. office-managed
	• Collaboration with administration
	  – The more examples before we start the year the better; fewer what-ifs
	• Clear systems of support
	  – Instructional facilitators
	  – Administrators
	  – Professional learning
	• Clear and timely communication from administrators
	  – Close the loop!
	  – Follow through
	  – ALL staff
	• Empathy
	• Strategies and professional learning around communicating with families

Families
• Clear/timely communication from staff and administrators
• Positive feedback early on to help ensure behavior does not derail learning
• Clear expectations for students
• Caring staff
• Kind tone on phone and in person- not talking at/ not telling them how they should have parented
• Meet parents/adults where they are
• Flexible meeting times—not scheduling meetings so they miss a full day's work when they are hourly
• Phone conversations if those work better
• Awesome front office secretary is bilingual
• Will speed up parent contact with Spanish-speaking families
• Empathy
	Administrators
	• Clear/timely communication from staff
	• Communication with parents
	• Communication with ALL staff (classified)
	  – Discipline expectation for students
	  – Hallway expectations for students
	  – Schoolwide expectations for students
	  – Included in meeting that may affect them and/or written information
	• Empathy
	• Concerns to be brought to admin about discipline in a productive way

To support students in the classroom, a problem-solving form was created for teachers and staff members to use before sending a student to the office. By allowing students time to pause and reflect on what was happening in the situation, there were opportunities for the student to regulate without having to be removed from the classroom completely. By providing supports for the users closest to the occurrence (teachers, classified support staff), the adults working with the student were able to build deeper relationships with students and problem-solve in ways that showed students they were their advocates.

In addition, a new referral form was created in collaboration with the neighboring middle school to align practices between the two schools. One of the biggest changes made was requiring the staff member who wrote the referral to be the first point of contact at home. The assistant principal knew the key to supporting students in behavioral changes was building relationships with the adults who worked with them the most.

PDSA Cycle 1

In the first 6 weeks of school, the assistant principal tracked the disciplinary conversations she had with students who were sent to the office (see Table 7.2)

She also noted that students who were Latinx and received SPED services and/or identified as active ELL and/or dual identified for both SPED and ELL were disproportionately receiving failing grades (Ds and Fs; see Table 7.3).

The data were based on live grades rather than summative grades that had been finalized at the end of a grading term, but they foretold negative academic outcomes for these students if something did not change quickly.

Seeing the disparities for both grades and discipline caused alarm for the leaders in the building. They knew they needed to analyze what was happening in their school: "Effective problem-solving demands that a premium be placed not just on what needs to be fixed but also analyzing why systems currently work as they do and learning how they might be reformed for the goal of greater efficacy at scale" (Bryk et al., 2015, p. 32). The assistant principal continued to monitor the data, looking for trends with the disciplinary referrals that were written and trying to better see the system as it currently existed. By midyear, the referral data continued to show a similar pattern (see Table 7.4).

Table 7.2. Discipline Referrals: First 6 Weeks

	Number of Referrals/ Total	**Percentage**
Female	15/84	18
Male	69/84	82
6th Grade	14/85	16.7
7th Grade	24/84	28.6
8th Grade	44/84	52.4

Table 7.3. Demographics of Students Receiving Failing Grades

	Percentage of Student Population	**Percentage of Total Failing Grades**
Total student population	100	20
Latinx	26	27
Receive SPED services	15	40
Active ELL	21 Ever English?	55
Dual-identified	% of overall population?	69

Note: SPED = special education; ELL = English-language learner.

Table 7.4. Demographics of Discipline Trends

	October Percentage	**January Percentage**	**Percentage Change**
Female	18	20.9	+2.9
Male	82	79.1	−2.9
6th Grade	16.7	21.2	+4.5
7th Grade	28.6	32.1	+3.5
8th Grade	52.4	46.7	−5.7

Decision: Adopt, Adapt, or Abandon the Change Ideas

The assistant principal sat down with the team and other administrators to brainstorm what next steps might be. Through the collaboration, the secondary team determined there was a need to

- identify strategies for staff to use that will support discipline work with male students specifically. As a staff, we continued to disproportionately discipline male students compared to female students.
- increase the use of Collaborative Problem Solving (CPS) strategies as those had helped build partnerships among general education teachers, special education teachers, counselors, and administration noting the clear guidelines and boundaries with consistency had improved student behavior across the school.
- improve guidance and professional learning for support staff who struggled with student behavior and who did not utilize CPS strategies. Some staff did this naturally, with or without training, but some struggled with empathy and in making ways to work with students in culturally responsive, individualized ways that ensured success.

PDSA Cycle 2

The changes identified after PDSA Cycle 2 were implemented at RMS in the second semester by the assistant principal with the support of the discipline team. Because the assistant principal supervised many of the classified staff, relationships had already been formed and goals for supporting students were set for the remainder of the year. Classified staff met with the assistant principal regularly and when the team identified students needing additional behavioral supports, the team determined who had the best relationship with the student; that adult provided structured support proactively and reactively. Breaks were given, safe spaces were offered, and positive behavioral intervention and strategies allowed the team to identify incentives students were willing to work toward.

By the end of the year, the focus on grade-level supports seemed to be working. Although eighth graders were disproportionately receiving referrals early on in the year, the referral count matched the grade-level demographics, within a few percentage points, at the end of their first year (see Table 7.5).

Table 7.5. Discipline Data by Demographics: End of Year

	October	January	October–January Difference	June	October–June Difference
Female	18%	20.90%	+2.9%	17.1%	−0.9%
Male	82%	79.10%	−2.9%	82.9%	0.9%
6th Grade	16.7%	21.20%	+4.5%	28.8%	12.1%
7th Grade	28.6%	32.10%	+3.5%	35.4%	6.8%
8th Grade	52.4%	46.70%	−5.7%	35.8%	−16.6%

Seeing the System: What Worked and What Did Not Work

Although we improved our disproportionate referral of eighth-grade students, we did not improve our disproportionate referrals for boys. Data about discipline outcomes for students based on racial demographics had not been closely studied over the full year, and end-of-year disaggregation of data by race was not completed, a serious mistake in our equity work.

At the end of the year, we conducted a postmortem and determined that classrooms were not set up as a system conducive to support students with an active learning style. We still had much to learn about trauma-informed practices for staff. The responses to male behaviors were reactive and not proactive. Male students continued to be disproportionately written up for referrals at a rate of nearly nine to one and specific male students were receiving a significant number of referrals as staff "documented" behavior concerns:

- five male students had over 30 referrals each
- six male students had between 20 and 29 referrals each
- eight male students had between 10 and 19 referrals each
- one female had 11 referrals

These 20 students received 424 of the 948 overall referrals, or 44.73%. The demographics of these students included Latinx (40%), African American/Black (5%), and White (55%).

There were also inconsistent procedures and staff support:

- five different secretaries input referrals into the online tracking system
- data input did not occur in a timely fashion
- the discipline committee and data review process did not occur throughout the year to identify formative and proactive steps
- nearly one third of licensed staff were new to the building

PDSA Cycle 3

Looking back on the previous year, the assistant principal identified what she could do to move the work forward. She adjusted the discipline team meeting schedule to mirror the attendance team schedule, meeting biweekly. She identified a timeline for making student schedule changes before the end of the first quarter to better match student learning with teachers' teaching style. She scheduled break times for students whose past behavior indicated that they needed this time to catch their breath, regulate, or just pause for a few minutes. She scheduled times for increasing family partnerships. She used summer months to increase training in trauma-informed practices; these trained staff members would become members of the trauma team and discipline team. She increased training and support for the attendance/discipline secretary to ensure data were entered and reports prepared prior to regularly scheduled team meetings. Students who needed a better balance of activities received personalized schedules, including walk–talk time with adults with whom they connected and felt safe. She recommitted to her antiracist, culturally responsive leadership beliefs to ensure data were reviewed regularly by gender, ethnicity/race, and grade level. Meetings were scheduled with families for any student receiving three referrals. Teacher training on alternatives to referrals continued. The team met regularly to review data and adjust their change ideas to support student behavior. At the end of the year, the data revealed that boys continued to be disproportionately referred for discipline, and Latinx students were disproportionately referred for discipline. Despite these changes, we had made no significant improvement (see Table 7.6).

Before heading into the next year, the assistant principal engaged in empathy interviews with students with multiple referrals and

Table 7.6. Change in Referrals November to June

	November	February	November–February Difference	June	November–June Difference
Female	15.98%	12.78%	–3.20%	12.13%	–3.85%
Male	84.02%	87.22%	3.20%	87.87%	3.85%
6th Grade	38.36%	34.20%	–4.16%	36.29%	–2.07%
7th Grade	18.26%	22.11%	3.84%	20.04%	1.78%
8th Grade	43.38%	43.70%	0.32%	43.67%	0.29%
Latinx 17% of total population	39.27%	38.77%	-0.50%	36.50%	–2.77%
White 76% of total population	56.62%	57.72%	1.10%	57.17%	0.55%

students who had not received a referral in 3 years at RMS. She also sought out staff members who wrote the most and the least number of referrals for the year to better understand their experiences in the classroom. Through these empathy interviews, teachers, students, and families shared what supports were improving students' behavior and what was keeping them in the classroom learning. The major theme in each of the conversations was the importance of relationships.

PDSA Cycle 4

A key learning was that we should have conducted empathy interviews with our students of color during our first PDSA cycle. Empathy interviews revealed that culturally responsive relationships were making the difference for our students of color and for the Latinx students specifically. By identifying the support staff who had the best relationships with students and their families before the year began, plans were proactively placed for push-in supports and scheduled connections to foster the continued connections.

There were also unplanned beneficial outcomes from the conversations after PDSA Cycle 3. Staff members started asking each other about their practices around writing students up for behavioral infractions. Professional learning communities by grade and content area asked for supports specific to the issues they were experiencing in their classrooms and teachers experienced what Perry et al. (2020) notice: "As a working professional, you want your work to make a difference, to spread, and to be useful to others and yourself" (p. 23). The initial conversations with a few students and staff had created a ripple effect. Now disciplinary practices were part of ongoing conversations, not just relegated to once-a-year or even to the disciplinary team meetings.

Additionally, time to collaborate with the discipline team allowed the staff to make adjustments to the referral form and define discipline terms for consistency and alignment to the trauma-informed care and culturally responsive practices. The team also created and led professional development around best practices for classroom management with staff to target specific behavioral needs and lagging skills for students. These professional development opportunities were geared toward the behaviors being documented the most consistently across the larger system.

During the empathy interviews, we noticed another variation in performance: who was writing the referrals. Reflecting on these data, the assistant principal met with multiple staff members to identify what worked and when so the staff could adapt at scale what was being successful within this specific context. Through partnerships with the counselors and administration where specific behavior concerns persisted, staff learned and grew. Identified staff received Child Protective Services training along with training in trauma-informed care to support their own growth and to grow the leadership of key staff in the building.

Looking to the system, support staff schedules were solidified and communicated to all staff, with intentionality around which classified staff were assigned to specific classrooms based on both student need and licensed staff strengths. This opportunity to build stronger relationships allowed the classified staff to better support the behavior of the students they served. Knowing our students more deeply allowed the team to write behavior plans and put behavior contracts in place earlier in the year, proactively seeking supports that would keep students in the classroom and support teaching staff. The team also changed the schedules in first semester for students who were struggling behaviorally, with counselors and support staff focusing deeply on building relationships with new sixth graders.

RMS also established the Wellness Space with planned breaks, sensory options, movement breaks, and quiet activities to meet student needs. We created a consistent staffing schedule so students knew who they would see in our two offices and who was available to support them. Students would seek out specific adults they had built relationships with, including the secretaries, custodians, and kitchen staff.

At the end of the first quarter, each grade level identified two or three students who were struggling the most behaviorally. Once identified, the entire staff was made aware who the students were, regardless of whether the student was in their classes or not. Throughout the building, staff sought to give positive affirmation and behavioral support every change they got. This schoolwide "dosing" of positivity saw much lower referral rates as a result. The referral count decreased more than 40%. Grade-level referrals were within a few percentage points of their population proportion as well. Most important, students of color were receiving referrals at a rate that was proportional to their enrollment. The focus on supporting students through culturally responsive relationships was reducing the referral counts and addressing our equity goals.

PDSA Cycle 5

The discipline team met again in February 2020 to review these data. As a team, they made predictions using a discipline prediction tool.

Working with partners, each team reviewed the discipline data presented in different ways, including data disaggregated by special population, comparing the 2018–2019 and 2019–2020 school years, and considering students with multiple referrals and by types of infractions. The most significant conversations came from reviewing the data disaggregated by gender, race/ethnicity, and receiving services for ELL or SPED (see Table 7.7).

Table 7.7. Discipline Data Disaggregated

	Referral	RMS Population	Difference
Female	24.62%	50.28%	−25.66%
Male	75.38%	49.53%	25.85%
6th Grade	36.92%	36.10%	0.82%
7th Grade	29.23%	35.14%	−5.91%
8th Grade	33.85%	28.76%	5.09%
Latinx 17% of total population	29.23%	27.22%	2.01%
White 76% of total population	60.77%	65.25%	−4.48%
SPED 15% of total population	17.69%	12.90%	4.79%
TAG 5%	2.31%	4.86%	−2.55%
ELL 21% of total population	6.15%	5.05%	1.10%
Monitored 18%	12.31%	9.53%	2.78%

Note: SPED = special education; TAG = talented and gifted;
ELL = English-language learner.

The team recognized that the changes in the first semester had significantly reduced the number of referrals overall but had the greatest impact on reducing referrals for male students. All other special population referral counts were within about 5% of the population proportion.

Lessons Learned

Although we decreased disparities in our third year, it was clear that it took too long to address racial disparities and there was still more to do. Bryk (2020) contends that improvement requires believing strongly in what you are trying to accomplish and building a community that advances agency for these changes. But simultaneous with that, improvement also entails challenging what you are doing and questioning where you may be coming up short. (p. 98)

In our case, we needed to focus on culturally responsive teaching practices as well as other systems issues. The team understood that and identified a few areas to focus their energy for the second semester:

- reviewing referral language to determine biases for disciplining Latinx and male behaviors
- finding ways to proactively support monitored students who had been transitioned out as active ELL supports
- teaming with SPED teachers to identify proactive supports for students receiving three or more referrals that had also been identified as needing SPED services
- reviewing staff data to see who was or was not writing disciplinary referrals to identify potential biases

The team recognized barriers to greater improvement were

- traditional classroom settings and instructional decisions that have not adjusted to meet the needs of our changing demographics and student needs, are not culturally responsive, and result in racial and ethnic disparities
- inconsistent classroom and hallway expectations from all staff
- work requests for students in in-school suspension or out-of-school suspension were not being met
- the large proportion of new staff, both new to teaching and new to RMS; changing staff at RMS makes consistency difficult, with 60% of our licensed staff at RMS having been at the school for less than 3 years

Pausing the Work During COVID-19

As the second semester began, the team was not able to continue their work. Schools were shut down with the COVID-19 global pandemic. Although the classroom moved to virtual screens, the discipline team committed to continuing their work when students returned to the building. There is still more work to do, particularly regarding anti-racist and culturally responsive teaching practices (Gay, 2010), but the conversations started through exploring data from different perspectives and stakeholders allowed proactive supports for behavioral concerns to be implemented. As Bryk et al. (2015) explain, "harnessing multiple forms of expertise, so that they joined together as something considerably more than a sum of random parts, is essential for meaningful change" (p. 140). Moving forward, staff will continue to use culturally responsive practices, trauma-informed practices, collaborative problem-solving, and relationship-focused tactics to support all students to achieve the goal of being both academically and socially successful in our school.

Discussion Questions

1. How might you use empathy interviews to better understand the experience of students and families from all backgrounds and to gather actionable information as you investigate your system and biases within your system?
2. How do you create intentional teams of stakeholders to value multiple perspectives in analyzing the system as it currently exists and understanding who the system advantages and disadvantages?
3. Where are change ideas improving the system, and where are change ideas stagnating or worsening outcomes for students, particularly students of color and other historically underserved populations?

References

Bryk, A. S. (2020). *Improvement in action: Advancing quality in America's schools* (Continuous Improvement in Education Series). Harvard Education Press.

Bryk, A. S., Gomez, L. M., Grunow, A., & LeMahieu, P. G. (2015). *Learning to improve: How America's schools can get better at getting better.* Harvard Education Press.

Gay, G. (2010). *Culturally responsive teaching: Theory, research, and practice* (2nd ed.). Teachers College Press. file:///Users/dpeterso/Downloads/reyourbook chaptereditsrequestedbysept_13/ Geneva Gay – Culturally Responsive Teaching - Central ... https:/www.cwu.edu › sites › files › documents

Perry, J. A., Zambo, D., & Crow, R. (2020). *The improvement science dissertation in practice: A guide for faculty, committee members, and their students* (Improvement Science in Education and Beyond). Myers Education Press.

Peterson, D.S. & Carlile, S.P. (2019). "Preparing school leaders to effectively lead school improvement efforts: Improvement science." (pp. 167–182). In R. Crowe, B. N. Hinnant-Crawford, & D. Spaulding (Eds.), *The Educational Leader's Guide to Improvement Science: Data, Design and Cases for Reflection.* Myers Education Press.

Thonstad, C. (2019). Growth and grading: Overcoming "grades don't matter" in middle school. In R. Crow, B. N. Hinnant-Crawford, & D. Spaulding (Eds.), *The educational leader's guide to improvement science: Data, design and cases for reflection* (pp. 257–275). Myers Education Press.

CHAPTER EIGHT

Improving Our Response to Intervention Program: Improvement Science

VICTORIA BROWN

Eagle Elementary School (EES; pseudonyms used throughout) is one of five elementary schools in a school district in the Willamette Valley in Oregon. Led by one administrator, it is the only dual-language school in the district and with a population of 550 students, is the largest elementary school in the district and the third-largest school in the district following the high school and one of the two middle schools. Admission to the dual-language program is a lottery process, open to all students outside the school's boundaries, with half of the students Hispanic and half non-Hispanic. The goal of the dual-language program is to improve outcomes for speakers of other languages (SOLs).

With more than 95% of students qualifying for free and reduced-priced lunch, EES is a Title I school offering services to support students living in poverty. EES has multiple community partnerships, including a daily free breakfast and lunch program. A resource room run by the community provides students access to clothing, school supplies, and personal hygiene items as needed. However, what sets the elementary school apart from most Title I schools is that it offers free after-school care for all students through a partnership with a local church. A local university also has preservice teachers that provide after-school academic support for students falling behind. EES is known for forging relationships with community partners that benefit the student population.

Improvement Science Team

EES uses the response-to-intervention (RTI) system to support student success. The Tier II behavior intervention team consists of the building administrator, one counselor, one special education (SPED) teacher, and myself. As a principal intern, I chose this team because of their existing leadership responsibilities for specialized services for students. Using improvement science (IS) methods, we could increase our services to students without placing additional burdens on their already overworked and understaffed departments. We met every 6 weeks to discuss data on our interventions, talk about referral data, review teacher requests for assistance, and problem-solve. I then met with my administrator to discuss the IS-specific topics in order to refine our process and track the small changes that the IS process requires. In the first year of its creation, the Tier II behavior intervention team was a big change for our school. I engaged in numerous follow-up meetings with my administrator to focus on the driver diagram and to refine the IS process. Our formal meetings had agendas that we followed very closely and the unofficial meetings were leadership mentoring sessions to guide me in the IS process. Our next step was to complete the fishbone diagram and identify a focus for our improvement efforts.

Need for Improvement

I chose to use the Frattura and Capper (2007) equity audit template in order to have disaggregated data reveal trends in student behavior data. The equity audit data helped us identify our problem of practice: Our interventions for behaviorally challenged students do not address their needs. However, we needed more information on which kids needed additional interventions. We noticed that most referrals were for boys who are White. We also needed additional data regarding which teachers were writing discipline referrals and for which students.

We know as educators that students with adverse childhood experiences and resulting trauma (Romero et al., 2018) demonstrate behaviors reflective of their trauma. Although we understand this, it is difficult to know how to best address a student's dysregulation in the classroom. Teachers can end up frustrated and at their wit's end. It was important to develop a team of behavior specialists that support students' sense of physical and emotional safety in the classroom, provide additional services based on need, and refer students for SPED services if needed. This is a tiered intervention model that supports students as well as teachers. Our behavior intervention team examined the root causes of student behavior.

Empathy Interviews

In addition to making sure we were addressing root causes of student behavior, we wanted to understand the perspective of staff. Empathy interview data revealed that a large part of our specialists' days focused on addressing student behavior. We discovered that 50% of one SPED teacher's work in the previous year was spent managing the behavior of kids who were not on his caseload. As a result of our previous improvement process, he has been able to spend 90% of his time working with students solely on his caseload; our principal also saw a decrease in time spent managing behavior. The person who has not experienced a decrease in their duties or responsibilities is the person who is responsible for Tier II interventions, our counselor. He continued to address misbehavior for 50% of his day; while the improvement effort was an improvement for others, it was not for him. However, he identified the biggest benefit of the improvement work was improved systems for support. He indicated he would like to see our next improvement effort focus on the capacity of teachers to manage Tier II behaviors without always having to rely on our team members.

Theory of Improvement

The initial working theory of improvement came from our district's work around RTI and tiers of support. The district had started by focusing on reading and had a pretty solid foundation developed in this area. However, with the district moved to increasing the inclusion of students receiving SPED services in general education classrooms, we found that there was a need for behavior interventions that also were supported by RTI. We got together and identified the barriers that we faced when it came to systematically supporting student behavior. We found that teachers, staffing, interventions, identification, and not having a system were our primary drivers. Secondary drivers that were within our locus of control included increasing our responsibility for our school's break space for students receiving SPED services, known as "the Falcon's Nest," and tracking our data through our check-in, check-out (CICO) system. Finally, we were able to focus on what we needed to do when a student was not responding to the prescribed Tier II intervention, which led us to look at systems that were in place and how we tracked functional behavior assessments (FBAs) and behavior intervention plans (BIPs).

Our plan to address equity during this process was twofold. First, we knew that boys were disproportionately identified as needing additional behavior supports to be more successful in the classroom. Second, we knew that there was an additional burden placed on our counselor due to the sheer number of students we have and the responsibilities placed on him. Each of our cycles focused on what students needed and then how each team member could create a broader system of support.

Testing the Change

With each Plan–Do–Study–Act (PDSA) cycle, we found additional aspects of the plan that needed to be developed in order to address student needs. I had initially thought that if we had a strong Tier II intervention system in place, all would be solved. During each PDSA cycle, we ensured that we were continuously monitoring our systems and determining what needed to happen when a student was not responding.

Tier II interventions are designed to meet the needs of approximately 15% of the school population. We were serving 7% of the school population in a Tier II intervention, so our goal was for Tier II interventions to be successful with 15% of the population. We considered various components of our informal interventions, whether they were a fit for our formal interventions, and if they also resulted in teachers feeling supported. We also wanted to know if we were under-identifying students.

Our next steps in this project were to have another meeting during which we modified our plans for students based on our underutilization of the CICO system and increased staffing in our break spaces. Additional steps were looking at Tier I supports and student identification measures. Next, I share what we learned through our PDSA cycles.

PDSA Cycle 1

In PDSA Cycle 1, we implemented a data-based intervention by taking responsibility for the Falcon's Nest, our school break space. This was not a small change, and we found that multiple secondary drivers had to be addressed, but our easiest measure was comparing the number of students served over the past years in the Falcon's Nest. In 2019–2020, we had a 44% increase in the number of students being served in the Falcon's Nest over the 2018–2019 school year. Traditionally, the Falcon's Nest was only accessible to kids being served by individualized education plans (IEPs), and therefore, we were able to open the room up to other students not served by IEPs to provide support they needed.

Empathy interviews and comparisons of data from the previous year were used to evaluate success in PDSA Cycle 1. The Tier II team taking over the Falcon's Nest allowed us to find ways to use classified staff as behavior interventionists. To maximize student usage of the Falcon's Nest, we moved the room to another classroom in the building, requested grant money, and purchased supplies for the various stations in the room. We needed to develop the data tracking system for students based on the zones of regulation that we were using schoolwide to develop emotional literacy in kids and help them identify their emotions. In addition, we needed teachers to collect data to determine how kids were returning to class. Although the data were helpful in our Tier II team meetings, we had no comparative data from the previous year. However, because the project started out as a way to assist the administrator and licensed support staff so that they were not continuously putting out fires, empathy interview data and the number of students served were used to determine if we should adopt, abandon, or adapt this change idea. At the end of PDSA Cycle 1, we decided the data indicated we should adopt this as a change for our school.

PDSA Cycle 2

In PDSA Cycle 2, we needed to refine how we tracked data for the CICO system to ensure that the system was being implemented schoolwide and that it was an effective intervention. We used continual tracking of students who were on CICO plans to determine if the program was being followed. We analyzed their daily points, tracking graph, and other student data to determine if it was an effective intervention for specific kids, noticing that three of the four students met their target 80% of the time. This PDSA cycle created the most discussion and reflection. The CICO system is considered to be a research-based Tier II intervention designed to meet the needs of 15% of students, yet CICO was only serving 7% of our students. We decided to try a new change idea: identify more mentors to check in with kids, develop a better data tracking system, and add students to the program. A social work intern volunteered to enter data into our system for mentor use. We added to our team meeting agendas a data discussion to ensure that we were focusing on what we do when kids are meeting, not meeting, or exceeding expectations. We wanted to be able to tailor students' plans to meet their individual needs.

At the end of this PDSA cycle, we used an audit of our CICO intervention program to determine next steps for the process. We found that students not responding were not regularly being tracked and followed up with when referred for an FBA. This became the focus for our next PDSA cycle.

PDSA Cycle 3

We began PDSA Cycle 3 in the spring of 2021, shortly before the COVID-19 school closure. We had our interventions in place but did not have an effective system for next steps when a child was not responding. Office referrals continued to mount, and everyone was trying to help, but we weren't sure who was doing what. Formal behavior evaluations needed to take place, and we did not have a system for tracking this. Our change idea was to add to every meeting agenda a discussion of student FBAs. This was highly effective. For the first time, we had all the information in one place and were able to share responsibilities when it came to ensuring we were following federal and state guidelines regarding FBAs and doing what was best for children. We listed which students needed a formal evaluation and behavior plan in place and who was responsible for which students. We tracked the change in their status every 3 weeks.

Once schools reopened, FBA discussions continued to be on every agenda.

Implementation Challenges

The Tier II behavior intervention team started and began testing changes through PDSA cycles because of the high number of students and teachers needing support with student behavior and the limited number of staff able to address these needs. The most important part of this project was making sure that the team met regularly to track how students were doing and to adapt, adopt, or abandon our change idea based on our data and our context. At every team meeting, we tracked changes, monitored progress, evaluated success criteria, and agreed on modifications going forward. We used empathy interview data, CICO data, and systems review feedback from the team to determine our next steps.

We began the 2019–2020 school year with a focus on improving student outcomes in the classroom based on behavior interventions at the Tier II level. The school district is an RTI participant and our interventions needed to be research-based and measurable. In order to provide interventions that were measurable, we expanded participation in our Falcon's Nest program, improved our CICO data tracking system, and created a system for tracking students who were not responding to our Tier II interventions. There were many successes in this project that allowed for students to better receive what they needed to be successful in school. However, there are some future considerations to keep in mind when moving forward into the school years that follow.

It is going to be important for leaders to determine if these behavior interventions equate to an improvement in academic achievement. A school's role in a student's life is changing, and there is a heavy focus on social-emotional awareness and support; however, a school's main objective still remains academic achievement for all students. It will be essential to consider how these changes have impacted student achievement and determine if there is a loss of learning or an improvement in student achievement. During the course of this project, it was not possible to correlate interventions to test scores or grades. However, with data from this year and report card data, it will be possible in the coming years to consider how a student's academic performance is being affected through Tier II behavior supports.

Furthermore, wellness rooms are being developed in many schools; however, there is limited research on whether the time spent out of the class is negatively impacting a student's academic performance. Time out of the classroom is instructional time lost. How do we balance the emotional state and mental health of students while ensuring that they receive high-quality instruction at the same time? These are important considerations because they could potentially decrease student achievement if not planned well. In our case, we decided to schedule time in the wellness room around direct instruction time, which was not always easy to do.

Finally, we have to consider all tiers of intervention when recommending students for a specific intervention. We need to do this by tracking who is being referred. Are there more boys than girls? Are students of color or recent immigrants referred more often than others? These are important considerations when analyzing referral data. If we fail to recognize that we are underserving or overidentifying historically underserved students, we are perpetuating a system of oppression.

Discussion Questions

1. What could contribute to your team's ability to adapt, adopt, or abandon a change after a PDSA cycle?
2. What sociopolitical issues would you need to consider when implementing an improvement project in the area of student behavior?
3. How could your team go about conducting an equity audit?
4. What data, disaggregated by gender, race, ethnicity, socioeconomic group, or ability group would be hard for your teaching staff to address? What resources would be of help?

References

Frattura, E. M., & Capper, C. A. (2007). *Leading for social justice: Transforming schools for all learners*. Corwin.

Romero, V., Robertson, R., & Warner, A. (2018). *Building resilience in students impacted by adverse childhood experiences: A whole-staff approach*. Corwin.

CHAPTER NINE

Increasing Academic Success Through a High School Advisory Program

BRYCE BENNETT

South High School (SHS; pseudonyms used throughout) is a traditional public school with Grades 9 to 12 and 1,300 students, located in a small town of 52,000 residents an hour outside a major urban area. Approximately 90% of families speak English in the home, while 8% speak Spanish and 2% speak other languages; students of color compose 35% of the population, and 14% of students receive special education services. Almost half the families receive free or reduced-price lunch services.

SHS is an AVID Demonstration School (AVID, n.d.), one of three demonstration schools in Oregon. SHS is recognized for removing barriers to success in education, its high-level instructional practices, and student growth. Most professional development activities are related to AVID strategies. SHS also completes a student needs assessment every year. The data give us information on school culture and climate, as well as to identify if students' individual needs are met. This survey, completed by the entire student body, provides a data set for the school on which to base preventative work, as well as identify obstacles to social-emotional and academic success. Students are brutally honest in this survey, and the school supports individual students who are exploring their gender identity, have suicidal ideation, struggle with addiction, or other personal conditions that impact their success. The data identify systemic issues related to equity in the school and provide information related to the experiences of adolescents in our school and community.

Advisory Programs

High school advisory programs are frequently implemented by schools as a way to strengthen connections between adults and students to foster a personalized and supportive school culture. Unfortunately, most schools have developed advisories with the reliance upon intuition and anecdotal evidence rather than empirical data (Shulkind & Foote, 2009). Due to this lack of empirical evidence and the fact that many advisory programs are difficult to maintain and fund, school advisories are constantly modified and often removed from the school schedule after inconsistent outcomes. Evidence of academic and social-emotional improvement is inconsistent or negligible. Due to lack of structure, advisories become classroom teacher-dependent. Although it is clear that in any given building, some teachers develop highly successful advisories in which students feel connected to teachers and peers, other advisories become a place where students get a "break" from education and use the time as a study period or as time to connect with friends. Typically, when schools attempt to make advisories more focused on academics, they select a "one size fits all" scripted program that does not address educational disparities appropriate for their environment.

SHS was not an exception. Data collected over time regarding advisory success indicated a disconnect between the established goals and current practice. The school needed a program that provided academic interventions for students who were failing and who were not on track to graduate in four years. One of the components of the school's improvement plan was based on academic success defined by "on track for graduation," as reported by the Oregon Department of Education. Using these data, the Principal Advisory Committee and site council established the goal that 90% of 9th- to 11th-grade students would be on track to graduate at the end of the 2019–2020 school year. The school support teams defined *academic success* as having the required credits and college-ready grades at the end of the 2019–2020 school year. The school needed a means of completing this goal.

Need for Improvement

The SHS advisory period is called "FLIGHT," and during summer planning, the FLIGHT team created a plan that acknowledged the school's excellent tools for academic intervention that were already in place while also recognizing that the current advisory system was not performing the way that it was originally designed. As an example, the FLIGHT class, a 35-minute period that meets Monday through Friday, was used basically as a homeroom/study hall. Based on teacher and district support feedback and student outcome data, the team believed that adding more structure to FLIGHT classes in the form of academic interventions and assistance was needed.

The Plan–Do–Study–Act (PDSA) Cycle: Planning

The Improvement Science Team. The initial improvement science team consisted of 12 members. The team included the principal, an assistant principal, a school counselor, and eight teachers that represented every department in our school, as well as our AVID director. The team also included the coordinator of our after-school tutoring and mentoring program called RISE. These members were selected in order to get a wide perspective from people who are already school leaders and/or were willing to embark on a change initiative. The goal was to get a wealth of information about what was working in the current advisory model as well as identify the goal for change. This task force was challenged with creating a new structure for advisory that was effective in disseminating information regarding social-emotional development and college and career readiness. The principal, the assistant principal, and an administrative intern selected the team members based on their significantly different roles and backgrounds in the school. School involvement and a growth mindset were also factors.

Data Collection and Analysis

This initial group met over a 3-day period. Day 1 was used to assess the current issues, address the school bell schedule, and address the problem of an inefficient advisory. Day 2 focused on exploring other models of advisory used in similar schools, collecting information about successful practices, and gathering information from other staff members. Day 3 was spent compiling the information and creating a new bell schedule and system for advisory that would be productive and was equitable for all students.

A smaller subsection of the core team had numerous follow-up meetings and narrowed the improvement science team to five people. This team consisted of the principal, the assistant principal, an AVID team member who also coordinates our freshmen success class called Pre-flight, a new 0.5 full-time-equivalent staff member who helped coordinate the new advisory team called FLIGHT, and an administrative intern. This team met every Monday morning before school to discuss the plans for the FLIGHT class for the next week, as well as to examine future changes that might need to be incorporated.

Obtaining accurate qualitative and quantitative data was problematic early on. The district data warehouse was not the most user-friendly program, and the variables related to the qualitative data it supplies were already set. It was also very early in the school year, and there was a limited data set. The team was initially challenged to gather useful information from this program and use it to determine the successes of the new schedule and advisory. However, other data sources, including the equity audit and the empathy interview data were collected and reviewed in the design stages of this improvement effort.

Empathy Interviews

In order to get a clear picture of the issues at SHS, several sources of data needed to be collected. Data included district-generated information on grades, credit recovery, graduation data, attendance data, referral information, and needs assessment information. We also conducted empathy interviews with educational leaders, community partners, and teachers who had the most interactions with the historically underserved students at SHS. These empathy interviews helped guide this improvement science project as well as increase cultural awareness of underrepresented students.

Using this information, a staff-wide survey was conducted related to these academic issues. The survey asked questions related to current schoolwide practices related to grading and perceptions regarding student understanding of grading practices. Questions were also asked about how teachers and staff work with students who were falling behind.

The results of the survey and school data were confirmed with a group of students chosen as a representative group of the student population. This group was asked similar questions and encouraged to share what they thought would make a difference in their own academic success. These students were interviewed to see if the educators truly understood their students, as well as to connect both groups, with teachers and students working together to understand the academic needs of historically underserved students.

The team concluded that certain academic success interventions were missing. There was not a successful means of helping historically underserved students understand their grades, grading practices, and a means of understanding how to improve grades once they were failing or fell far behind. Ultimately, the FLIGHT core team hypothesized that the school needed to do a better job of teaching students about academic success, and needed a way to incorporate grade checks, establishing academic goals, and another system for academic support for the students who were behind and felt defeated.

Equity in Academic Success

We read numerous articles to gather more information related to equity and the usefulness of advisory programs. We explored topics such as youth development through social and emotional learning (SEL) interventions, programs supporting English learners (Alvarez et al., 2012) and special education (Edmonds & Spradlin, 2010), examined the relationship between academic growth and social-emotional development (Taylor et al., 2017), and identified culturally responsive teaching strategies.

SEL is one of the interventions that the FLIGHT core team considered a critical component for academic success. On-site collaboration, coaching, and time are essential for widespread changes in teachers' practices across a school or district. Changes in teacher practice require investing time and resources in teachers' learning so that they can develop the expertise needed to improve teaching and learning for English-language learners (ELLs). Students (and their teachers) learn new content and language through participation in activities in which they use and engage with the target language, concepts, and skills. We explored Quality Teaching for English Learners (QTEL, n.d.), which emphasizes the importance of inviting students to engage in challenging disciplinary activities (Alvarez, 2012). We believed that teaching English-language development and incorporating some of the QTEL strategies in all classrooms would increase student engagement, success, and academic accomplishments. If QTEL strategies were related to active participation and were culturally engaging, students would feel that they are part of the learning community. Cultural and preferred language factors would have to be incorporated in our classrooms and be a part of the structure of advisory.

The core team also read research indicating that adults, in general, are not necessarily the answer, but the adults who can also identify with the student culturally and racially can have the most impact on academic gains (Zaff & Malone, 2020). Zaff and Malone (2020) showed that when we have more adult interaction and influence with youth, there are more positive academic and social-emotional outcomes, particularly in predominantly Black or African American communities. When a culture of making connections to students is expected, then positive outcomes will increase. When teachers have the ability to bring community members who reflect their race and ethnicity into the classroom, this is another potential positive influence. Our FLIGHT program was designed to build such relationships between adults and students. However, the typical teacher is White, a native English speaker, and of middle-class background. In order to increase academic success for historically underserved students, we needed to increase our diversity and our cultural responsiveness.

Next we examined research indicating that high-performing districts shared "ownership" of students with disabilities, primarily in the area of collective responsibility for student success and leadership. Teachers who were genuinely concerned with providing students with the skills they would need for their future endeavors, not just skills to pass the state accountability test, also had more academically successful students receiving special education services. When special education teachers worked closely with general educators and had the ability to share their expertise for the benefit of all students, not just those receiving special services, they became better educators.

Teaching with cultural relevance is a vital part of academic growth (Wyatt, 2014). Because of the federal No Child Left Behind legislation, several companies have attempted to create cookie-cutter curriculum in order to achieve higher test scores. Currently, this has morphed into other scripted programs for not only Common Core but also social-emotional development and academic success curriculum. SHS has implemented several of these programs over the last decade, many of which are not culturally sensitive.

Theory of Improvement and Testing the Change

The core team had researched other schools and programs, as well as academic data from schools with similar demographics. The team reviewed the times and placements of current FLIGHT classes and how that time was utilized. Furthermore, the team decided that the school needed to incorporate academic success components in professional development and department teams, with the hope of it influencing the configuration of FLIGHT and ultimately academic success. Finally, they wanted to introduce character-building components addressing academic prowess and motivation in FLIGHT classes. Our aim statement was that by June 2020, the advisory program will enhance its current curriculum to define *academic improvement*, provide resources related to academic improvement, and understand character traits related to academic improvement for all students.

The core team focused on possible change ideas that could improve the FLIGHT advisory program. To best understand the barriers to academic achievement in FLIGHT, the core team constructed a fishbone diagram (see Figure 9.1).

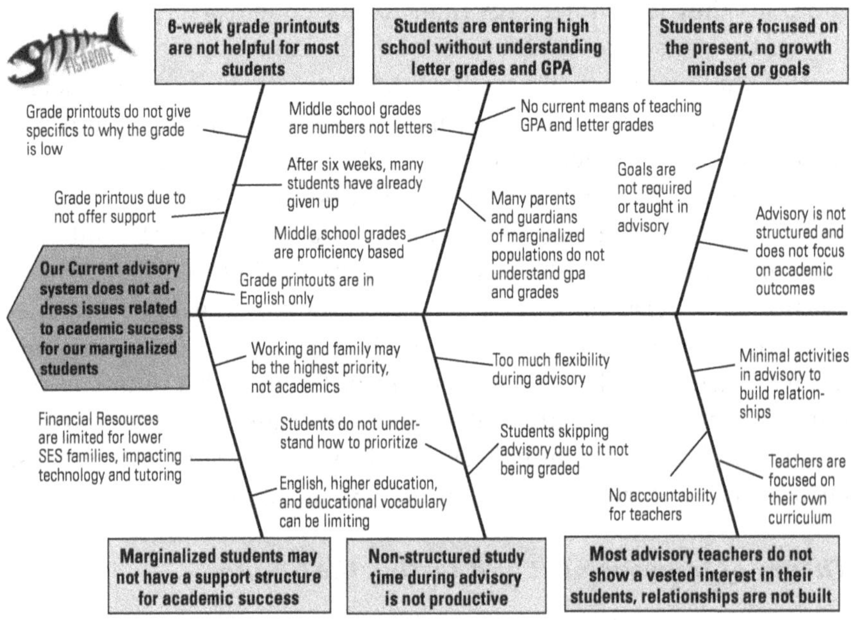

Figure 9.1. Fishbone Diagram

The FLIGHT core team identified the following barriers to student academic success: (a) 6-week grade printouts are not helpful for most students; (b) we don't have a support structure for academic success for historically underserved students; (c) students are entering high school without understanding letter grades and grade point average; (d) nonstructured study time during advisory is not productive; (e) students are focused on the present, with a limited growth mindset or goals; and (f) most advisory teachers do not show a vested interest in their students and relationships are not built.

Change Ideas

The core team decided to focus on three change ideas related to academic success: a review and placement of an advisory period with structure, the incorporation of academic success components in teacher professional development and department teams, and the introduction of social-emotional components related to increasing academic prowess and motivation (see Figure 9.2).

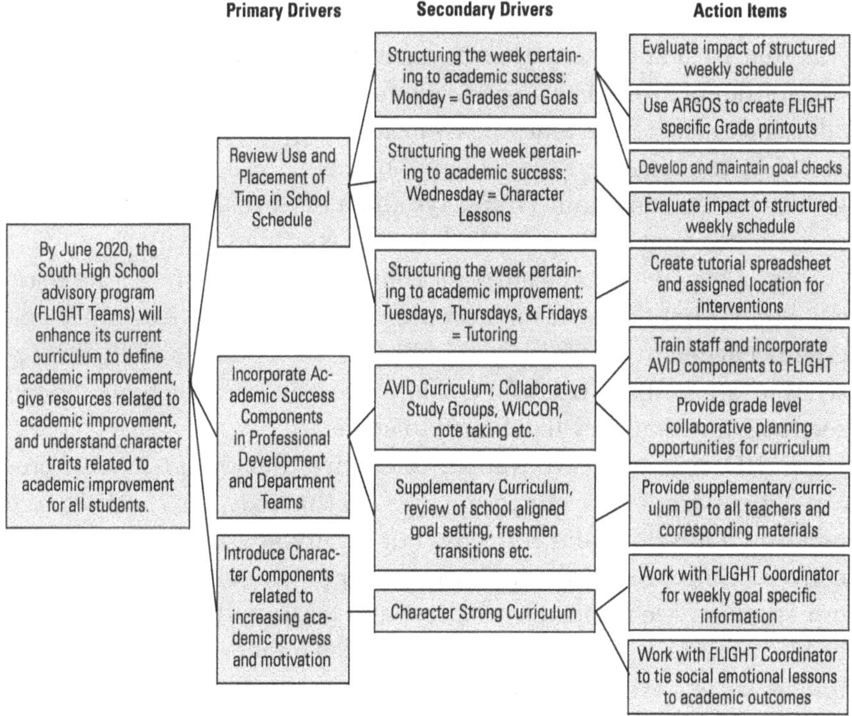

Figure 9.2. Driver Diagram

PDSA Cycles

All the PDSA cycles were research-driven, and data were collected from district data systems related to letter grades and credit recovery.

Data were also gained through empathy interviews with 30 students, more than half of the school staff, and 12 parents. We also conducted a teacher and student survey. All PDSA cycles included discussions of whether we should adopt, adapt, or abandon our change ideas, using grades, credit data, and student evaluations of the Character Strong program to inform our decisions.

PDSA Cycle 1

The first PDSA cycle was established by the FLIGHT core team with the intent of adding more structure to the FLIGHT schedule. The hope was that by adding structure to each day with academic interventions, students would be more academically successful. This included adding a grade check and weekly academic goal development every Monday, tutoring, test makeup, lab makeup, or collaborative study groups on Tuesdays and Thursdays and a brief relationship-building social-emotional activity on Wednesdays (see Figure 9.3).

After reviewing data, surveys, and empathy interviews, the team concluded that there was a brief improvement in failing grades and credits earned in credit recovery, moving from 82% to 84%, respectively, of students on track for graduation. However, the team did not see the gains that they had hoped to achieve.

In PDSA Cycle 1, we wanted to ensure that the process of creating a system for weekly grade checks, tutorials, goal setting, and emotional development reflected our equity goals. After numerous conversations around the best process for getting this information to our students, we decided the easiest and least costly response would be to have each student use technology, cell phones, or Chromebooks to check their grades. However, we only had enough Chromebooks for two thirds of the student body, and many students do not have phones. Also, by taking the time to log in during FLIGHT, we would take time away from goal setting, which was a major part of the intervention that the team wanted to incorporate. The only solution was weekly grade printouts for each student. Therefore, a faculty member needed to oversee this process, and a schedule needed to be followed. This staff member would also need to add lessons for social-emotional development on Wednesdays and oversee the pullout tutorial process.

PDSA Name: Structure of Weekly FLIGHT Schedule to Enhance Academic Success		
	Test cycle: 1 2 3 4 __1_	**Start date: September 2019** | **June 2020**

PLAN	**What change is being tested?** Will there be higher opportunities of academic success by adding structure to our FLIGHT schedule. Whereas Monday will be grades and goal oriented, Tuesdays and Thursdays will be structured tutorials and help sessions, and Wednesdays will be social emotional development lessons.

What is the goal of the change? To assess whether adding structure to FLIGHT will increase the number of students who are academically "on track" for graduation based on ODE standards and school data. 90% of the SHS student body will be on track at the end of second semester of the 2019/2020 school year

Details of implementation plan (who, what, where) Implemented by the FLIGHT team coordinators starting the third week of first semester in the weekly calendar by FLIGHT Team teachers.

What is your first question?	**What are your additional questions?**
Will adding structure to the FLIGHT schedule increase academic success?	1. What percentage of teachers are adhering to the structure, broken down by day?
What is your prediction? Due to the lack of structure in FLIGHT during previous terms, several FLIGHT classes were not utilized as hoped for increased academic development. This added structure will hopefully increase students' awareness of their current grades, establish goals for academic achievement, give resources for academic support/tutoring, and increase social emotional development to recognize the need for academic success.	2. Is there a specific part of the structure that is more meaningful for academic success than the others? 3. Are these structural components enough to increase schoolwide academic success for 90% of SHS students to be on track for graduation in 4 years?
What are the measures? Student's success in making up credits for failed classes, and percentage of students with failing grades.	**What are your additional predictions?** 1. 75% of FLIGHT teachers will adhere to the structure plan generated by this team. 2. The academic interventions and tutorial will be a better indicator of academic growth and grade change than the other two factors. 3. Other school wide interventions will need to be added in order to achieve our target goal of 90% of SHS students being on track for graduation.
Details about data collection (Who is responsible for data collection? When? How?) Two measures of data will be collected at six week intervals and compared to the 2018/2019 school year. This will be accessed by Bryce Bennett by pulling ARGOS and Odysseyware data for quantitative data. There will also be a student survey completed at week six and empathy interviews of students, teachers, and parents throughout in order to gather qualitative data.	**What are the measures?** 1. Student survey related to teachers following the FLIGHT plan. 2. Pulling data from which FLIGHT teachers are utilizing the FLIGHT Pass system(Google FLIGHT Pass Spreadsheet) for requesting students to attend tutorials and other academic support interventions. 3. Six week grade and credit recovery checks in order to see if the structure alone is the best intervention for academic success. Student survey about usefulness of the structured interventions broken down by day. **Details about data collection (Who is responsible for data collection? When? How?)** Administrative Intern, Assistant Principal and FLIGHT Coordinator will pull the six week data from ARGOS, Odysseyware, and Google Sheets. Administrative Intern will create the student survey and reconcile the data.

	Test cycle: 1 2 3 4 __1_	Start date: September 2019	June 2020
DO	**Was implementation of the change carried out as intended?** The structure and FLIGHT plan calendar was implemented as planned. There were multiple initial setbacks related to grade checks and goal setting on Mondays. Pinnacle was not able to generate a student specific report that could be separated by FLIGHT teams. Without this report separation, this would create massive man power to sort by FLIGHT each Friday leading into the next week. We were able to create a grade printout from ARGOS that could be separated but needed to have the report created through the ESD with this specific intention. The goal was also to list missing assignments etc., but the data report was not able to generate this information. There was also some confusion among staff related to the FLIGHT passes. The first week was a bit rocky, but we were able to have a fully functional system by week 3.		
STUDY	**What were the results?** Did the results match the prediction? The data was actually a bit surprising. More than 75% of the teachers were utilizing the FLIGHT Pass successfully (92%). Whereas, according to the student surveys, most teachers (63%) were only handing out the grade printouts on Mondays and were not connecting with students on an individual level to set goals. There were also only slight improvements in students being on track compared to the previous year up from 82% to 84%.		
	What did you learn? It appears that some parts of this structured week are successful. According to the student survey, they appreciate the grade checks and goal development more than the other structured components. However, 37% of our student body is not getting the same information and support with establishing weekly and long term goals. It would also be important to see if there is a specific component to the FLIGHT structure that is more successful than the others.		
ACT	**What will you do?** Adapt **What is the rationale for that decision?** There is merit to adding the structure but we need to do more evaluation. The long term goal of 90% of our students being on track at the end of the 2019/2020 school year, gives us more time to tweak this system. Empathy interviews by teachers have suggested that we might want to adjust which days are assigned to grade checks, social-emotional development and tutorials. The relationship building/goal establishment factor is still neglected by some teachers. Is the structure the piece that adds too much rigidity to teachers?		
	What will you do next? More evaluation and empathy interviews. Data needs to be gathered through teacher surveys as well. It is also pertinent to sort through data to see which components of the structure are successful and which are not.		

Figure 9.3. PDSA Cycle #1 Overview

PDSA Cycle 2

The team's research concluded that many teachers were underutilizing certain aspects of the FLIGHT advisory plan. The biggest factor was related to student engagement and relationships with their peers in FLIGHT and with the FLIGHT teacher. This was very evident on Mondays when printed grades were handed out to students with minimal feedback/support.

As an AVID Demonstration School, our natural response was to add more AVID strategies to the FLIGHT curriculum, with a major emphasis on high-leverage teaching strategies and impactful relationship development, both of which are proven pieces of the AVID curriculum and are apparent in the academic growth of the school's AVID classes. Therefore, these strategies became a major part of department time as well as in the school's professional learning communities (see Figure 9.4).

PDSA Cycle 3

The research and data from PDSA Cycles 1 and 2 concluded that to truly impact academics, the school needed to embrace a more structured form of social-emotional development and relationship building within the FLIGHT curriculum. Most of the FLIGHT classrooms were showing academic gains, and students enhanced their relationships with their peers and teachers. Goals on Mondays were becoming a normal part of the classroom experience, and teachers were impactful in the goal-setting process by establishing a growth mindset. However, some classrooms and students were being neglected due to the teacher engagement and/or the lack of connection to the social-emotional growth practices within FLIGHT. Due to this variability, the majority of staff and the FLIGHT core team decided to research and eventually invest in the Character Strong curriculum.

PDSA Name: Adding components related to Academic Success Through PLCs and Departmental Teams Team members: **Undisclosed**			
	Test cycle: 1 2 3 4 __2_	**Start date: November 2019**	**June 2020**
PLAN	**What change is being tested?** Will adding AVID strategies (WICCOR, Collaborative Study Groups, and relationship building factors) to FLIGHT contribute to academic success of South High School students?		
	What is the goal of the change? To assess whether adding AVID strategies to FLIGHT will increase the number of students who are academically "on track" for graduation based on ODE standards and school data. 90% of the SHS student body will be on track at the end of second semester of the 2019/2020 school year.		
	Details of implementation plan (who, what, where) Implemented by the AVID core team and administration during PLCs starting the seventh week of first semester and strategically added to departmental time and schoolwide collaborative groups including PRIDE and the freshmen transitions committee.		

	Test cycle: 1 2 3 4 ___2_	**Start date: November 2019**	**June 2020**
PLAN	**What is your first question?** Will adding AVID strategies to FLIGHT increase academic success? **What is your prediction?** If FLIGHT teachers use passion and relationship building skills as well as AVID strategies in FLIGHT instruction, students will show academic gains. **What are the measures?** Students' success in making up credits for failed classes, and percentage of students with failing grades. **Details about data collection (Who is responsible for data collection? When? How?)** Two measures of data will be collected at six week intervals and compared to the 2018/2019 school year. This will be accessed by Bryce Bennett by pulling ARGOS and Odysseyware data. There will also be a teacher survey related to relationships with FLIGHT students given before winter break and empathy interviews with teachers, students, and parents throughout.	**What are your additional questions?** 1. What percentage of teachers are using these taught strategies in their FLIGHT classes? 2. Is there a specific part of the introduced strategies that are more meaningful for academic success than the others? 3. Are the teacher directed components enough to increase schoolwide academic success for 90% of SHS students to be on track for graduation in 4 years? **What are your additional predictions?** 1. 80% of teachers will use at least 3 of the relationship building factors taught during PLCs. 90% of teachers will be using other AVID strategies to increase factors related to academic success in FLIGHT. 2. Relationships with FLIGHT students will be the biggest indicator of academic success by FLIGHT teacher. The teachers who connect with their FLIGHT students will be more academically successful. 3. Administrators will need to actively observe FLIGHT classes in order to evaluate if our strategies and goals are being implemented successfully. **What are the measures?** 1. Teacher surveys need to be gathered in order to establish which strategies are being utilized. Note: What will be implemented to ensure that we have a high percentage of teachers taking the survey? 2. Pulling data from which FLIGHT teachers are utilizing the FLIGHT Pass system (Google FLIGHT Pass Spreadsheet) for requesting students to attend tutorials and other academic support interventions as well as teacher survey and empathy interviews of students. Six-week grade and credit recovery checks in order to see if the structure alone is the best intervention for academic success. Student survey about usefulness of the structured interventions broken down by day. 3. Plan for the administrative and FLIGHT team to visit, observe, and connect with teachers and students during FLIGHT time. **Details about data collection (Who is responsible for data collection? When? How?)** Administrative Intern, Assistant Principal and FLIGHT Coordinator will pull the six-week data from ARGOS, Odysseyware, and Google Sheets. The principal will create the teacher survey and reconcile the data. Whole team will complete and compile empathy interviews.	
DO	**Was implementation of the change carried out as intended?** For the most part, this was implemented as planned. However, there were multiple teacher meetings (3) that had to be rescheduled due to a variety of reasons, snow day, district initiative, etc.		
STUDY	**What were the results? Did the results match the prediction?** The data was not surprising. The teachers who reported "high quality" relationships and used AVID strategies with their students had a higher percentage of students who are academically successful (92% on track at the end of the first semester according to ARGOS and Odysseyware data). Student and parent empathy interviews also reflected a similar outcome.		

	Test cycle: 1 2 3 4 __2_	Start date: November 2019	June 2020
STUDY	**What did you learn?** Building relationships with students and using high leverage teaching strategies in FLIGHT classes increased academic success. The combination of adding structure and teaching relationship building and incorporated AVID strategies had a higher outcome than structure alone.		
ACT	**What will you do?** Adapt **What is the rationale for that decision?** We still have numerous teachers who are only marginally using the skills they were taught and created during FLIGHT classes. We must further evaluate data in order to see if these strategies can be used efficiently in all FLIGHT classes. From an equity level, some students are still not receiving the support that they need in order to garner academic success and to be "on track" for graduation.		
	What will you do next? More evaluation and empathy interviews. Data needs to be gathered as to why some teachers are not utilizing these strategies.		

Figure 9.4. PDSA Cycle #2 Overview

The hope was that this curriculum would enrich all students by giving a strong framework for social-emotional lessons and bonding activities that were easy for the teacher to incorporate (see Figure 9.5).

Implementation and Challenges

The implementation of these academic interventions in advisory was a smooth process, primarily due to the structure of improvement science. This improvement process was started through the selection of a core team that represented multiple academic areas and included staff members who are passionate and have dedicated resources for other successful interventions. People were strategically selected for the FLIGHT core team with the hope that all the departments would have a voice and collectively would see a need for change. If this team were not selected with these factors in mind, we believe dissent among staff would have been high. Even though most staff viewed the advisory as an intervention and information dissemination system, prior to this improvement process, there had been a huge push to remove advisory completely and just add more time to classroom instruction. The core team was able to evaluate the data, recognize the need for academic interventions, and test potential change ideas through the improvement science process. Through the surveys and

PDSA Name: By adding social emotional development and structure infused relationship building strategies through the "Character Strong" curriculum, increase academic success Team members: **Undisclosed**			
	Test cycle: 1 2 3 4 __ 5_	**Start date: January 2020**	**June 2020**
PLAN	**What change is being tested?** Will there be higher opportunities of academic success by adding Character Strong lessons to our FLIGHT schedule on Wednesdays. Will the increase in social emotional development and relationship building skills increase academic success?		
	What is the goal of the change? To assess whether adding the Character Strong structure to FLIGHT will increase the number of students who are academically "on track" for graduation based on ODE standards and school data. 90% of the SHS student body will be on track at the end of second semester of the 2019/2020 school year.		
	Details of implementation plan (who, what, where) Implemented by the FLIGHT team coordinators and the Character Strong team starting the first week of January.		

What is your first question? Will adding Character Strong to the FLIGHT schedule increase academic success?

What is your prediction? The implementation of structure and AVID strategies has increased academic success for most teachers. Adding in a structured curriculum related to social emotional development and relationship building will increase academic success for students.

What are the measure(s)? Students' success in making up credits for failed classes, and percentage of students with failing grades.

Details about data collection (Who is responsible for data collection? When? How?) Two measures of data will be collected at six week intervals and compared to the 2018/2019 school year. This will be accessed by Bryce Bennett by pulling ARGOS and Odysseyware data for quantitative data.

There will also be a student survey/evaluation completed through Character Strong at the end of the school year. There will also be empathy interviews of students, teachers, and parents throughout in order to gather qualitative data.

What are your additional questions?
1. What percentage of teachers are adhering to the structure created by Character Strong? Is there going to be pushback for more structure?
2. Are the lessons in Character Strong easily utilized and adaptable?

What are your additional predictions?
1. 80% of FLIGHT teachers will adhere to the structure plan generated by this team.
2. There will need to be some tweaks to the curriculum in order for it to be utilized effectively.

What are the measure(s)?
1. Student evaluations and Character Strong survey in June.
2. Empathy interviews with FLIGHT teachers and a small trial evaluation performed by the FLIGHT core team.

Details about data collection (Who is responsible for data collection? When? How?) Administrative Intern, Assistant Principal and FLIGHT Coordinator will pull the six-week data from ARGOS, Odysseyware, and Google Sheets. Character Strong will provide the student evaluation survey and data.

DO	**Was implementation of the change carried out as intended?** The Character Strong Implementation was created successfully and added to the FLIGHT curriculum as planned. There were major issues related to the "ease of use" by the Character Strong team. The lessons needed to be adapted to meet our students needs and additional resources were needed to make the changes. The platform for the lessons also needed to be adjusted so that substitutes could gain access to the lessons.

	Test cycle: 1 2 3 4 __3_	Start date: January 2020	June 2020
STUDY	**What were the results? Did the results match the prediction?** Disrupted by Covid 19		
	What did you learn? The Character Strong lessons had to be adapted to fit the advisory time frame as well as adjusted for cultural responsiveness. Some of the social emotional factors could be a factor for academic gains, as well as potential decreases in disruptive behaviors and truancy.		
ACT	**What will you do?** Core team will meet in the summer to discuss plans related to revamping advisory for possible distance education in the 2020/2021 school year. More data will be required to see if social emotional skills impact academic gains.		
	What is the rationale for that decision? School closure due to Covid 19		

Figure 9.5. PDSA Cycle #3 Overview

empathy interviews, the core team was able to formulate a plan and recognize which areas of FLIGHT were least productive and where changes needed to occur. By gathering information and collaborating with students and staff, a framework for change was established, and the school community was in support of the implementation.

Creating a structure for advisory was daunting and challenging. Although there are numerous models in other schools, it was important to find a model that would work best for our school's unique bell schedule and for our students in our context. The biggest factor that had to be considered was the cultural and socioeconomic backgrounds of our students and families. A model for advisory had to be created where resources were not assumed to already exist; we needed to provide resources to students in order to increase academic success. Fortunately, the school administrators understood this need and allocated resources.

Out of the three cycles, PDSA Cycle 2 had the fewest implementation challenges. Professional development was already on the school calendar, and the desire to focus on developing relationships in advisory, and in classes in general, was highly supported by the administration. In addition, the school already had the framework for this intervention by incorporating AVID and Upward Bound strategies. AVID and Upward Bound both focus on relationship building, and these teachers are experts in this area. Time to implement these strategies just needed to be incorporated into the school professional learning communities.

The core team could have adopted our change ideas and brought them to scale in our district after PDSA Cycle 2 as academic gains increased during the first two cycles. However, the core team felt that they could continue to increase academic success by adding elements of the Character Strong program for social-emotional development. The hope was that this scripted program would be culturally responsive and fit into our advisory period smoothly. This would remove some of the coordination and process by the FLIGHT coordinator, and it would bring equity to each class by having a similar script. Unfortunately, we discovered we needed to condense the curriculum into shorter periods and modify the curriculum to reflect the cultural backgrounds and language needs of our students.

Learnings

Unfortunately, the COVID-19 school closure resulted in the end of advisory for the 2019–2020 school year. Some of the relationship skills taught in professional learning communities are being implemented through distance education but not specifically in the advisory program. Providing grade printouts and offering social-emotional lessons abruptly stopped due to the school closure, precisely at the time when the need for social-emotional support for our students increased dramatically.

The goal of this team was to use data for the entire school year in order to see the potential academic gains from all three cycles. The 2% gain from 82% on track to 84% on track for graduation after the first cycle showed that there is a possibility that the structure, tutorials, and grade printouts were effective. The teachers and students who reported "high quality" relationships and used AVID strategies had a higher percentage of students who were academically successful (92% on track at the end of the first semester according to district data sources). Student and parent empathy interviews also reflected a similar outcome. However, the impact of the change idea of implementing Character Strong lessons and relationship skills into advisory is unclear.

Our plan is to continue this important work, using PDSA cycles to continuously improve our work, adjusting how we support students through a pandemic using distance education, or a hybrid approach. Technological needs and cultural sensitivity and responsiveness will have to be considered for this potential new format. We do know that during the time of our increased focus on relationships, prior to the pandemic, we had had an 18% decrease in behavioral incidents and a 9% increase in attendance. So although we don't know if FLIGHT is responsible for these improvements or whether they are due to other curricular changes, systems for supporting credit recovery, or a change in school demographics due to slight boundary changes, we do know we improved our support to our students.

Discussion Questions

1. What structured interventions could potentially help students in poverty in your school be more academically successful? How would you begin your improvement science efforts?
2. How could you focus on culturally responsive change ideas in your context? What supports and barriers exist?
3. Which learnings from our improvement process would be the most beneficial, for the population you work with, specifically related to increasing students' academic achievement?

References

Alvarez, L., Catechis, N., Chu, H., Hamburger, L., Herpin, S., & Walqui, A. (2012). Quality teaching for English learners (QTEL) impact study. https://www.sausd.us/cms/lib/CA01000471/Centricity/Domain/5397/QTEL%20 Impact%20Study.pdf

AVID. (n.d.). *Oregon snapshot.* https://www.avid.org/cms/lib/CA02000374/Centricity/domain/8/snapshots/AVID%20Snapshot%20Oregon.pdf

Edmonds, B. C., & Spradlin, T. (2010). What does it take to become a high-performing special education planning district? A study of Indiana's special education delivery service system. *Remedial and Special Education, 31*(5), 320–329. https://doi.org/10.1177/0719325083274451

Quality Teaching for English Learners. (n.d.). *Resources.* https://www.qtel.wested.org/resources

Shulkind, S. B., & Foote, J. (2009). Creating a culture of connectedness through middle school advisory programs. *Middle School Journal, 41*(1), 20 27. https://doi.org/10.1080/00940771.2009.11461700

Taylor, R. D., Oberle, E., Durlak, J. A., & Weissberg, R. P. (2017). Promoting positive youth development through school-based social and emotional learning interventions: A meta-analysis of follow-up effects. *Child Development, 88*(4), 1156–1171. https://doi.org/10.1111/cdev.12864

Wyatt, T. R. (2014). Teaching across the lines: Adapting scripted programmes with culturally relevant/responsive teaching. *Pedagogy, Culture and Society, 22*(3), 447–469. https://doi.org/10.1080/14681366.2014.919957

Zaff, J. F., & Malone, T. (2020). Moving beyond academics. *Youth and Society, 52*(1), 55–77. https://doi.org/10.1177/0044118X17725970

Improving Ninth-Grade On-Track Rates in an Urban Public High School

BRIAN RAHAMAN

In December 2018, Capitol High School (pseudonym) was faced with a problem: The ninth-grade on-track rate was a dismal 7% nearly halfway through the school year. This troubling statistic portended an equally troubling graduation rate three years down the line. The problem was identified during a quarterly meeting with the school's board of trustees. When pressed by board members on why the on-track rate was so low, the principal did not have answers. It was clear that there was an urgent problem, but nobody understood the root causes of the problem nor how to fix it. As it turns out, this was exactly the type of problem that is best addressed using improvement science principles and techniques. A central office staff member, who later assumed a leadership role at the school, proposed that he work with school leaders to improve the ninth-grade on-track rate. The board agreed, and within the next few days, the work commenced.

The ninth-grade on-track indicator was first developed by the University of Chicago's Consortium on School Research. In Chicago, a student is considered on track if they fail no more than one semester of a core course and earn at least five credits by the end of freshmen year (Allensworth & Easton, 2005). However, because school districts have varying promotion and graduation policies, the definition is sometimes modified depending on the school district context. For example, the School District of Philadelphia (SDP) defines *ninth-grade on-track* as earning at least one credit in each of the four core content areas (English, math, science, history) plus one additional credit in any course (Wills, 2018). The latter definition was used at Capitol High School because it aligned better with the school's graduation requirements and grading policies.

The ninth-grade on-track indicator has proved to be one of the best predictors of on-time high school graduation. For example, the University of Chicago researchers found that being on track at the end of the ninth grade was a better predictor of high school graduation than a student's race/ethnicity, prior school achievement, or socio-economic background (Allensworth & Easton, 2005). In Philadelphia, researchers found that students who were on track at the end of the ninth grade were between 40-45% more likely to graduate from high school within 4 years (Wills, 2018). The ninth-grade on-track indicator is an important metric both because of its ability to predict which students will graduate from high school and because it is an indicator that is available early in a student's high school career, which provides time for intervention and support.

School Context

Capitol High School is a small college-prep school whose mission is to prepare historically underrepresented students for success in college. To achieve its mission, the school offers a college preparatory curriculum, such as Advanced Placement and dual-enrollment courses, as well as opportunities to participate in enriching extracurricular programs, including sports, theater, and international trips. The school enrolls approximately 250 students in Grades 9 through 12. Approximately 99% of students are African American and 1% are Latinx. Nearly one out of four students receives special education services, and all students qualify for free or reduced-priced lunch.

Despite its college-prep focus, however, Capitol High School has struggled with student performance for many years. For example, during the 2018–2019 school year, only 2% of students were proficient on the state English language arts (ELA) assessment, and 7%

were proficient on the math assessment. During the year in which the improvement project was implemented, the school was on its fourth principal within 5 years. Needless to say, the school was in desperate need of improvement, and the ninth-grade on-track problem provided school leaders with an opportunity to prove that they could develop and execute a plan to achieve better student outcomes.

Improvement Science in Action

Problem of Practice

Our problem of practice was evident. We needed to dramatically improve the ninth-grade on-track rate, which was in the single digits nearly halfway through the school year. We viewed this problem as an equity issue because virtually all Capitol High students were from historically underrepresented groups. We knew that the ninth-grade on-track rate was a key indicator in predicting graduation outcomes. We needed to get our students back on track for an on-time graduation and a solid grade point average if they were going to matriculate to college after high school. To improve the rate, however, we first needed to understand why so many students were failing classes. Our first step was to form a team to investigate the problem.

The Improvement Team

To guide our team development process, we asked ourselves one question: Who must be a part of the improvement team to give us our best chance of improving the ninth-grade on-track rate? We chose to limit our team membership to the individuals whom we felt needed to be part of the process, albeit for different reasons. We could have easily included many other people, including the department chairs, the assistant principal, or a ninth-grade counselor. However, we decided that there were better ways to involve other key people than to make them a part of the team. In a later section,

I describe some of the tools we used to solicit feedback from other stakeholders during the planning process.

The improvement team for the ninth-grade on-track project included a central office employee, the principal, the director of student support services, and the health teacher. The central office employee initiated the improvement project and served as the team lead, but he needed school-based partners to support the effort. The principal was a natural choice for the team because it was the principal who would make on-the-ground decisions about the instructional program, including any interventions that might be implemented. It was also important to include the director of student support services to ensure that the project was equitable for all students, including those with special learning needs. This person was able to provide background information about specific students as well as cohorts of students, which was helpful for selecting an intervention group that was representative of the entire student population.

The team member who was not an obvious choice was the health teacher. This teacher taught dance and health as ninth-grade elective courses. The health class turned out to be an excellent option for implementing the intervention because it was one of only two classes that enrolled all ninth-grade students (ELA was the other). The health course also had more curricular flexibility compared to ELA, and it had a teacher who the team felt would be able to execute the intervention plan with fidelity. This last point was important because, without adherence to the intervention as it was designed, we would not be able to determine the efficacy of the intervention.

We deliberately kept the improvement team small so that we could act quickly. Our initial goal was to develop and implement a change idea that could positively impact student grades during the current semester, which only had about 5 weeks remaining. We also wanted to test the change idea in as little time as possible so that we could expand the intervention if it proved to be effective. The problem with large, unwieldy teams is that they require more time for nearly every aspect of the improvement process, including identifying the problem, determining which data to collect to better understand the problem, analyzing and interpreting the data, formulating a working theory of improvement, and developing and selecting change ideas.

The other reason that we wanted to keep the improvement team small was to retain some degree of control over the outcome of the planning process. We knew that each additional team member would alter the group's thinking and ultimately change the improvement plan. Although some degree of differential thinking is important, too much can slow the planning process down and lead to compromises on the quality of the work. In the end, our team was small, but it included the right mix of experience and know-how, and we found alternative ways of capturing and incorporating the perspectives of others.

Our Approach to Improvement

Once the problem was identified and the improvement team was formed, we were ready to launch our improvement process. Our basic approach to improvement was taken from Langley et al. (2009) and involved answering three questions:

1. What are we trying to accomplish?
2. How will we know that a change is an improvement?
3. What changes can we make that will result in improvement?

The first question is straightforward: The goal of the improvement team was to improve the ninth-grade on-track rate. Our goal was specific, measurable, attainable, relevant, and time-bound. The second question, "How will we know if the change is an improvement?" was more difficult to answer because it required that the improvement team think in detail about which metric to use and how to quantify improvement. The team needed a clearly defined method of evaluating the impact of their change idea so that they knew how to proceed in the final phase of the improvement project. Finally, the third question, "What changes can we make that will result in improvement?" required the improvement team to brainstorm and select change ideas to test. Our change ideas could have emerged from research literature or from a careful analysis of the system that produced the current outcomes.

After answering each of these questions, we then engaged in the Plan–Do–Study–Act (PDSA) cycle to test our change ideas.

PDSA Cycles

The PDSA approach to improvement provided a structure for the process without limiting our ability to add other important elements. For example, one member of the improvement team completed an online course in improvement science offered by the University of Michigan. Several concepts from that course were used in our improvement project, including the establishment of a team charter and the development of an aim statement and a theory of improvement. These tools were used to guide the entire project from start to finish. In the pages that follow, I describe the tools and processes we used at Capitol High School as we embarked on a learning journey to improve ninth-grade outcomes in our school.

Team Charter

As we began our planning process, we decided to create a team charter to document the details of our work. The team charter served three purposes. First, it functioned as a contract among the members of the improvement team by outlining the agreements that we made throughout the project. No team member could say that they did not know what they needed to do, because it was documented in the team charter. Second, the charter served as a running record of our work together. It outlined our collaborative thinking, discussions, and decisions. In this way, the charter was served as our meeting minutes, except with a better organizational structure. Finally, the team charter kept our team on the same page about our improvement project. It both eliminated confusion and highlighted aspects of the project that needed to be clarified.

We created the team charter inside of a Google document so that the most recent version of the charter would always be available to review. We reviewed the charter at the start of each meeting to remind the team of our prior agreements and to assess our progress along the way. The charter included a project overview and purpose, a list of team members, an aim statement, a list of data sources used during the diagnostic process (as well as the data itself), our interpretations of the data, our working theory of improvement, a description of the change ideas, our plan and timeline for implementing the change ideas, a description of the metrics that would be used to evaluate the change ideas, individual team member responsibilities, and potential roadblocks. It was a comprehensive document that included all the information we needed throughout the project.

Diagnosing the Problem

The first step in solving any problem is to understand the underlying causes of the problem. In medicine, this is referred to as the diagnostic process. However, physicians are not the only professionals who need to diagnose problems. Organizations, including schools, are faced with problems every day, and the leaders in these organizations must continually engage in diagnostic processes to pinpoint the causes of problems in order to find effective solutions. According to McFillen et al. (2013), the diagnostic process includes five steps, which are illustrated in Figure 10.1.

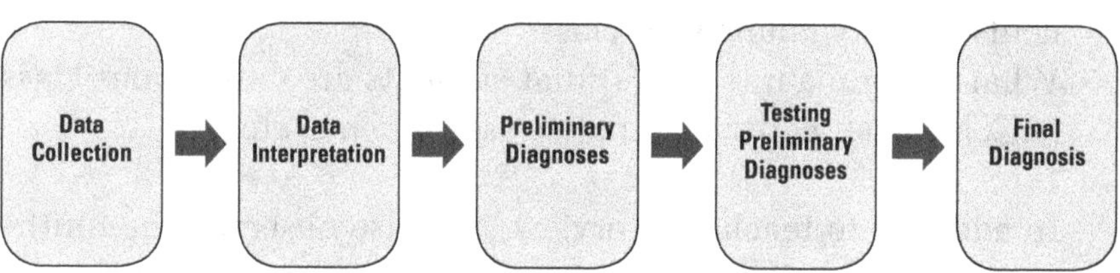

Figure 10.1. The Diagnostic Process

Data Collection

Our first challenge within the diagnostic process was to determine the data that we needed to collect. Based on our knowledge of the systems within the school, as well as the problem we were trying to solve (i.e., ninth-grade course failure), we decided to collect four types of data. First, we thought it was important to collect and analyze course grades to identify patterns in the data. We analyzed the grades from various perspectives, including by gender, by teacher, and in terms of how far students were from passing courses.

Second, we interviewed all ninth-grade teachers using a semi-structured interview format. We developed a standard set of open-ended questions, and we asked follow-up questions based on their responses. We considered developing a teacher survey, but we chose interviews as our data collection method because there were only nine teachers across the grade level. It was a small enough group that we were able to conduct the interviews within a few days. In a larger school, we may have chosen to administer a survey and then followed up with individual teachers to learn more. The primary teacher interview questions follow:

- What percentage of students is passing your class?
- Why do you believe that some students are failing?
- How much of a student's grade is based on each of the following components: classwork, participation, assessments, projects, and homework?
- What intervention strategies have you attempted with the students who are failing your class?
- What is the main reason(s) that students are failing your class (e.g., low test scores, incomplete assignments, etc.)?

In addition to teacher interviews, we also observed the ninth-grade classes to understand the classroom culture and the quality of instruction. The observations gave us a sense of how lessons were structured. For example, we wanted to know whether lessons included clear learning goals, models of how to perform skills, opportunities for students to practice under the watchful eye of the teacher, opportunities for the teacher to check for student understanding, and opportunities for students to receive feedback about how they were doing as well as how they could improve. The observations also gave us insight into the general classroom culture. Most importantly, it helped us to know what students did during class and whether there was a problem with student engagement.

Finally, we interviewed a sample of students who were failing classes to find out why they believed they were failing. We organized the complete list of students who were failing at least one class and randomly selected twenty students for interviews. Two of the students were not interviewed, however, and we ended up with a total of 18 interviews. The student interviews were invaluable because they provided us with insights about the problem that came directly from those who were experiencing the problem. Although each student's experience was unique, there were clear patterns across interviews that pointed toward specific root causes of the problem.

Data Interpretation

Once we collected the data, we needed to analyze and interpret it. The purpose of the data interpretation stage is to formulate a working theory of practice improvement (Bryk et al., 2016). First, we organized the data in a Google spreadsheet and asked each team member to review the data on their own. This ensured that everyone had a chance to make sense of the data without being influenced by anyone else's perspectives. Each team member was asked to write a short summary of their initial interpretation and to note questions that they had.

Next, the team met and shared their interpretations while the others listened. One team member recorded notes on a whiteboard during the share-out, which allowed us to eventually move from individual interpretations to group interpretations. For example, based on what was shared, we began to identify patterns across the team. We then developed a fishbone diagram to help visualize the problem and the various factors that we believed contributed to the problem. From there, we developed a driver diagram, which included our problem of practice—ninth-grade course performance—along with the primary and secondary drivers of the problem. With the aid of these processes and tools, we were beginning to form a working theory of improvement.

Preliminary Diagnoses

In the diagnostic model proposed by McFillen et al. (2013), the working theory of improvement is referred to as a preliminary diagnosis. This is the stage of the process where hypotheses are formed, debated, and discarded. Our working theory of improvement included three related components. First, we believed that students did not completely understand how the high school credit system worked. In high school, students must pass specific classes to earn credits for graduation. For example, students in Washington, D.C. must earn a total of 24 credits to graduate, including four credits in each of the core content areas (see Table 10.1). Through student interviews, we found that students did not understand that they needed to earn credits in specific courses and that failure to earn a credit would require summer school or some other credit recovery process to get back on track for graduation.

Table 10.1. Graduation Requirements for Washington, D.C., Public School Students

Subject	Credits
English	4.0
Mathematics (including Algebra I, Geometry, and Algebra II)	4.0
Science (including three lab sciences)	4.0
Social Studies (including World History 1 & 2, U.S. History, U.S. Government, and District of Columbia History)	4.0
World Language	2.0
Art	0.5
Music	0.5
Health and Physical Education	1.5
Electives	3.5
TOTAL	**24.0**

The second part of the credit system that students did not seem to understand was the calculation of the final grade. There are four marking periods at Capitol High School, which are averaged together at the end of the school year to determine the final course grade.

Students did not realize that a failing grade in one marking period meant that they needed to score even higher in subsequent marking periods to earn a passing score. For example, if a student earned a grade of 60% in one marking period, they would need to earn at least an 80% in the next marking period to have a passing grade in the course, which was 70% at Capitol High.

The last component of our working theory of improvement related to how grades were determined at the individual class level. All teachers adhered to a schoolwide system for determining student grades that included five types of points, each worth a standard percentage of the final grade:

1. Class assignments—20% of the total grade
2. Class participation—10% of the total grade
3. Homework—10% of the total grade
4. Projects—20% of the total grade
5. Assessments—40% of the total grade

We learned through classroom observations and teacher interviews that students were failing, in large part, because they were not participating in class, not completing class assignments, and not completing homework. These components accounted for forty percent of a student's final grade, and most teachers awarded points based on effort and completion rather than accuracy. Surprisingly, most students had no idea that their grades were determined based on specific types of points and that they were missing out on accumulating points simply by not trying. This insight suggested potential change ideas. First, though, we needed to clarify our goal for the project.

Aim Statement

An aim statement is a specific, measurable, and time-bound goal that provides direction for the entire improvement process. After we developed a solid understanding of the problem through the first three phases of the diagnostic process, we were ready to develop an aim statement. Our aim statement was as follows: To increase the percentage of ninth-grade intervention students (those receiving the change ideas) who are on track for graduation from 6% to 60% by the end of the third marking period. This was an ambitious goal, but we believed it was possible because the problem was largely about effort rather than an inability to learn. We would not have been so confident if we had found that students understood the grading system and were putting forth their best effort but were still failing. Because we knew that this was not the case, we believed we could improve significantly with a well-developed and well-executed set of change ideas.

Testing Preliminary Diagnoses

In order to test our preliminary diagnoses, we needed to develop specific change ideas that could be tested. Our working theory of improvement rested on the notion that students did not understand how the credit and grading systems worked in high school. If our theory were true, then we had to improve our students' understanding of the system to achieve better outcomes. We devised a plan to educate students about the credit and grading systems. Before we implemented the idea, though, we talked to students about their post-secondary goals. We asked them to reflect on and write about what they wanted to do after high school. We wanted students to develop a tangible vision of what they hoped their life would be like 5, 10, and 20 years in the future. As expected, most students wanted to attend college, they desired professional careers, and they aspired to an upper middle-class lifestyle. Once students had a vision of their future, we helped students make the connection between their academic performance and their future goals.

The next step was to educate students on how to get there. Students needed to understand how the credit and grading systems worked in high school. We designed a series of lesson plans that walked students through the credit requirements for high school graduation as well as how individual course grades were determined. We included practice for students to ensure the lessons made sense. For example, we provided students with their grades through the first two marking periods of the school year and asked them to calculate the number of points they needed to earn during the final two marking periods to pass each class. This component of the change idea was important because it was personalized for each student. It also provided students with a specific number to aim for in each course rather than simply stating that they needed to improve.

Once students knew what grades they needed to earn for the next marking period, we helped them find ways to improve their grades by making small adjustments to their daily routines. For example, we helped students see that they were losing many points by not completing homework and not participating in class. Because these points were based on effort, they could improve their grades simply by completing the work and turning it in. To earn these points, students identified specific changes they planned to make, such as going to sleep earlier and setting aside an hour each night to get their homework completed. Students checked in with their peers once per week for the remainder of the marking period to reflect on their progress and to identify additional changes they would need to make the following week.

The final change idea that we implemented was to standardize how participation grades were being awarded across classrooms. During our interviews, we learned that teachers were using class participation points in a variety of ways, and many teachers were using the points to manage student behavior. We needed this part of the grading system to be consistent across the grade level so that students knew what to expect and how to earn the points. With the help of the teachers, we developed a standard policy for awarding class participation points.

Improvement After Implementing the Change Ideas

We launched our change ideas during the final week of the second marking period. This was the week before students would get a fresh start in the grade book. We observed the execution of the change ideas throughout the marking period and believed things were going well. When we analyzed course grades in the middle of the third marking period, however, we found that students' grades had not improved nearly as much as we had hoped. We considered abandoning our change ideas at that point and implementing new strategies. However, we decided to be patient and wait until the end of the marking period to evaluate the impact of our change ideas on the target outcome. When we analyzed the final grades for the marking period, we found substantial improvement within our intervention group. More specifically, the change ideas improved the percentage of students who were on track for graduation from 6% to 76% in one marking period (see Figure 10.2). The improvement far outpaced the comparison group, which suggested that our change ideas had made the difference.

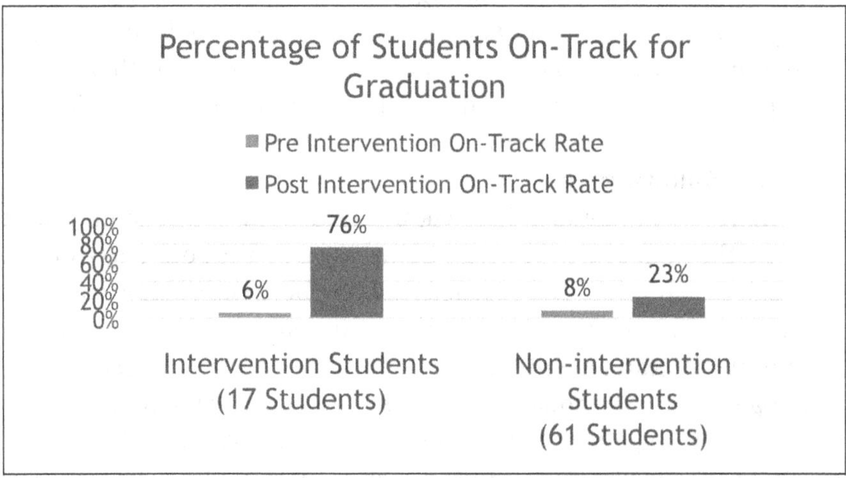

Figure 10.2. Final Diagnosis and Adoption of the Change Idea

The results showed, without a doubt, that our change ideas had worked. They may not have been the *only* factors that contributed to this important student outcome, but they were certainly a key part of the improvement. With these data in hand, it was now time for the last step of the process. We needed to determine what to do based on the results of our project. The standard options at this point in the process include abandoning the change ideas, adopting the change ideas, or revising the change ideas and testing again. For us, it was an easy decision to adopt the change ideas and to implement them with the other students. We did so during the first week of the fourth marking period, and once again, the change ideas led to significant improvement in the percentage of students who were on track to graduate by the end of the school year. In fact, by the end of the summer, more than 90% of students were on track to graduate, an impressive feat given where we started 7 months earlier.

Lessons Learned for Increasing Equity in Schools

Lesson 1: Build a Culture to Address Inequity

One of the first and most important steps to creating more equitable schools is to create an organizational culture where inequity is routinely identified and investigated. Without a supportive school culture, there is little chance that individual members of the school community will feel comfortable identifying equity issues and even less of a chance that those issues will be adequately addressed. To create this type of culture, it is important for school leaders to model the behavior that they wish to foster. At Capitol High School, it was notable that the principal and a central office administrator were directly involved in planning and implementing the project. This was a good first step in creating a culture that deals head-on with inequity. However, in retrospect, there was much more we could have done to normalize this process.

One of the key missteps we made during our improvement project was that we did not communicate what we were doing with enough people. Although we benefited in several ways from having a small team, the other side of that coin is that fewer people had insight into what we were doing, both in terms of understanding our goal as well as our approach to improvement. We should have been more deliberate about sharing our work with others in various ways, including through email, newsletters, and updates at staff meetings. If we had shared more information with school faculty throughout the project, we could have used the experience as a springboard for additional improvement projects since collective learning from one project to another is how a culture of improvement ultimately develops.

Lesson 2: Prioritize the Equity Issues That Matter Most for Students

Once a school organization develops a habit of identifying inequitable outcomes, the next challenge is to determine which problems to target first, which is easier said than done. As Elmore (2003) put it, "knowing the right thing to do is the central problem of school improvement" (p. 9). Not every problem affects students of diverse backgrounds in the same way or to the same degree. Some problems are more important to solve than others. One way to prioritize equity issues, then, is to start with the end in mind. Determine exactly what you hope to accomplish with students, and then identify the specific student outcomes that your school hopes to achieve. Once those outcomes are known, you will have a set of key performance indicators that you can monitor to assess your school's progress. These indicators provide a lens for identifying important equity issues.

At Capitol High School, we developed a set of metrics that tell us the extent to which we are achieving our mission of preparing students for success in college. The set of metrics includes the percentage of students passing all their courses, average achievement on math and reading curriculum assessments, attendance rate, and the percentage of students who immediately enroll in a 4-year college or university, among others. We collected and monitored these data throughout the year, and we specifically looked for inequitable outcomes among student groups. For example, when we shifted to remote learning due to the pandemic, we noticed that boys were much more likely than girls to disengage from school and fail courses. We were able to identify the issue quickly and begin working to resolve it. We had a school culture that focused on data and looked for inequities, and we had a method of prioritizing certain equity issues over others.

Lesson 3: Use Improvement Science to Develop and Test Change Ideas

Having a school culture focused on equity and improvement is necessary, but not sufficient, to eliminate inequity within a school organization. You also need effective methods to develop and test change ideas. Improvement science offers a proven set of practices and tools to do just that. The first step for school leaders is to learn about improvement science. There are many books that describe the core principles and techniques of improvement science, including *The Improvement Guide* (Langley et al., 2009) and *Learning to Improve* (Bryk et al., 2016). While these books provide a foundational understanding of improvement science, this current volume makes an important contribution because it provides concrete examples of improvement science being applied in real school settings. In essence, these school-based examples are case studies that can be used to foster learning and to spark ideas for improvement projects in your own school.

Once you understand the basic components of improvement science, the best way to deepen learning is to simply get started. It is a good idea to start with a project that targets a manageable problem. The ninth-grade on-track improvement project at Capitol High was an excellent place to start because it was a problem that needed to be solved and that seemed solvable. If we had chosen an intractable problem as our first foray into improvement science, we could have easily been discouraged and failed to build buy-in and momentum for additional improvement projects. Instead, our improvement project led to remarkable improvement in the ninth-grade on-track rate and a collective belief that improvement science could help us solve other problems.

However, it is important to note that not all improvement projects lead to improvement. If everything worked, you would not need to run any tests. You would simply implement ideas and observe the improvement. The whole purpose of testing change ideas is to determine what works in a specific context and why. However, with improvement science, even failed tests are opportunities for learning. You test ideas and then use the feedback, or the outcome, to inform subsequent tests. It is an iterative process that often goes through multiple cycles before the best solution is found. This is precisely what we did to improve our ninth-grade on-track rate at Capitol High School.

Discussion Questions

1. What are the most important student outcomes in your school?
2. Are there any equity concerns across those outcome measures?
3. Which outcome, if improved, would have the largest positive impact on your school and your students?

References

Allensworth, E. M., & Easton, J. Q. (2005). *The on-track indicator as a predictor of high school graduation.* Consortium on Chicago School Research.

Bryk, A. S., Gomez, L. M., Grunow, A., & LeMahieu, P. G. (2016). *Learning to improve: How America's schools can get better at getting better.* Harvard Education Press.

Elmore, R. (2003). *Knowing the right thing to do: School improvement and performance-based accountability.* NGA Center for Best Practices.

Langley, G. J., Moen, R. D., Nolan, K. M., Nolan, T. W., Norman, C. L., & Provost, L. P. (2009). *The improvement guide: A practical approach to enhancing organizational performance.* Jossey-Bass.

McFillen, J. M., O'Neil, D. A., Balzer, W. K., & Varney, G. H. (2013). Organizational diagnosis: An evidence-based approach. *Journal of Change Management, 13*(2), 223–246. https://doi.org/10.1080/14697017/2012.679290

Wills, T. (2018, May). *Defining 9th grade success: A new 9th grade on track definition* (District Focus Series). School District of Philadelphia. https://www.philasd.org/research/wp-content/uploads/sites/90/2018/05/On-Track-Focus-Brief_May-2018.pdf

Addressing Equity Issues for Long-Term Multilingual Learners: Using Improvement Science Practices to Improve Understanding and Services

BILL EAGLE AND SUSAN CONNOLLY

Educational equity means that every child receives whatever she/he/they need to develop to her/his/their full academic and social potential and to thrive, every day.

Elena Aguilar (2020, p. 6)

Washington State serves approximately 135,000 students identified as multilingual/English learners (m/ELs). These students represent more than 100 distinct languages and comprise nearly 12% of the total student population. Districts strive to ensure m/ELs achieve proficiency in English as well as meet challenging state standards, which is not only the goal of transitional bilingual instructional programs (TBIPs) but also both a federal and state legal requirement. However, despite well-intentioned efforts, m/ELs remain among the most underserved, marginalized, and lowest performing groups of students within the state. As seen in Table 11.1, m/ELs lag behind in multiple categories. The gap between m/ELs and non-m/ELs is disturbingly wide.

Table 11.1. Washington State Report Card Diversity Report

Washington State Report Card 2018–2019	ELA	Math	Science	9th-Grade On Track*	Graduation (2020)	Drop Out (2020)
m/ELs	13.3%	14.5%	7.3%	86.8%	68.4%	16.8%
Non-m/ELs	64.9%	52.8%	50.4%	89.7%	84.3%	8.3%

Note: ELA = English language Arts; m/Els = multilingual/English learner.
* Ninth-grade on-track indicator measures the rate of credits students earned relative to credits they attempted in ninth grade. Students who end ninth grade on track are four times more likely to graduate on time.

Long-Term English Learners—Addressing Needs With Equitable Practices

The quantity, quality, and consistency of programs and instruction English Language Learners receive can move them towards English proficiency and content mastery or relegate them to long term status.

—Laurie Olsen, PhD (2014, p.8)

The journey toward English proficiency and academic achievement for m/ELs progresses through common stages yet is also highly individualized and nonlinear. Each student's journey will be unique precisely because each student's needs are unique. The time frame for students to achieve academic proficiency in English when being educated in English-only environments is, on average, 5 to 7 years (Collier & Thomas, 2009). Although this applies to students entering U.S. school systems at any age, for m/ELs entering the system as kindergarteners, this 5- to 7-year time frame makes the early elementary years critical. During these early years, m/ELs need appropriate and explicit instruction in reading foundational skills not unlike their monolingual English peers. However, as August and Shanahan (2006) note,

Instruction in the key components of reading is necessary—but not sufficient—for teaching language-minority students to read and write proficiently in English. *Oral proficiency in English is critical as well* [emphasis added]—but student performance suggests that it is often overlooked in Instruction. (p. 4)

Throughout their journey toward acquiring English proficiency, m/ELs need specific, intentional focus on both the interpretive (listening, viewing, reading) and expressive (speaking, writing) modes of communication with specific attention to the development of oral language proficiency as the foundation to developing literacy—reading and writing. Without intentional instruction addressing oral language development (listening and speaking), m/ELs risk plateauing in their English-language development and slipping into long-term status at the secondary level. Students not acquiring proficiency in English within the typical 5- to 7-year time frame experience what has become known as long-term English learner (LTEL) status.

Students experiencing LTEL status share several common characteristics, including the following:

- a lack of oral and literacy skills necessary for academic success
- fossilized features of home language infused with social English (such as Spanglish or Chinglish) which do not support academic English necessary for school
- habits of passivity and nonengagement (it is safer to remain quiet and hope to pass through unnoticed)
- A majority aspire to attend college
- an internalized sense of failure (i.e., sense that their struggles are their fault) results in a disproportionate rate of dropout, estimated at four times greater than average (Olsen, 2014)

Improvement Science Approach to Change Initiatives

Research asserts that the unique language and literacy needs of m/ELs can be effectively addressed, given appropriate, robust systems of instruction and services aligned to best practices for m/ELs. This includes addressing the dual obligation of designated English-language development as well as meaningful access to rigorous, grade-level content, appropriate staffing ratios, ongoing job/embedded professional learning, and adequate/sufficient allocation of resources. But putting research into practice in school settings is not always easy.

The careful design constructs, control of variables, and complex statistics involved in many types of research often leave schools with the impression that simply engaging in a "best practice" with "fidelity" will lead to measurable results. However, such approaches have not led to the systemic changes needed to ensure all m/ELs are receiving what they need every day in order to "develop to their full academic and social potential" (Aguilar, 2020, p. 6). Improvement demands consideration of context as well as research-based best practices. What works for one group of students, in a particular school, with a particular teaching staff, may not work as well or at all in another setting. Districts must build an understanding of current program structures, organizational norms, policies, and practices that influence the outcomes for multilingual learners that result in high numbers of LTELs.

This is where improvement science poses an appealing alternative to the manner in which schools typically advance change initiatives. Improvement science offers a practical approach to identifying impactful change ideas generated for a particular context by the teachers, students, administrators, paraprofessionals, and other staff who daily work and learn within that context. Job-embedded measures based on pragmatic evidence are a tenet of the improvement science approach. Such measures permit rapid testing and refining of change ideas leading to important learning about their impact on the system.

Figure 11.1 outlines key markers in the improvement science journey. This process guided the work in which the authors engaged with a variety of districts across central Washington State, each on its unique trajectory toward equitably addressing the LTEL phenomenon.

Central Washington School District

The Central Washington School District (CWSD; pseudonyms used throughout) represents a compilation of the various districts and schools with which the authors collaborated. In this part of Washington, the dominant language is English, followed by Spanish, Russian, and Ukrainian. While other languages are also represented, by far the two most common are English and Spanish. Program models that develop language and literacy in two languages, English and the student's primary language, are highly effective and the priority model for Washington State. These programs focus on developing bilingualism and biliteracy for all students, including monolingual English speakers as well as bilingual speakers of English and the partner language. However, English-only models remain more common. Of the 77 school districts in this part of the state, only 12 offer dual-language or developmental bilingual language programs. The remaining 65 districts provide English-only programs. The goal of English-only program models is English proficiency in the least amount of time.

In what follows, we share the experiences of the CWSD as they leveraged improvement science methods and tools to address the needs of m/ELs.

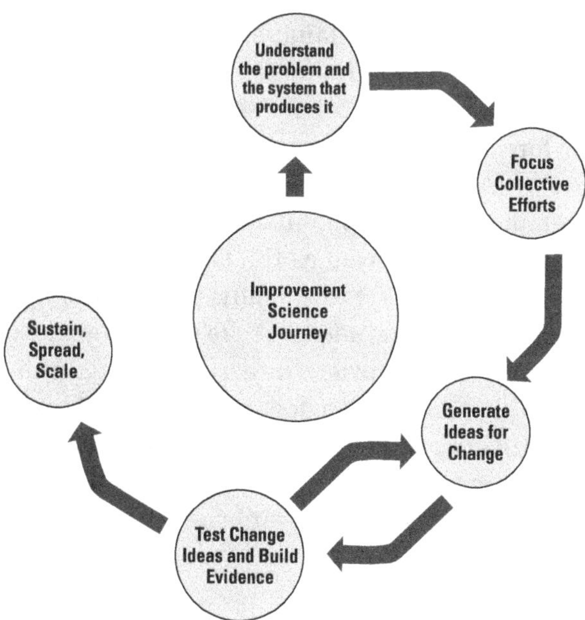

Figure 11.1. Improvement Science Journey

Understand the Problem and the System That Created It

Based on its state English Language Proficiency Assessment (ELPA21) and the number of students still in the bilingual program after 5 years, CWSD elected to take a close look at their English-only program for m/ELs, in particular those students who had not exited the program after 5 years who may be experiencing LTEL status. They discovered that not all identified m/ELs were receiving designated English-language development. In addition, meaningful access to content was inconsistently provided across the district. This information guided the creation of a blueprint for working with district administrators to deepen their understanding of the language acquisition process and collectively begin to address the systems-level changes needed. Because they had recently received some training in improvement science strategies, administrators decided to put together teams to investigate systems across the K–12 environment.

As an initial step, CWSD engaged in a data dive with all district administrators. Through a facilitated process modeled after data-driven dialogue (Wellman & Lipton, 2017), administrators analyzed student-level data in English language arts (ELA), math, science, ninth-grade on-track status, graduation rate, length of time identified as m/EL, and attendance. Two 3-hour sessions allowed teams to make observations, formulate ideas, and pose questions regarding the comparative performance outcomes of m/ELs and non-m/ELs.

In an attempt to uncover potential root causes leading to gaps in performance outcomes, as well as the large percentage of students demonstrating likely LTEL status, teams utilized the five-whys protocol. They discovered that students at the elementary level were only receiving pullout services provided by a paraeducator utilizing a technology software platform, which does not meet minimum civil rights requirements. Meaningful access to core content occurred primarily in classrooms where teachers were either endorsed in English learner (EL) and/or received ongoing, job-embedded professional learning, and follow-up coaching.

One elementary team opted to conduct empathy interviews with both classroom teachers and EL students. Empathy interviews gather information regarding needs, concerns, barriers, and successes via direct dialogue with individuals close to the issues you want to address. The process allowed for both staff and student voice regarding pathways to English-language proficiency through the school's current m/EL program. After carefully crafting several questions designed to encourage the sharing of stories and perspectives, the team conducted multiple interviews over a short time and came together soon afterward to consolidate their learning. A few key findings began to emerge: (a) Students indicated that reading was something they found difficult about school, and (b) classroom teachers wanted increased collaboration and planning time with the building's EL specialist.

The middle and high schools noted inconsistent approaches in the delivery of English Language Development (ELD) services, resulting in a lack of support for some groups of qualified students. For example, at one high school, only students identified as newcomer m/ELs (which accounts for 10% of the total identified m/ELs at the high school) received any designated ELD. Instructional strategies to provide meaningful access to core content only occurred in classrooms where teachers had received ongoing, job-embedded professional learning along with follow-up coaching to support the implementation of the strategies.

After completing the data-dialogue process, the following guiding question emerged: "How can we create a system in which all students identified as m/ELs received both designated English language development instruction provided by a certificated teacher as well as ensure meaningful access to rigorous grade-level instruction?"

Focus Collective Efforts

The core improvement belief that systems produce the results they are designed to produce led teams across the district to apply methods designed to give deeper insight into the experiences of teachers and students. Empathy interviews (introduced earlier) can help identify leverage points for teams seeking to focus their collective efforts. Seeking answers to questions about "Who is involved?" and "Who is impacted?" guides improvement for equity and embraces the core of a user-centered, problem-specific approach to designing potential solutions (Hinnant-Crawford, 2020). In order to understand the problem from the perspective of those closest to instruction and provide opportunities for voice from a variety of perspectives, teams agreed to conduct empathy interviews with bilingual programs students as well as classroom teachers and English as a second language (ESL) support staff. Empathy interviews, therefore, introduced student voices into the investigation process. In addition, the interviews gave both staff and students opportunities to share needs, experiences, barriers, and bright spots.

Teams across the district agreed to conduct empathy interviews using the same set of carefully designed questions to elicit important information about potential bright spots and areas of concern, as well as barriers to learning. Each team took responsibility for completing a targeted number of interviews over a period of one week. Multiple interviews were conducted with a representative set of core classroom teachers, ESL staff, and bilingual program students. At the end of the week, the teams gathered to consolidate their learning. Looking across responses, a central theme began to emerge from the teaching staff: the concern that their m/EL students were not engaging in academic-content classroom discussions at the same level as their native English-speaking peers.

In order to focus their efforts on increasing the percentage of EL students using academic vocabulary, the team then used a driver diagram to help articulate a theory of learning. Driver diagrams provide a visual link between change ideas, drivers, and aim statements. When read from left to right, a driver diagram expresses the link between a change idea and an aim statement—in other words, it tells us the "how." Reading from right to left, a driver diagram explains "why" we are implementing a particular change idea.

The driver diagram (see Figure 11.2) led the team to articulate the following theory: If we want to increase the percentage of EL students using academic vocabulary, we need to engage more ELs in classroom discussions. One way to do that is by incorporating the use of sentence frames.

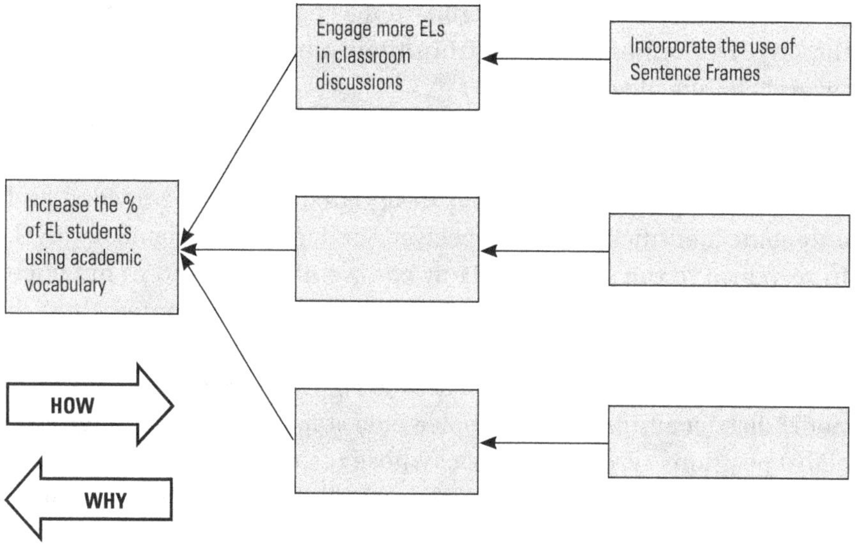

Figure 11.2. Driver Diagram (4 boxes intentionally left blank)

Generate Ideas for Change

The trick to improvement is to find what works for your context and under what conditions. As teams sought to develop potential change ideas, they considered several common sources available to schools. Asking the questions below helped them generate potential changes to address their identified root causes:

- What does the research say about effective practices to support language acquisition?
- What ideas have helped other districts our size in supporting language acquisition?
- What have we learned through our investigation of our system that might help us determine how to support language acquisition?

In addition to illuminating priority concerns through the voices of those involved in the system and those impacted by it, empathy interviews can serve as a springboard for change ideas. For teams in the CWSD, themes resulting from their empathy interviews led to several change ideas.

Prior to beginning this work, paraeducators at the elementary level had been tasked with supporting m/ELs while they engaged on a tech-based platform. No other designated ELD was provided and only some identified students received services at the secondary level. In response to the question, "How can we create a system in which all students identified as m/ELs received both designated English language development instruction provided by a certificated teacher as well as ensure meaningful access to rigorous grade-level instruction?" district administrators took a bold step to create language specialist positions across the district whose responsibility will be to provide designated ELD and to collaborate with core/content teachers. They utilized a staffing ratio protocol to equitably assign staff as the distribution of m/ELs is not consistent from building to building.

At one high school, the administrative team, in conjunction with the authors and the language specialist, designed a new course that focused specifically on students demonstrating LTEL status. The goal of the course was to identify and target the unique language development needs of each student and design instruction to unblock their language development. The primary target area was oral language development, specifically in the form of academic discourse and expressing one's ideas using academic language verbally and in writing. The first year resulted in one section of the course offered to incoming ninth graders who were demonstrating LTEL status.

Test Change Ideas and Build Evidence

At the heart of learning to improve is the idea of testing small changes, collecting evidence of the impact those changes produce in the system, and using that evidence to inform further tests. These small Plan–Do–Study–Act (PDSA) cycles can lead to rapid improvement through refinement of change ideas. In addition, teams can determine early on whether a change idea is not producing promising results and may need to be abandoned.

Recall that at one elementary school, empathy interviews revealed a desire among classroom teachers for increased collaboration and planning time with the building's EL specialist. In order to learn more about the amount of collaboration time needed, as well as the types of information that might be beneficial to discuss during this time, the group decided to create a draft collaboration protocol and asked the EL specialist to try it out with the building's third-grade teachers. Several short PDSA cycles were implemented to test and refine the protocol. As a result, collaboration time between third-grade teachers and the building EL specialist became more intentional with a focus on planning for instructional activities and greater coordination between the core classroom and support for ELs.

Middle school teams decided it would be important to share with each student their language proficiency scores and engage them in identifying goals around targeted language development needs. As mentioned earlier, the middle school also elected to incorporate the use of sentence frames in order to engage more EL students in classroom discussions. They felt this idea would lead to a greater percentage of EL students using academic vocabulary. To initially test this change idea, a small group of seventh-grade teachers consistently incorporated the use of sentence frames in their instruction for a period of 2 weeks. During that 2-week period, to measure the impact of this strategy, teachers collected anecdotal data from classroom discussions regarding the use of academic content vocabulary by m/EL students. In addition to the anecdotal evidence, students were given a short survey asking whether they felt the use of the sentence frames had positively influenced their ability to participate in classroom conversations. Initial results from this small group of teachers indicated the sentence frames were useful to students, and classroom discussions were becoming more robust. Based on this evidence, the middle school staff resolved to continue testing the incorporation of sentence frames with a larger group of staff and students across a variety of grade levels.

Sustain, Spread, and Scale

During the first year of the specialized course for students demonstrating LTEL status at one high school, the results indicated an increase in the number of students achieving English proficiency as demonstrated on the annual summative language proficiency assessment. The anecdotal data indicated increased confidence in the students and a deeper understanding of their unique journey toward English proficiency and how it was impacting their academic achievement. For the second year, the number of sections of the specialized course for students demonstrating LTEL status was expanded from one to seven. A team consisting of administrators, language specialists, a facilitator, and teachers met and analyzed the individual data on all identified m/ELs and created individual learning plans for each, placing students strategically in this course or in an ELA course taught by trained and supported teachers. In order to staff this, the administrators examined the credentials of all the teachers in the building, identifying those with EL/bilingual endorsements. Two teachers were identified as highly interested in changing their workload to include sections of this new course. Although the results of the annual summative assessment are not available at the time of writing of this chapter, the anecdotal evidence strongly indicated the positive outcomes of the courses. Teachers reported that students seemed happy to be in the course and expressed concern that they would have to leave the course if they passed the summative assessment, stating, "It helps me in my other classes as well." In the coming school year, plans were made to offer additional sections based upon the identified needs of the incoming ninth-grade students. The team of teachers were proud of the impact of their improvement work and presented their learning at the Washington Association of Bilingual Educators annual conference in 2021.

The basic components of the improvement science processes utilized in CWSD and some of the related concepts and actions specific to addressing the unique needs of the LTELs are presented in Figure 11.3.

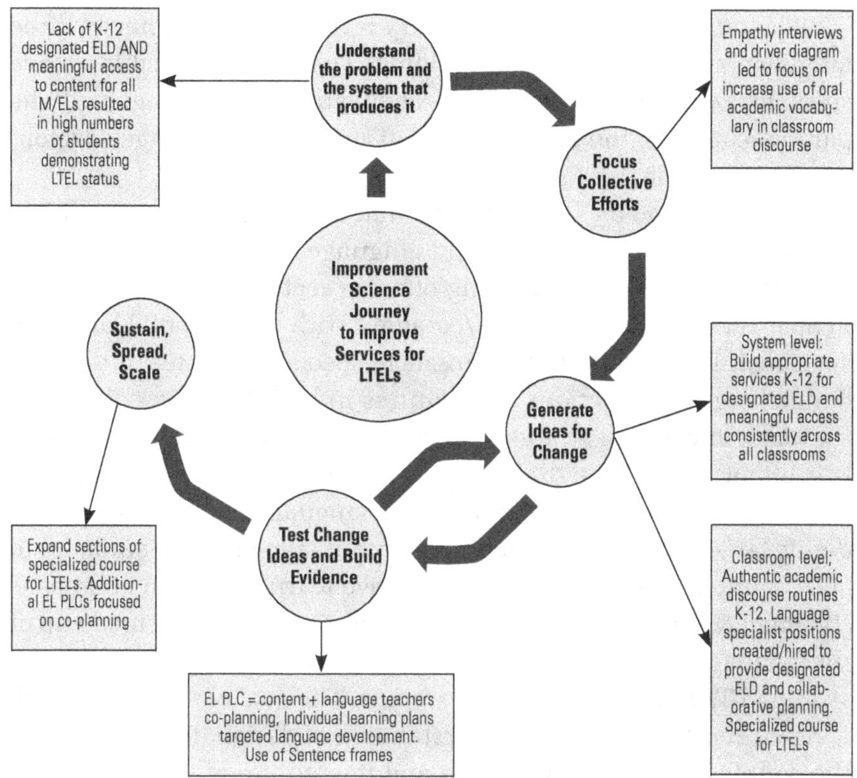

Figure 11.3. Improvement Science Journey for Improving Outcomes for English Learners

What's Next on This Journey?

CWSD continues to improve their TBIP by striving to ensure all K–12 m/ELs receive appropriate language development instruction and meaningful access to content. In addition to continuing the PDSA cycles outlined earlier, the administration created a districtwide team to begin the process of designing a K–12 dual-language program model. This process requires one to two years of planning prior to launch. Dual-language programs begin at the kindergarten level at one elementary building and add grade levels as students progress through the system.

The next steps at the elementary level include the newly hired language specialists for each building. These certificated language specialists will be supported by paraeducators, but no longer will the paraeducators be the sole providers of support or language development instruction.

At the secondary level, professional learning community (PLC) collaboration among content and language specialists continues to increase. We are now discussing offering sections of algebra taught in Spanish that are co-planned/cotaught with the bilingual language specialist. In this design, the language specialist will teach the academic language functions and features in both languages, bridging the academic language and content from one language to the other. It is important to note that bridging is not translation but a process that utilizes contrastive analysis of the language features of the academic language used to teach the content, allowing the students to access and discuss the content they have learned in both languages (Beeman & Urow, 2013). A newly created EL PLC will be made up of the language specialists and ELA teachers who have students demonstrating LTEL status in their classrooms. The goal of the EL PLC will be to strengthen teachers' understanding of designated ELD within the context of their content area and how to target these students' unique language development needs, utilizing improvement science processes and protocols.

Conclusion

Equitably addressing the language and literacy development needs of m/ELs requires an intentional design of systems and instruction with this student group's unique needs at the forefront. It is vital, therefore, that actions include

- evaluation and improvement of the language program to ensure both designated ELD as well as meaningful access to content are provided for all K–12 m/ELs.

- ensuring that the most qualified, certificated educators are providing designated ELD and that core/content teachers are trained and supported in understanding language acquisition as well as appropriate instructional practices and strategies. This requires drawing on collaboration with language specialists and, as much as possible, coteaching within core/content classroom teachers.
- an intensive focus on oral language development, with extensive, supported opportunities for students to discuss the content they are learning using the targeted language functions and linguistic features in all classrooms.
- individualization in the form of targeted goals based on the student's unique language development needs. This involves formatively monitoring students' language use and development, then adjusting targets based on evidence collected.

Educators can easily fall into a common belief that focusing on universal goals designed to support all students will, in turn, close opportunity gaps for m/ELs. However, m/ELs bring a unique context and set of needs that require targeted and specific approaches to develop language and content simultaneously. Schools must, therefore, set goals targeting improvement for specific subgroups of students versus generalized goals aimed at "all" students.

Improvement is highly contextual. We must find what works for whom, and under what conditions. As Aguilar (2020) notes, "Educational equity means that every child receives whatever she/he/they need to develop her/his/their full academic and social potential and to thrive, every day" (p. 6). For students demonstrating LTEL status, this means identifying and targeting the individual, unique challenges that each student faces in order to equitably address this educational system problem. This includes addressing designated English-language development as well as meaningful access to rigorous, grade-level content; appropriate staffing ratios; ongoing/job-embedded professional learning; and adequate/sufficient allocation of resources. Improvement science methods and tools allow districts to carefully examine systems to better meet student needs.

Discussion Questions

1. How might empathy interviews assist your staff in determining the unique needs of multilingual learners?
2. What are some examples of change ideas to support multilingual learners in your school's context?
3. How do you decide when to spread and scale change ideas within your system?

References

Aguilar, E. (2020). *Coaching for equity: Conversations that change practice.* Jossey-Bass.

August, D., & Shanahan, T. (2006). *Developing literacy in second-language learners: Report of the National Literacy Panel on Language Minority Children and Youth.* Erlbaum.

Beeman, K., & Urow, C. (2013). *Teaching for biliteracy: Strengthening bridges between languages.* Caslon Publishing.

Collier, V. P. & Thomas, W. P. (2009). *Educating English learners for a transformed world.* Dual Language of New Mexico Fuente Press.

Hinnart-Crawford, B. N. (2020). *Improvement science in education: A primer.* Myers Education Press.

Olsen, L. (2014). *Meeting the unique needs of long term English learners: A guide for educators.* National Education Association.

Wellman, B., & Lipton, L. (2017). *Data-driven dialogue: A facilitator's guide to collaborative inquiry.* Miravia.

CHAPTER TWELVE

Improved Outcomes for All: Students With Disabilities and Improvement Science

KRISTINE J. MELLOY AND TOBY KING

We share the experiences of teachers and administrators in rural and urban K–12 schools who enthusiastically adopted problem-solving practices that resulted in increased academic, behavioral, and social achievement among students receiving special education services reflecting the Individuals with Disabilities Education Improvement Act (IDEIA, 2004) expectations for inclusive school settings. Improvement Science in education is a way for educators to "uncover 'what works' in education, but also is a way to understand 'what works where, when and for whom'" (Hobbs, 2018, The Edge section). Used as a problem-solving approach, improvement science in education involves six core principles (Hudson, 2018). Table 12.1 illustrates each of the core principles with an example of how these principles apply in addressing systems change related to the delivery of special education services in inclusive school settings.

District Context

The School District of Sunshine River (SDSR) serves 23,000 students with 1,200 full- and part-time teachers and staff in 25 schools. The student population consists of 60% students eligible for free and reduced-price meals, 70% students of color, 20% English learners (EL), and 10% students with disabilities (SWDs). Sunshine River is

Table 12.1. Six Core Principles of Improvement Science and Examples of Their Application Related to Delivery of Special Education Services in an Inclusive School Settings

Improvement Science Core Principles (Hudson, 2018, paras. 3–8)	Examples of Application of Core Principles Related to Delivery of Special Education Services in an Inclusive School Setting
1. "Make the work problem-specific and user-centered" (para. 3). **Questions to guide thinking:** "What specifically is the problem we are trying to solve?" "How do we know it is a problem?"	**Problem:** Black and Brown SWDs segregated from general education (inclusive) classrooms. **How we know:** Academic and social competence gaps keep Black and Brown SWDs from growing academically, behaviorally, and socially.
2. "Focus on variation in performance" (para. 4). **Questions to guide thinking:** "What works, for whom, and under what set of conditions?"	**What works:** SWDs who are not Black and Brown grow academically, behaviorally, and socially in inclusive classrooms.
3. "See the system that produces the current outcomes" (para. 5). **Questions to guide thinking:** "How do local conditions shape work processes and resulting outcomes in various systems in the school?"	**Systems:** • Educator capacities • Critical mindsets (e.g., SWDs can't/can learn grade-level content) • Multitiered systems of support

4. "We cannot improve at scale what we cannot measure" (para. 6). **Questions to guide thinking:** "What data are being collected and analyzed to determine if strategies are working?"	**Data:**
	• Formative
	• Summative
	  - Data digs
	  - Data teams
	  - Data-driven instruction

5. "Use disciplined inquiry to drive improvement" (para. 7). **Questions to guide thinking:** "What are the results of the PDSA cycles related to the problem of practice?"	**Aim statement:** Culture and Climate By the end of the school year, teachers and staff implement effective systems that support social and emotional learning opportunities for all students, so they engage in healthy learning environments as measured by their responses on a survey about culture and climate, and Black and Brown SWDs increased time spent in inclusive school settings.
6. "Accelerate learning through network improvement communities (NIC)" (para. 8). **Questions to guide thinking:** "Who are outside experts or researchers we should connect to the most effective teachers in our school to discuss how we can create change that lasts?"	University faculty experts in equitable special education services joined K–12 effective special and general education teachers to discuss: • What questions are we seeking to find answers about our school? • Are those the right questions? • How do we know? • What are the problems of practice we face?
7. "Make the work problem-specific and user-centered" (para. 3). **Questions to guide thinking:** "What specifically is the problem we are trying to solve?" "How do we know it is a problem?"	**Problem:** Black and Brown SWDs segregated from general education (inclusive) classrooms. **How we know:** Academic and social competence gaps keep Black and Brown SWDs from growing academically, behaviorally, and socially.

Improvement Science Core Principles (Hudson, 2018, paras. 3–8)	Examples of Application of Core Principles Related to Delivery of Special Education Services in an Inclusive School Setting
8. "Focus on variation in performance" (para. 4). **Questions to guide thinking:** "What works, for whom, and under what set of conditions?"	**What works:** SWDs who are not Black and Brown grow academically, behaviorally, and socially in inclusive classrooms.
9. "See the system that produces the current outcomes" (para. 5). **Questions to guide thinking:** "How do local conditions shape work processes and resulting outcomes in various systems in the school?"	**Systems:** Educator capacities • Critical mindsets (e.g., SWDs can't/can learn grade-level content) • Multitiered systems of support
10. "We cannot improve at scale what we cannot measure" (para. 6). **Questions to guide thinking:** "What data are being collected and analyzed to determine if strategies are working?"	**Data:** Formative Summative – Data digs – Data teams – Data-driven instruction
11. "Use disciplined inquiry to drive improvement" (para. 7). **Questions to guide thinking:** "What are the results of the PDSA cycles related to the problem of practice?"	**Aim statement:** Culture and Climate: By the end of the school year, teachers and staff implement effective systems that support social and emotional learning opportunities for all students, so they engage in healthy learning environments as measured by their responses on a survey about culture and climate, and Black and Brown SWDs increased time spent in inclusive school settings.
12. "Accelerate learning through network improvement communities (NIC)" (para. 8). **Questions to guide thinking:** "Who are outside experts or researchers we should connect to the most effective teachers in our school to discuss how we can create change that lasts?"	University faculty experts in equitable special education services joined K–12 effective special and general education teachers to discuss: • What questions are we seeking to find answers about our school? • Are those the right questions? • How do we know? • What are the problems of practice we face?

Note: SWD = student with disability; PDSA = Plan–Do–Study–Act.

located in the Mountain West of the United States and has a population of approximately 106,000. The district's mission is to engage every student in a personalized, well-rounded, and excellent education, preparing students to be college- and career-ready.

State standardized test data from the last three years in math and English language arts (ELA) show students are making progress at the elementary, middle, and high school levels with an increase in ELs on track for English-language proficiency, increased graduation rates, a decrease in dropout rates, and increase of SWDs who spend

80% or more of their day in the general education classroom as their least restrictive environment (LRE).

Equity Focus

Kozleski et al. (2020) indicate that SWDs are the most likely candidates for being underserved in schools even though IDEA (2004) requires every student to have a free and appropriate public education (FAPE) and despite equity goals (Melloy & Murry, 2019). Often, educators have a lower set of expectations for SWDs (Jung et al., 2019).

The Improvement Team

Although SDSR experienced some impressive improvements, SWDs still achieved below state expectations for math and ELA. Black and Brown SWDs were included in general education classrooms 80% or more of their day at a lower rate than their White peers with disabilities. The district focused on two major improvement strategies: instructional strategies and professional development support to achieve its mission.

In establishing this mission, the superintendent and the district improvement team set a clear vision that all teachers in the district receive training to use improvement tools to create classroom learning communities. With priority performance challenges focused on SWDs, the district improvement team posited that using improvement science tools to increase training, support, and understanding of grade-level expectations aligned with standards would increase outcomes. Teachers bought into the mission because the process engaged them and their students.

All administrators in SDSR are deeply involved in carrying out the districtwide instructional improvement master plan to improve academic growth for SWDs, especially Black and Brown students. Principles are becoming embedded in the system as leaders, teachers, and staff aim to (a) prepare students who will engage in a challenging, personalized, well-rounded education, preparing every student to be college and career ready; (b) increase engagement and interest in learning through community and school partnerships with students, families, and community to enhance student success; (c) cultivate a safe and supportive learning environment for all, embracing diversity, honoring and engaging all stakeholders and promoting safety; and (d) be innovative and accountable to the community through measurable outcomes and continuous improvement.

Our Problem of Practice

Janiece is a ninth-grade student at Central High School (pseudonyms used throughout) in an urban city in the U.S. Midwest. Janiece, who identifies as a cisgender female, goes by the pronouns *she/her/hers*. She is eligible for special education services and has an individualized education program (IEP) to address her learning disabilities and emotional and behavioral disorders. Early in Janiece's education career, she received much of her special education and related services in resource settings, resulting in significant gaps in content mastery and social competence. Janiece and her IEP team developed a plan to address her support needs in ELA and social-emotional learning (SEL). The team wrote Janiece's IEP to provide her services 100% of the day in inclusive classrooms with peers with and without disabilities. Janiece's personalized learning plan includes the goal of being college- and career-ready by high school graduation. Her IEP supports her special learning needs.

Janiece's story is typical of SWDs in U.S. schools that follow the principles of improvement science (Bryk et al., 2010) and whose faculty, staff, and administrators have critical mindsets (DeHartchuck et al., 2019). By following the principles of improvement science, Janiece and her IEP team find solutions to help Janiece meet the standards for high school graduation; improvement science provides an effective, efficient, and equity-focused process for solving problems. The faculty, staff, and administrators in Janiece's school established critical mindsets as an essential system change to allow for effective inclusive education for SWDs. McLeskey et al. (2014) describe effective inclusive schools as those "with classrooms where students with disabilities get the support they need to succeed in academic, social and extra-curricular activities" (p. 4). The assertion that a child must be able to perform academically on grade level or behave in such a way to be able to receive instruction in the general education setting, indicates the erroneous belief that SWDs must earn a place in the inclusive school setting (Jung et al., 2019). The multitiered systems of support (MTSS) and response-to-intervention (RTI) movements, in part, are designed to replace the implicit or explicit biases that exist in schools related to the deficit perspective of disability, including beliefs regarding access to general education by SWDs (McIntosh & Goodman, 2016). Students identified with a disability in SDSR are performing below state expectations in math and ELA. Black and Brown SWDs are denied their civil rights to an FAPE and equitable access to general education content and SEL opportunities with peers without disabilities.

Based on an equity mindset, the problem of practice we focus on in this chapter required responding to questions such as those presented in Table 12.2.

Table 12.2. Questions to Address Educational Needs of Students With Disabilities

> - How can school leaders, teachers, and staff be proactive in addressing students' instructional needs with the most continuous learning and behavioral challenges?
> - How can school leaders, teachers, and staff be more effective and efficient with the deployment of human capital so that system improvement is sustainable and students' needs are met?

To improve equity among SWDs, schools must increase time in the LRE. Increasing time in the LRE improves access to peers without disabilities, general education curriculum, and college- and career-readiness opportunities (Kozleski et al., 2020).

The Problem

State education agencies (SEAs) are required to monitor the LRE rates of each local education agency (LEA) because these rates coincide with SWDs' achievement (Bateman & Cline, 2019b). To that end, details get lost in the aggregate. For example, it might not be of concern if a state had 75% or more of students with disabilities placed in the general education classroom. However, when the SEA analyzed the data, some placement figures were well below 75%, while others were over 75%. SEA analysis of the LRE data by schools within each LEA revealed a completely different story than the picture based on aggregated data. In collaboration with teachers and staff, school leaders can begin to make systemic improvements based on the shared aim (Bryk et al., 2010) that all SWDs will be included in inclusive classrooms 80% or more of the day and that a targeted percentage will graduate from high school.

Teachers must provide standards-based instruction to students. Additionally, teachers must provide personalized and differentiated instruction for each of the students in their classrooms. In many cases, however, teachers lack personalized and differentiated instruction preparation. Students of color often attend schools where their teachers are newer to the profession and less experienced. These issues exacerbate an already strained system of educating students so they can become college- and career-ready.

Investigate Root Causes of the Problem

To identify the problem and its root causes, our school leaders, in collaboration with teachers, staff, students, and families, began investigating the root causes of persistent performance challenges for SWD by asking these questions:

- What do we expect our students with disabilities to know and be able to do?
- Where does instruction occur on what we expect our students to know and be able to do?
- How much time do students with instructional gaps spend in classes where the instructional expectations are aligned with standards?
- Does our system typically segregate students with instructional gaps and learning difficulties for remediation?

- What are our schoolwide expectations for students with instructional gaps?
- How much access do students with identified instructional gaps have to our most skilled educators?
- What is the system for providing teachers and staff access to professional development/technical assistance opportunities to support them in meeting their needs related to instruction, culture, and climate?

Problem-Solving Process for Continuous Improvement

Once school teams identify the problem, a problem-solving process for continuous quality improvement is implemented to address problems efficiently and effectively. Identifying the problem of practice and instituting the core principles associated with improvement science helps implement and sustain effective practices that lead to systems changes that affect student achievement (Hobbs, 2018; Hudson, 2018).

Plan–Do–Study–Act (PDSA) Cycles

The tools used in the improvement science process for improving systems that provide educational services for SWDs allow for ongoing inquiry and learning. A primary tool of improvement science is the PDSA inquiry cycle. A detailed description of the PDSA is found in the next section of this chapter. The tools described in this section of the chapter provide ways for the school improvement team (SIT) to identify specific problems, review IDEA requirements for the delivery of special education services concerning school systems, engage in activities designed to illuminate biases and root causes of problems, and have student-centered discussions. These tools are used in the PDSA cycles to gather information and data needed to develop the aim statements and primary and secondary drivers for the change of ideas based on the theory of improvement. Table 12.3 provides an example of often used tools, purpose, and resources for continuous improvement in education in the PDSA improvement science process.

Table 12.3. Tools Used in the Improvement Science Process: Tool, Purpose, and Resources

Tool	Purpose and Resources
Equity Audit	This tool helps school leaders assess whether or not the school provides the processes and information that create a positive learning environment so students and staff can perform at their highest level.
Root-Cause Analysis	Root-cause analysis helps identify, select, and plan for implementing specific evidence-based practices or interventions that are likely to remove the root cause or mitigate the chances of root causes.
Empathy Interview	Empathy interviews with students and others are designed to help educators dig deeper than surface questions that prompt general responses. The empathy interview helps educators identify not only the current state of students, but it also helps them gain an understanding as to what students' needs are and how students can be supported.

A way to improve outcomes for SWD is to employ the PDSA cycle process. PDSA cycles provide a way for teachers and others to repeat the process to test an initial hypothesis (Plan), collect data on how the plan is going (Do), analyze that data (Study), and make data-driven decisions about implementing the next cycle to broaden the improvement's impact (Act) (Hudson, 2018).

Plan

In changing the system of delivering support for SWDs, the first step (Plan) to consider is the individual support needs in various contexts (e.g., consultation, coteaching lite, coteaching, resource/separate class). Considering the context allows educators to plan where and how these supports will best meet students' needs. Table 12.4 illustrates consideration of context for each student's support needs in a typical elementary general education classroom. The IDEIA (2004) requires that the general education classroom is the first place considered for SWDs to receive specially designed instruction and related services to meet their needs.

Table 12.4. Continuum of Supports for Students With and Without Disabilities: Contextual Consideration

Instructional Area	Consulting	Coteaching Lite	Coteaching	Resource/ Separate Class
	Students need indirect support to access content in this context.	Students need access to direct support periodically (every other day) in this context.	Students need access to direct support daily in this context.	Students need direct support in an alternative location (this is not about the educators or the supplies).
English Language Arts (ELA)	Jaclyn Allison Alexandra Connor	Alex Kacie Theresa Jack S.	Carissa Brooklyn Zachary Coco Beau	Tyler
Math	Eric	Kelli Matt Peter Carter	Cole Megan Luke	Ashley
Social-Emotional	Elizabeth Mackenzie Grace	Ryan Michael Alex	Madelyn Jack H. Lindsey	James

Do

After summarizing the students' contextual instructional needs, the next step is to cluster students with like support needs in classrooms for elementary schools or sections for middle and high schools (Fisher et al., 2021). Clustering (Do) is an important next step. It enables the building administrators to identify staff who have the skills and dispositions to work collaboratively in the best interest of the students they serve.

Study

Identifying teachers and staff who have skills and dispositions in line with the students' best interest allows for studying (Study) the school's culture and climate and who may need professional development to address critical mindset issues. The study step of the process gives the team opportunities to discuss the environmental context and meet the students' instructional needs. There may be temptations to place students with disabilities in more restrictive environments based on their past performance. However, making decisions based on past performance rather than on data that indicate otherwise presupposes where students' needs are best supported. There may also be a temptation to place students into LREs without support. FAPE and LRE, based on the student's IEP, ensure needed support (Bateman & Cline, 2019b). In the following sections, we share several ideas that effectively solved common school problems in our work with teams developing systems that supported SWD and their peers without disabilities in inclusive schools.

Student Assignment to Classrooms. There are many ways to create classrooms that are rich in diversity and embrace inclusion. In this chapter, we provide a suggestion for an equitable way to assign students to classes. The special and general education teams collaborate to identify the students' instructional support needs by grade level/content and assign students with disabilities to classes based on their needs. Students with similar needs are "clustered" into classes before assigning students without disabilities and the educators. This strategy enables the teacher to be more efficient in delivering instruction. In secondary schools, the modus operandi uses the Student Information System scheduling function to place students into their classes by section. Using the alternative method previously described in secondary schools enables the scheduling team to know how many sections of each core content area, for example, would require more in-class support than another section. School teams are prepared to develop their service delivery schedules for implementation on the first day of school and eliminate segregation and modification, except based on student needs, and provide more contextual remediation aligned to the class's instructional expectations.

Staff Assignment to Classes/Sections. Once student needs are identified, imagine a scenario in which staff skills and expertise align with the student's needs in the given content class or grade level. Additionally, special educators may be assigned to specific classrooms during content-specific times or intervals to co-deliver instruction, offer small-group instruction (along with the general education teacher), and support all learners in the class. Using data to assign students and staff, the school ensures that their students with identified instructional gaps are in classrooms where the instruction is aligned to the standards, taught by highly skilled teachers, and staffed with special service providers when necessary to meet the instructional needs of the students assigned to such classes.

Act

The final step in the PDSA cycle is to act on the improvement idea, adapting, adopting, or abandoning the change idea as needed based on repeated cycles. PDSA cycles completed in short time frames (e.g., seven to ten days) allow adjustments to interventions and practices based on formative data. Designing classroom/section teacher and staff assignments to meet identified SWD support needs and equipping educators with the skill and the will to deliver effective instruction are two practices that positively affect SWD achievement (McLeskey et al., 2019). Furthermore, the PDSA process enables the school to assign specialists to collaborate with classroom teachers to design and deliver instruction that is more responsive to the students' identified support needs in the classroom.

PDSA—Beyond the "Do"

It is well documented that educational initiatives often do not go beyond the "Do" part of the PDSA cycle (Bryk et al., 2010; Hudson, 2018). Emerging evidence suggests that personal beliefs, behaviors, and people's values when implementing improvement strategies can affect the quality of implementation, and therefore, the outcomes (Park et al., 2015). The PDSA cycles of improvement science are meant to avoid "stalling out at the do phase of the cycle" (Hudson, 2018, para. 7) through repeated cycles.

Aim 1

The SDSR continuous improvement plan was based on two major improvement aims: quality instruction and culture and climate.

Culture and Climate. By the end of the school year, teachers will use effective Tier 1 instructional strategies to allow all students access to grade-level content with the support of Tier 2 interventions as measured by increases in academic achievement.

- Root causes:
  - Some educators lack the belief that all students can learn on grade level and all content, creating barriers for student access to appropriate content.
  - MTSS has not been fully implemented to establish universal, targeted, and intensive support to meet all students' needs.
  - Some staff lack the understanding of grade-level expectations with the standards; therefore, students are not accessing grade-level learning standards.

Strategies. Several action steps were completed as part of the SDSR model for improvement. A continuous improvement consulting agency was hired to build a technical support team consisting of a layered coaching system to train teachers and build capacity. The first level of coaching included one-to-one discussions with teachers in which they shared information about their learning goals, learning requirements, and student data. Then teachers engaged in PDSA cycles, particularly around improving academic instruction for SWDs and the inclusion of Black and Brown SWDs through coteaching and Universal Design for Learning (CAST, 2021) strategies. The second level of coaching involved teachers observing instructional coaches in a "train the trainer" structure. This model builds an internal capacity to ensure the improvement work continues even if teachers change.

Aim 2

Culture and Climate. By the end of the school year, teachers and staff will implement effective systems and practices that support social and emotional learning (i.e., CASEL SEL Framework) (CASEL, 2021) opportunities for all students to engage in healthy learning environments as measured by responses to a culture and climate survey, and increased time in the general education classroom for Black and Brown SWDs.

- Root causes:
  - See Aim 1

Strategies. Several action steps were completed as part of the SDSR model to address the culture and climate improvement strategy. A district equity leadership team was established to support each building's equity team development as they supported the cultural proficiency work at the building level. District staff collaborated with community partners and district family and student support team members to support families and students' SEL needs. The district and building equity teams ran PDSA cycles focused on the following:

- SEL supports
- procedures and routines focused on a culture of learning
- systems and professional development support that focus on attendance and behavior

For each of the continuous improvement aims, the PDSA cycles ran approximately 7 to 10 days. During this time, district leaders, teachers, and others collected student and teacher data (e.g., helpful strategies, tweaking, needing to be scrapped) to track their progress toward the aim. Sharing data with students and teachers motivated them to focus on their learning and supporting their peers.

Lessons Learned for Increasing Equity in Schools

Change using improvement science resulted in many lessons learned. In this chapter's approach, the big takeaway is that it takes active, informed, and knowledgeable leadership and collaboration among teachers and staff to identify the problem, develop a plan, implement the plan, check the progress on the plan, and make refinements to the plan. SDSR made progress toward the continuous improvement aims for quality instruction focusing on professional development supports, which resulted in academic growth in ELA for students without disabilities. However, SWDs did not experience academic growth.

Increased time in the general education classroom for SWDs indicated progress toward achieving the culture and climate aim. Figure
12.1 depicts the SDSR data for Black, Brown, and White SWDs in the
general education classroom 80% or more of the day between 2017
and 2020.

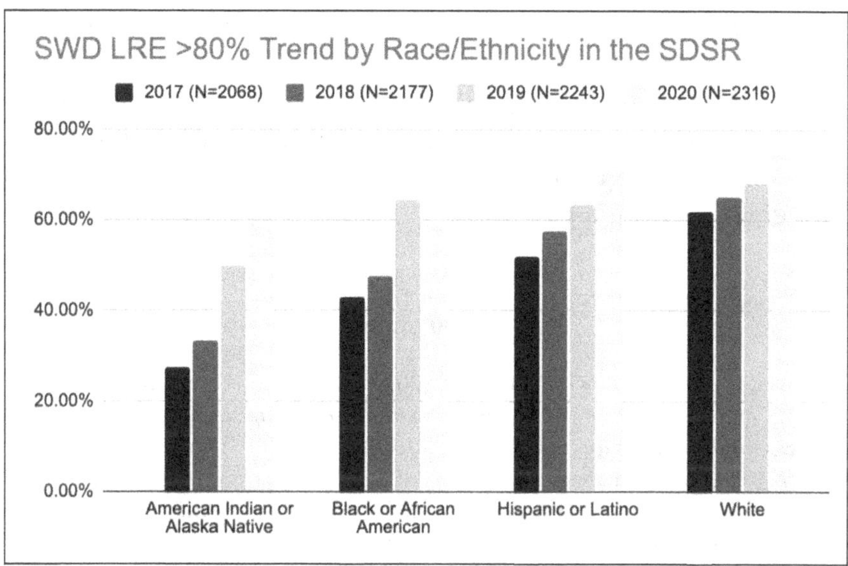

Figure 12.1. Students with Disabilities: Least Restrictive Environment
>80% Trend by Race/Ethnicity in the School District of Sunshine River

The administrators, teachers, and staff for the SDSR may celebrate
their achievements. However, they know that to sustain Black and
Brown SWD inclusion in general education classrooms, completing
additional PDSA cycles with additional change ideas is necessary.

Discussion Questions

1. Alignment of staff skills and expertise with the needs of SWD
   students in a given content class or grade level is essential for
   academic growth. How might leaders effectively support prac-

tices that promote this alignment? How might teachers collaborate to build this capacity?

2. In this case study, increased time in the general education classroom for SWDs indicated notable progress toward achieving the culture and climate aim and resulted in academic growth in ELA for students without disabilities. However, SWD did not experience academic growth. What additional PDSA cycles might address these issues?

3. What is an area of improvement in your school that would address the goal of SWD being included in inclusive classrooms 80% or more of the day and that a targeted percentage will graduate from high school?

References

Bateman, D., & Cline, J., with L. Matson. (2019b). Current and emerging trends facing special education. In *Special education leadership: Building effective programming schools* (pp. 228–243). Routledge.

Bryk, A. S., Gomez, L. M., & Grunow, A. (2010). *Getting ideas into action: Building networked communities in education.* Carnegie Foundation for the Advancement for Teaching. http://www.carnegiefoundation.org/spotlight/webinar-bryk-gomez-building-networked-improvement-communities-in-education

CASEL. (2021). Interactive CASEL SEL framework. SEL: What are the core competence areas and where are they promoted? https://casel.org/sel-framework/

CAST. (2021). Universal design for learning guidelines. About universal design for learning. https://www.cast.org/impact/universal-design-for-learning-udl

DeHartchuck, L., Kruse, L., & Whittaker, M. (2019). *Forward together: A school leader's guide to creating inclusive schools.* National Center for Learning Disabilities and Understood. https://www.ncld.org/wp-content/uploads/2019/12/Guide-to-Creating-Inclusive-Schools-12.9.2019.pdf

Fisher, D., Frey, N., Smith, D., & Hattie, J. (2021). *The distance learning playbook for school leaders: Leading for engagement & impact in any setting.* Corwin.

Hobbs, M. (2018, October 15). *Charting a science of improvement in education.* UNC School of Education. https://ed.unc.edu/2018/10/15/charting-a-science-of-improvement-in-education/

Hudson, E. (2018, September 20). *Six principles of improvement science that lead to lasting change.* https://medium.com/@ejhudson/six-principles-of-improvement-science-that-lead-to-lasting-change-c8015212c66

Individuals with Disabilities Education Improvement Act of 2004 (IDEIA), 20 USC § 1400 et seq. (2004).

Jung, L. A., Frey, N., Fisher, D., & Kroener, J. (2019). *Your students, my students, our students: Rethinking equitable and inclusive classrooms*. ASCD.

Kozleski, E., Stepaniuk, I., & Proffitt, W. (2020). In the eye of the storm: When retreat is an unacceptable option. *Multiple Voices: Disability, Race, and Language Intersections in Special Education, 20*(1), 16–31. https://doi.org/10.5555/2158-396X-20.1.16

McIntosh, K., & Goodman, S. (2016). *Integrated multi-tiered systems of supports: RTI and PBIS*. Guilford.

McLeskey, J., Maheady, L., Billingsley, B., Brownell, M. T., & Lewis, T. J. (2019). *High leverage practices for inclusive classrooms*. Council for Exceptional Children & Routledge.

McLeskey, J., Waldron, N. L., Spooner, F., & Algozzine, B. (2014). What are effective inclusive schools and why are they important? In J. McLeskey, N. L., Waldron, F. Spooner, & B. Algozzine (Eds.), *Handbook of effective inclusive schools: Research and practice* (pp. 3–16). Routledge.

Melloy, K. J., & Murry, F. R. (2019). A conceptual framework: Creating socially just schools for students with emotional and behavioral disabilities. *World Journal of Education, 9*(5), 113–124. https://doi.org/10.5430/wje.v9n5p113

Park, S., Hironaka, S., Carver, P., & Nordstrom, L. (2015). *Continuous improvement in education*. Carnegie Foundation for the Advancement of Teaching. https://www.carnegiefoundation.org/resources/publications/continuous-improvement-education/

CHAPTER THIRTEEN

Equitable Special Education Evaluation in the Time of COVID-19

KILEEN BIRMINGHAM AND JAMES SANDERS

Sequoia Creek School District (SCSD) is located in suburban Portland, Oregon. The school district surrounds a lake and is comprised of six elementary schools, two middle schools, and two high schools. It is an ever-growing and ever-diversifying school district. SCSD serves 7,000 students with an overall 4-year graduation rate of 95%, well above the reported statewide average of 80% in 2019. Of the 7,000 students, 690 students are identified as a student with a disability. The following reflect 4-year high school graduation and special education eligibility percentages defined by race and ethnicity. The Latinx high school completion rate is 94%, with 8% of total special education eligible students. The White high school graduation rate is 95%, with 76% of total special education eligible individuals. The Asian completion rate is 97%, with 6% of total special education eligible students identifying as Asian. The multiracial completion rate at 94%, with 8% of total special education eligible students identifying as multiracial. The other races subgroup, total graduation rate, and special education eligibility rate for Native American, Black, and Asian Pacific Islanders have been combined to protect student identity due to the low numbers of students in these groups. The total 4-year graduation rate for this group is 84%, with 2% of total special education eligible students. This high school completion rate is above the statewide average and substantially below the 4-year graduation rates for all other categories in SCSD.

Graduation rates for English-language learners (ELLs) and students eligible for talented and gifted (TAG) services are 100%, with ELLs qualifying for special education at 1% and individuals receiving TAG services qualifying at 5% of total special education eligible students.

SCSD has placed equity at the center of the work in schools. The district has adopted the SCSD equity policy driving how an equity lens can be applied to the daily work of educating and supporting youth. Specifically, guiding questions are used to consider how any decision may impact a student's access and inclusion in their education. Those questions consider the following: (a) How does the decision align with the equity mission? (b) Who does the decision impact? (c) Who does the policy ignore? (d) Does the decision worsen or disrupt existing disparities? (e) How does the decision contribute to a sense of inclusiveness? and (f) How will the team follow up to ensure the decision had the intended outcome? In support of equitable access, the district is utilizing a multitiered system of supports (MTSS) approach to address student academic and social-emotional/behavioral needs. Within that work, the school district has adopted a social-emotional learning curriculum that comes through the lens of equity, designed to support inclusion and community within our schools, as well as develop the social-emotional learning skills of all students. In support of adult learning, districtwide professional development on equity has been provided with building-level equity teams conducting monthly professional development for staff.

During the transition to online comprehensive distance learning (CDL), SCSD has provided technology tools, training, and curriculum for the online learning environment. Online resources to facilitate instruction and expand technology skills were available as well. The associated training for these tools is supported by in-district staff along with external consultant support. Students were given Chromebooks or iPads with Wi-Fi hot spots to address internet connectivity. Daily meal distribution was provided to all students regardless of eligibility criteria for the federal free and reduced-price lunch program. A new online K–12 reading curriculum was released with associated teacher professional development in conjunction with a new online math and reading assessment system for benchmark testing employed for fall, winter, and spring data collection. Schools are using these new resources and tools for a very different approach to teaching and learning.

Improvement Science Team

The improvement science (IS) team is composed of all those who have actively used the evaluation center since it opened in October 2020. Each person has been trained in health and safety protocols, as well as the use of a new online assessment system. The professionals are school psychologists, a special education teacher, an administrator, and a teacher on special assignment. Each person was selected based on their level of familiarity with the center and its use.

Need for Improvement

This chapter focuses on the accurate assessment of students for special education during the COVID-19 closure using an evaluation center in SCSD. During CDL in the spring of 2020, the district had to stop assessing students for special education eligibility due to the closure of schools. With the reopening of schools through hybrid instruction, school districts were required to reengage with the federal obligation for Child Find. Child Find is the requirement to assess and identify any and all students suspected of having a disability preK through 12th grade for special education services. To that end, SCSD felt it wisest to start small with a centralized evaluation center located in a community school in which students and assessors come to the center for testing. There are plans to move the assessment process back to schools for the 2021–2022 school year.

Equity Audit

To gain a better understanding of the distribution of special education eligibility among all students served in SCSD and how equity is playing into eligibility status, we consulted the Frattura and Capper

(2007) equity audit because it took a deeper dive into areas relevant to special education and considered important demographics as they relate to race and socioeconomic status. Coupled with questions from the Frattura and Capper audit, we pulled qualitative questions from the Smith et al. (2017) audit and developed an interview survey. The resulting survey was completed by members of the IS team.

When looking at district-level data through the lens of the equity audit, interesting and emerging patterns appear. For example, SCSD reporting indicated TAG students make up 17% of the total student population but only 5% of that total number are students eligible for special education. These data left the IS team concerned there may be an underrepresentation and under-identification of dual-identified students in the district. Parent advocacy groups have shared concerns that this specific student group has been underserved and under supported. School teams have reported difficulty knowing how to accurately identify TAG students in the specific learning disability category, for example.

Using statewide reporting data, eligibility rates for students of color are important considerations for this improvement project. During the 2016–2017 school year, Latinx students were twice as likely to qualify for special education services under the category of specific learning disability than were their White peers. However, in comparison, during the 2015–2016 school year, Latinx students were twice as likely to qualify for special education under the communication disorder category than White students. Finally, Black students in 2017–2018 were twice as likely to be identified under communication disorder, emotional disturbance, other health impairment, and specific learning disability than White students. A deeper dive into that data indicated the total number of students identifying as Black was 11, with seven of those individuals moving into SCSD in 2017–2018 with previously established eligibilities from prior school districts. When looking at more current eligibility data from 2018–2019 and 2019–2020 and disaggregated by race, it appears that in these years, all communities of color were proportionately made eligible for special education for the priority categories of autism, communication disorder, emotional disturbance, intellectual disability, specific learning disability, and other health impairment. Thus, SCSD has not been flagged by the Oregon Department of Education (ODE) for a disproportionate number of students of color made eligible for special education in the last 2 years. Although this is a positive trajectory for improvement, the district is compelled to maintain a vigilant stance when considering students of color for special education. Through data analysis using the equity audit and personal observations, the IS team felt the need to explore their perception of assessment accuracy given the historical context of overidentification of Latinx youth and the anxieties of using professional judgment when assessing students during the COVID-19 closure.

Empathy Interviews

Empathy interviews were developed to consider the experience of those using the evaluation center and to get a deeper understanding of what factors affect assessment accuracy. Respondents felt practice time and training in the use of the new assessment tools were essential to ensure the likelihood of valid and reliable assessment results especially in the new assessment environment. Assessors reported the need for strong online customer service support for the scoring system and test administration. Ease in scheduling the use of the centralized evaluation center was seen as a priority, as well as creating a sense of safety for families who were bringing their children back to a school for the first time since the closure of school due to COVID-19. Some respondents felt the district may not be assessing students who would benefit from special education services, while all respondents felt the district has received more requests for evaluation since the center has opened. Respondents reported both validity and reliability of assessments as being very important, but when asked to choose between the two, assessors indicated validity as the overriding priority given the assessment environment during a pandemic. Interviewees reported varying degrees of comfort in using professional judgment when guiding eligibility decisions, especially when using a broader array of assessments beyond standardized assessments. Respondents resoundingly indicated tutoring and outside school supports such as schooling in pods to be significant equity concerns across the district, particularly for students of color or those experiencing economic challenges.

Literature Review

The literature examining the special education assessment process and how assessment practices impact student supports and eligibility is considerable. Banerjee et al. (2014) found that assessment professionals preferred comprehensive evaluation data over limited or no assessment data for postsecondary students. Although this is not surprising information, it is clear that in the absence of comprehensive assessment data, providers expressed a preference for diagnostic and historical evidence to establish special education eligibility. Hanchon and Allen (2012) found examiners preferred standardized measures (e.g., Behavior Assessment Scale for Children 2 [BASC – 2] and the Achenbach System of Empirically Based Assessment [ASEBA]) over nonstandardized measures in understanding a student's presenting challenges. The perception of usefulness of the standardized measures over other points of data were perceived as four times more helpful than the other measures considered. Hanchon and Allen also examined how years of professional experience as a school psychologist influenced the use and understanding of the federal definition of emotional disturbance. Study results indicated evaluators with more than 15 years of experience felt a greater level of ease when supporting an emotional disturbance eligibility and clearly preferred standardized scales for collecting testing data. Assessment professionals in Sullivan et al. (2019) looked at special education eligibility rates by race to determine how examiner bias may play into eligibility decision-making. Researchers were looking at how preconceptions about race affect the likelihood that a student of color would qualify for emotional disturbance, intellectual disability, or autism spectrum disorder. Statistical analysis and survey responses indicated little evidence that students of color were disproportionately identified for special education over White students. In this study, evaluators reviewed testing data and eligibility decisions without knowing the race of the student. An interesting issue to consider is how knowing the race of the student influences data analysis or eligibility decision-making given there are data reporting the disproportionate number of students of color identified for special education. These studies, in conjunction with others, helped to frame the work of the IS team, providing direction and clarity around what may actively influence accurate assessments for special education.

Problem of Practice

The IS team sought to understand how they could ensure the assessments they were performing did not result in false-positive eligibilities for special education. This was especially relevant given several factors outside the control of the assessor given the altered assessment environment. The team arrived at the following problem of practice: given the constraints of the COVID-19 closure, we are not accurately assessing students for special education.

Theory of Improvement

In an effort to dig deeper and consider key factors contributing to the problem of practice the IS team conducted a root-cause analysis. This analysis examined both primary and secondary contributing elements that could increase the likelihood of inaccurate special education assessments. The fishbone diagram in Figure 13.1 is a distilled reflection of group brainstorming sessions.

Primary casual factors identified by the group were student comfort, reliability/validity, home factors, tools, and anxiety. The IS team focused on a single root cause on the fishbone analysis to narrow the scope of the work. The IS team felt anxiety was a good starting point in that this root cause had a greater likelihood of leading to actionable change ideas in the COVID-19 closure. Throughout the development of the root-cause analysis and the driver diagram development, the IS team used a series of equity questions drawn from Crow et al.

(2019) to guide their thinking and to raise awareness around personal bias in an effort to interrupt educational disparities during the brainstorming sessions. Periodic perception checks using the equity questions were utilized to support team members in asking themselves the questions and responding as they felt comfortable. From the fishbone exercise, the IS team crafted the driver diagram containing the aim statement, primary and secondary drivers, and change ideas (see Figure 13.2). The aim statement and the change ideas were designed to increase the likelihood of assessment accuracy. The improvement science team went through a few iterations of the driver diagram to ensure the drivers were directly linked to change ideas and the aim statement. The IS team landed on three change ideas as they related to the primary driver. The first two change ideas, articulated in the following section, address the examiners' needs for training and practice in using new online assessments. As the team examined the potential change ideas, there was a concern raised regarding examiner bias in the assessment process. A third change idea was crafted to address that concern.

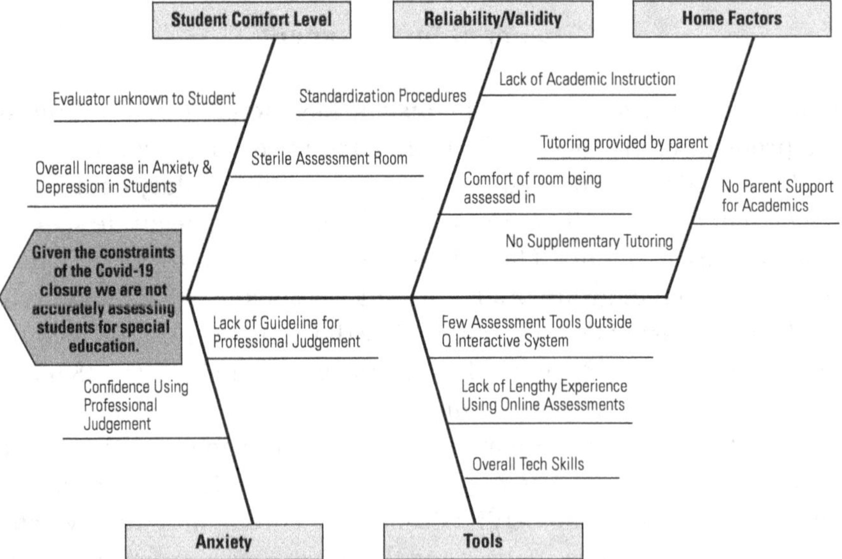

Figure 13.1. Fishbone Diagram

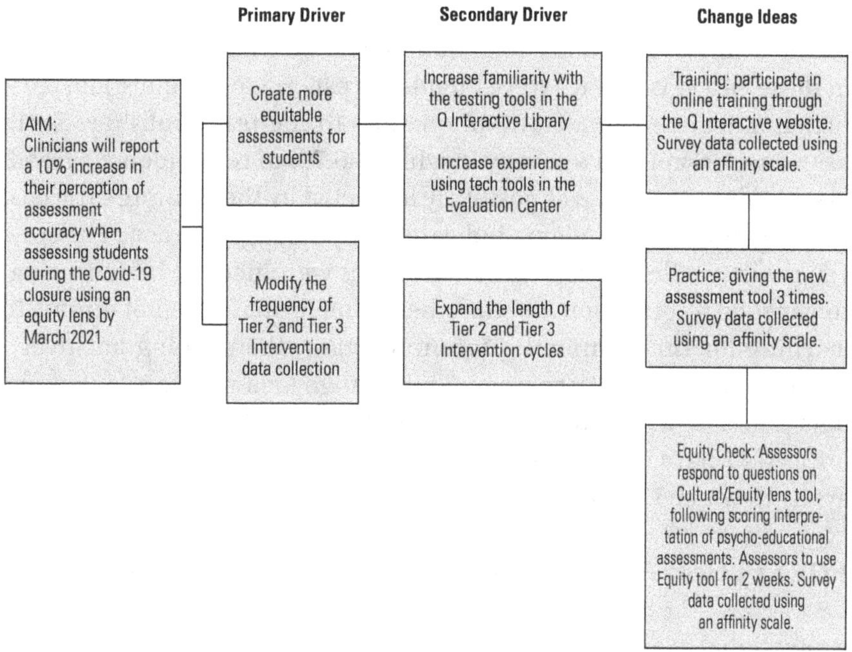

Figure 13.2. Driver Diagram

Testing the Change

Plan–Do–Study–Act (PDSA) Cycle 1: Participate in Online Training Using an Assessment Website

The assessment site utilizes familiar testing tools in a very new testing environment. To increase familiarity with the site and the tests, examiners were provided accounts and open access to online training. The goals of this PDSA cycle were increasing assessors' familiarity with the testing tools and to elevate assessment accuracy. This PDSA cycle ran from the second week in September 2020 through the third week in September 2020. The testing website included detailed tutorial videos on the use of the site itself as well as videos for all the tests available. Examiners were encouraged to view the tutorials at a time during the PDSA cycle that fit with their work schedule. Adjustments were made when some participants had questions that were not directly answered by the videos or were hard to locate on the website. Individual consultation was offered by the researcher in these cases. When we were unable to respond to the question, participants were given a 1-800 phone line to the test publisher. Each examiner completed a survey in which 66.7% of respondents agreed assessment accuracy was positively impacted by the training tutorials while 33.3% of respondents indicated they strongly agreed. The survey results indicated that online training was effective in delivering the needed information and that the online format does not diminish learning for the examiner. More important, the training positively impacted assessment accuracy. This change idea will be adopted for new assessors who enter the district and retained for existing examiners as they have unlimited access to the training modules for refreshers as they need them.

PDSA Cycle 2: Practice Administering Online Assessments

Professional examiners in the school district reported concerns about using a new online assessment suite for testing students. The tests within the suite are assessments the examiners were very familiar using, but administering them electronically was new territory. The new format involved using iPads instead of the traditional paper-and-pencil test administration. The goal of this change idea was to build assessor confidence in giving the tests electronically and, more important, increase assessment accuracy. The cycle took place for a 2-week period in late September and early October 2020. The PDSA cycle window needed to be adjusted due to challenges in scheduling availability of the evaluation center and a revised opening date for the center. Each assessor practiced giving the test and taking the test either with a colleague or independently at least three times before assessing a student. These practice sessions took place in the SCSD evaluation center or at the assessor's home. Examiners completed post–PDSA cycle surveys to determine how impactful the practice sessions were. Of the respondents, 83.4% strongly agreed or agreed that practice giving the test before a live administration increased assessment accuracy. Of the respondents, 16.7% strongly disagreed that practice using the online tools increased assessment accuracy. This was an interesting and surprising finding. It is possible the respondents incorrectly selected *strongly disagree* due to survey design issues. Examiners who participated in the PDSA cycle will no longer need to practice directly with another individual as they have gained the confidence they need to administer tests to students. For examiners new to the school district, this will be a newly adopted approach for onboarding new assessors.

PDSA Cycle 3: Assessors Respond to Questions on Equity Check

The IS team wanted to consider how cultural and racial bias of the examiner may impact the interpretation of assessment results. To that end, the team used the Equity Check to help develop new awareness around cultural and equity factors as they related to testing students for special education eligibility. PDSA cycle 3 was scheduled to take place from February 15 through February 26, 2021. Due to weather closures for the school district, an adjustment was made to extend the PDSA cycle to March 5, 2021, in order to allow for additional opportunities to utilize the Equity Check. Once an assessment was complete, the examiner answered a series of questions in the following three areas: (1) How well do I know my own racial identity? (2) How well do I know the cultural and racial identity of the student I have tested? and (3) How well do I know the students' experience of their culture within the classroom context? Once the PDSA cycle closed, the researcher sent an affinity survey to assessors for completion. Of the respondents, 100% agreed that using the Equity Check during the data analysis gave them an opportunity to explore how their race and culture could be impacting assessment accuracy. Of the respondents, 83.3% agreed while 16.7% strongly agreed the Equity Check helped them consider how assessment accuracy could be impacted by their level of knowledge of the racial and cultural factors at play in a student's life. Finally, 83.3% of respondents felt the Equity Check helped them see how assessment accuracy was influenced by classroom racial and cultural context while 16.7% strongly agreed. Important learning for this intervention cycle indicated the use of the Equity Check was supportive to examiners and provided new insights. The community of examiners are considering expanding the use of the Equity Check to the larger group of assessors within the school district.

Implementation and Challenges

All the school psychologists in SCSD were trained using the online testing tools and practiced using those tools. Additionally, school psychologists on the IS team participated in using the Equity Check for screening for cultural and racial bias in assessment results. The data from all three PDSA cycles indicated each intervention provided an overall benefit in ensuring accurate assessment results. Given the data quoted in the testing the change section of this chapter, the school district will retain the use of the training and practice procedures with the online assessments for new assessors. There are plans to include the remaining school psychologists in using the Equity Check. Additional professional development time will be needed for those who are new to using the tool.

Affinity surveys were used for data collection purposes for all three PDSA cycles. Each examiner was sent a survey following the cycle. Within each survey were questions addressing their perception of assessment accuracy. In PDSA Cycle 2, 16.7% of respondents indicated that they strongly disagree that practice using the online tools increased assessment accuracy. Each participant verbally agreed in the IS team meeting that practice made a significant difference in testing accuracy. Upon review of the survey format, it became clear that the order of the answer responses was not consistent among the questions. *Strongly agree* and *strongly disagree* were in different positions for different questions. Respondents could easily have inadvertently selected *strongly disagree* instead of *strongly agree*. With the expansion of the interventions and subsequent affinity surveys to a wider range of professionals within the district, revisions to the survey are necessary to ensure respondents correctly select the intended answer.

Several adjustments could be made to the different interventions themselves as the district considers applying their use to scale. For the Equity Check, developing a rubric for the responses on the tool to analyze response patterns would be a good next step. Additionally, the Equity Check could be used before testing the student to help assessors anticipate where bias could show up in the evaluation process. When considering the training intervention, survey data told the researchers that there was a need for more immediate responses to questions as they came up. Locating online resources to respond to urgent questions is needed.

Given the utility of the online assessment format, the district will be using this testing approach and expanding the assessor pool to special educators and speech pathologists in the fall of 2021. The data from PDSA Cycles 1 and 2 indicated the online training and practice sessions using the testing tools were effective in preparing staff to test students and obtain accurate assessment results. The next steps are expanding the intervention approaches more widely through the district by providing training in the online assessment tools and practice opportunities. This is under consideration for the 2021–2022 school year. Plans for this implementation include accessing accounts to online testing, additional teacher preparation time to do the training, and practice sessions with colleagues in the evaluation center. To ensure the efficacy of these interventions, additional PDSA cycles will be used to ascertain the benefit and impact on special education evaluations results.

Discussion

The 2020–2021 school year was anything but usual. Many of the established systems of care, pedagogy, and proven protocols for business as usual have been made irrelevant in the presence of the COVID-19 pandemic. Public education has been relegated to CDL in most counties and states. With this quick pivot to online instruction, numerous decisions were made with unintended consequences. At the same time, the responsibility of Child Find is essential in a public school's endeavor to provide a free appropriate public education

(FAPE) for all students regardless of ability, pandemic or not. Child Find at best is a complicated process, and it's become far more difficult during the pandemic. The lack of validity and a school psychologist's ability to follow established assessment measure norms places a tremendous emphasis on the school psychologist's professional judgment when helping individual education program (IEP) teams to make decisions regarding eligibility. For this reason, many districts simply chose not to evaluate students due to the complicated factors around assessment validity and the standardization process needing to be followed. In addition, and equally important, the effects of school closures have had additional and inequitable impacts on historically underserved populations. In SCSD, many families have the financial ability to provide tutoring services for their students at home to supplement CDL. Others have the financial ability for a parent to take leave from work to focus on their student while at home. And yet many of our students live in very different circumstances, without all those possible supplemental benefits to counteract the academic and emotional impacts of CDL. With this in mind, the evaluative process prescribed in Child Find elevates considerable inequities, with the possible overidentification of students from underserved populations. This improvement project aimed to find ways to maximize the validity of special education evaluations, minimize the anxieties that many school psychologists experience when circumstances require them to lean more heavily on their professional judgment, and minimize the obvious inequities inherent in the evaluation process during the COVID-19 pandemic.

Results indicated a strong relationship between a school psychologist's perception of an assessment's accuracy while utilizing appropriate personal protective equipment procedures. Their comfort level using alternate assessment protocols also increased substantially with peer-to-peer live-test administration practice and online training using new assessment tools. And finally, staff reported a significant increase in their level of knowledge around how racial and cultural factors might impact the accuracy of assessment results with the use of a developed Equity Check.

The unusual emphasis on using professional judgment on the part of school psychologists when helping teams navigate special education eligibility initially created a tremendous amount of anxiety for those assessing students. For many districts, the fear of under- or over-identifing students for services while in a pandemic was so great that they chose to curtail evaluations until conditions changed. The inclination to temporarily shut down the process is understandable. Assessment measures were not designed to be given in a pandemic environment with personal protective equipment and social distancing. In such conditions, they are arguably unreliable and invalid. And yet the impulse to not evaluate is fraught with complications and inequities as well. This improvement project, albeit limited in scope, demonstrates that there are things we can do to bolster the professional confidence level of school psychologists to pursue Child Find under these conditions. School psychologists felt the accuracy of their results improved with training and practice on the new assessment platforms. Psychologist training and ethical codes underpin a pervasive professional identity that emphasizes reliability, validity, and the replication of standardized processes. To alter these deeply held beliefs is understandably destabilizing. It was SCSD's belief that failure to consider evaluation would have led to numerous inequities that could result in the withholding of services due to unacknowledged disabilities.

Furthermore, this project demonstrated that school psychologists' self-perceived accuracy in the assessment process was increased through the use of the developed Equity Check. The Equity Check facilitated consideration of how racial and cultural factors, even further intensified due to the pandemic, could be influencing the identification process. The Equity Check was a set of questions designed to elicit thoughts and questions that are often overlooked due to our own identity biases. We are suggesting the continued inclusion of the Equity Check during the evaluation process beyond the time of COVID-19. Indeed, further review and revision would help improve the Equity Check, through a deeper look at the questions asked and the biases addressed. One can easily see how the utilization of such an instrument could lead to further examination of personal racial and cultural bias and how they relate to assessment interpretation and evaluation results.

With anxieties high, the fear of failure often leads to paralysis, and discussions with special educators around Oregon and in our nation during the early days of the COVID-19 pandemic looked no different. Equity-focused leaders in most districts were unsure how to best address the ethical dilemmas associated with Child Find under CDL. Questions of reliability and validity raised ethical questions regarding potential inequities associated with either under-identifying students or overidentifying students with disabilities. This was compounded with the inequitable impacts the pandemic had on traditionally underserved populations. Such leaders would do well to bring in stakeholders from impacted groups to consider problem-solving only after a complete picture of the ethical and equity dilemmas are clearly illustrated to all members.

The work fostered through this IS project facilitated the development of the evaluation center in SCSD, which proved to be a successful way to continue the district's charge of Child Find. The progress made in this area influenced numerous other districts within the county to adopt similar protocols, which undoubtedly impacted numerous students in a positive manner. And finally, in a time of indecision, and with many members of the IS team harboring thoughts of helplessness and frustration due to COVID-19 restrictions and the shutdown, this project offered members an opportunity to take charge, make a difference, and feel as though they were contributing to progress. Change can be difficult, but it can also be an opportunity for growth and a renewed sense of self-efficacy when the challenge is met. This holds true regardless of a pandemic or not and was an unexpected benefit of the work.

Discussion Questions

1. What steps do you take when bias is present in a special education to correct the situation?
2. What assessment tools or assessment processes have you used to interrupt cultural and racial bias in testing and reduce disproportionality?

3. What practices or polices can Tier 2 and Tier 3 intervention teams use to reduce disproportional referral rates for special education testing?

References

Achenbach, T. M., & Rescorla, L. (2001). *Manual for the Aseba school-age forms & profiles: An integrated system of multi-informant assessment.* ASEBA.

Banerjee, M., Madaus, J. W., & Gelbar, N. (2014). Applying LD documentation guidelines at the postsecondary level. *Learning Disability Quarterly, 38*(1), 27–39. https://doi.org/10.1177/0731948713518335

Crow, R., Hinnant-Crawford, B. N., & Spaulding, D. T. (2019). *The educational leader's guide to improvement science: Data, design and cases for reflection.* Myers Education Press.

Frattura, E. M., & Capper, C. A. (2007). *Leading for social justice: Transforming schools for all learners.* Corwin.

Hanchon, T. A., & Allen, R. A. (2012). Identifying students with emotional disturbance: School psychologists' practices and perceptions. *Psychology in the Schools, 50*(2), 193–208. https://doi.org/10.1002/pits.21668

Reynolds, C. R., & Kamphaus, R. W. (2004). *Basc 2, Behavior assessment system for children.* Pearson.

Smith, D., Frey, N., Pumpian, I., & Fisher, D. (2017). *Building equity: policies and practices to empower all learners.* ASCD.

Sullivan, A. L., Sadeh, S., & Houri, A. K. (2019). Are school psychologists' special education eligibility decisions reliable and unbiased?: A multi-study experimental investigation. *Journal of School Psychology, 77,* 90–109. https://doi.org/10.1016/j.jsp.2019.10.006.

CHAPTER FOURTEEN

Student Engagement Through Shared Power

JEFFREY R. WATERS

"But why is it shaped like a triangle?" Middle school students are often sharp like a knife, precise in their observations, curious in their questions. Here we were, teaching and learning about the Middle Ages and feudalism in a 21st-century classroom—serfs, nobility, and monarchs; things and people; structures without context—staring at the colorful social hierarchy model in our social studies textbook when students wondered aloud, "Why are we doing this?" I couldn't help but wonder the same thing.

"Good question," I responded. "Real Talk" is what my student Amari[1] called those moments when a question sent the class on an apparently urgent tangent, and he would often ask questions just to see if he could get the class going. It didn't matter whichever direction. It just had to be interesting, real, and relevant.

"Open up your social studies notebook and title the page: 'Feudalism.' Underneath that, write 'Social Hierarchy.' I want you to draw exactly what I draw—in your notes." I sat down at the document camera, made sure the projected image was focused, and titled a page, scribbling the heading and subheadings. On the page I drew a large empty triangle and a vertical line to its left with arrows on both ends. I labeled this line "power" and asked the class: "What is power?" There were a lot of blank stares. It was unclear whether the lack of engagement was because of how the question was framed or because students genuinely didn't have an answer.

---

1 Pseudonyms used throughout.

"Okay, write it down: 'power = who's in charge,' and let's put a plus sign by the top arrow and a minus sign by the bottom. What can you tell me about the people at the top based on the model?"

Amari raised his hand. "They have more power, so they're more in charge, but why is it a triangle?"

"Well, let's think about it this way: Who's in charge at our school?"

"That's easy—it's Mr. B," said Victor.

"How many of Mr. B is there?"

Students were uneasy, like it was a trick question. It wasn't. Maia shyly raised her hand. "One?" she said.

"Right—so let's draw a line across the triangle close to the top. Let's put a dot in it to represent Mr. B and let's title it. What is Mr. B?"

"He's the principal."

"But Mr. B isn't the only person who makes decisions at the school—who else?"

"Teachers," responded a student.

"But if Mr. B is in charge, how can teachers be in charge, too?" asked Amari.

"Maybe another way to think about it is 'who has the most say' about what goes on at the school," I wondered.

"Well, not all teachers have a say. Nobody listens to Mr. Maisel."

"You don't listen to anybody, Samiya," poked Victor.

"That's true," she said, grinning big.

"Okay—so we need more than one category of teacher," I suggested.

They seemed to be getting it: The model, mapping the social hierarchy of their lived experience in the organization of school, it was sinking in. Great! Feudalism! Standards! I was feeling good—like a real teacher, delivering content.

We drew some more lines, added some more dots. Each dot represented a person in the system.

As I prepared to move the students back toward vocabulary, the textbook, and the learning target, an uncomfortable reality settled over the class. In this attempt to draw on the prior knowledge of students and to connect their learning to their realities and contexts, in this model, students were peasants. The uncomfortable truth in that moment was that it resonated. It felt *true*. Administrators were monarchs who decreed, teachers were nobles who ran the kingdoms of their classrooms, and students were peasants who produced work, test scores, and results.

Students didn't have a say about what or how they learned, when they got to eat, when they went from class to class, who their teachers were, or even when they could use the bathroom. There was a lot of arguing over walking silently in lines, doing it over again, food in the classrooms, headphones, jackets, hoodies, dress code. There was a lot of conflict over what was "fair." Kids cracked jokes about "prison food" and were judged by their test scores and referral numbers. The system, as designed, was oppressive.

Complicating the dynamics of the conversation was race. In 2013, our school served the largest population of African American/Black-identifying families in the state of Oregon. The dynamics of a mostly White teaching staff teaching mostly Black students played out regularly across our building and in my class daily. As a White male teacher, trying to stay on top of the curriculum and deliver content, I was failing my students, and this was uncomfortably clear at the end of our lesson.

The hierarchical model our class mapped out together wasn't just inadequate; it was an example of institutional racism, patriarchy, and a fundamentally antidemocratic system: power concentrated in the hands of the few for the "benefit" of the many. If schools are reflections of society and society ultimately reflects the public education system, what are the consequences when we implement democratic principles into our systems? What are the consequences if we don't?

A pit grew in my stomach as we closed the lesson. *What am I teaching?*

Problem of Practice: Systems of Representation and Redress

Most public schools are rooted in systemic hierarchy. Those who have the most power (administrators) are the smallest stakeholder by volume. Those with the least power (students) are the largest stakeholder by volume. For better or worse, students are treated as victims of the system—without a say, without recourse, without the fundamental rights of democracy. At its worst, classrooms degenerate into workshops in which teachers "teach to the test."

Students see through this and often react by pushing back, their "misbehavior" rooted in resistance. How can they sit in classrooms that tell them that they live in a democracy but never get to choose when they go to the bathroom? How can they learn about the promises of America painted on the pages of textbooks written over 1,000 miles away, without ever reading about their neighborhood, their history, their excellence, or their grandmother?

Schools can degenerate into police states. Power struggles emerge: *us-against-them* mentalities that do further harm to the community. Tension can overwhelm cooperation: "Why do you let them listen to music in your class?" "They only get one bathroom pass a week." Administrators swoop in to handle "disrespectful behavior," "defiance," and "disobedience," as if standing in straight, quiet lines is the goal of school. There are fights and fists and tears, and the cycle continues—the hierarchy is maintained.

In such a system, students may leave school without the interest or expertise to engage in the processes of self-governance.

By centering student perspectives and inviting them to participate in decision-making on behalf of other students, we can increase engagement and improve outcomes. *Improvement science* opens the doors of possibility by inviting questions. Why are things as they are? How can shifts in our practice make positive change? How do we know if what we are doing is working? Why are we doing this? *What am I teaching?*

When we identify concerns or problems of practice, wonder about potential root causes, collect data, modify practices, measure results, and ask new questions, we can probe systems and outcomes while centering stakeholder voices. The process of conducting a cycle of inquiry as a community is fundamentally democratic. We solve problems together as a community for the betterment of the community (see Figure 14.1).

To respond to our wonderings about hierarchy in our school, our middle school teachers and students organized. In 2014–2015, we launched a Student Leadership class to promote student voice. The class spent that school year building on the eighth-grade social studies curriculum to form a government, write a constitution, and hold elections. We had fun in the process, toying with the idea of democracy and drawing possible models shaped like circles instead of triangles (see Figure 14.2).

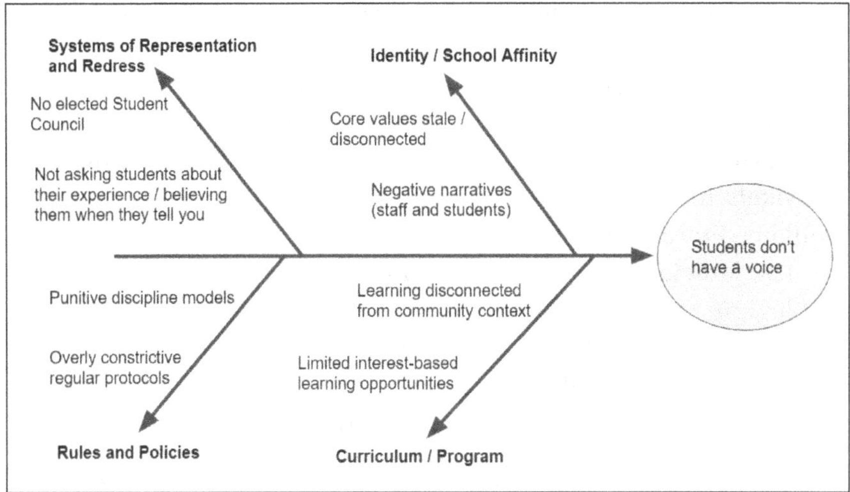

Figure 14.1. Student Voice Fishbone Diagram

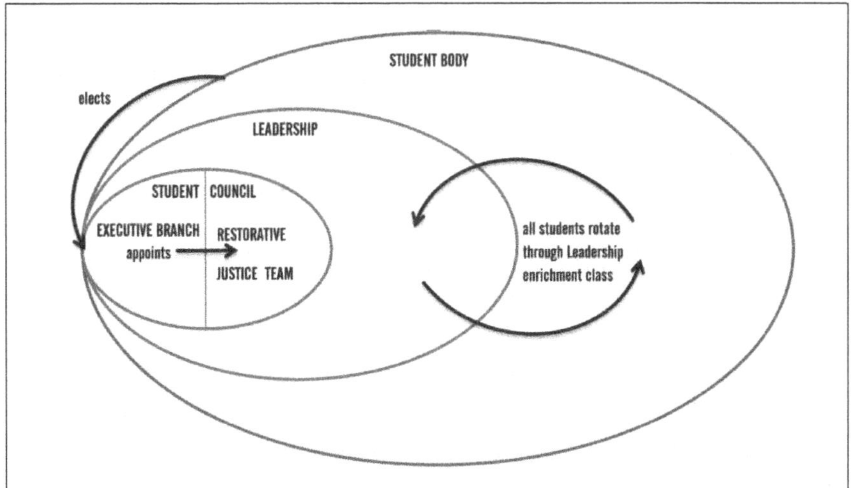

Figure 14.2. Student Council Model

Students devised a bicameral government with two houses that increased student responsibility and influence with age. The executive branch was elected. Students could vote for more than one student, with their choices weighted by rank. Sixth graders voted for two officers, seventh graders voted for three, and eighth graders voted for four. We wanted to embed the concept of *legacy* into the system—that we leave behind something for those who come after us to carry on—and determined that eighth-grade students would also get to vote in the sixth- and seventh-grade elections. This also served as a negotiated response to the adult argument that "student elections are just popularity contests." The idea was that eighth-grade students were less likely to have direct friendships with lower grade students and would be more impartial in their vote.

The judicial branch (later renamed the "reinforcement squad") would have equal representation, two representatives per grade level. Members of the reinforcement squad would be appointed by elected executive branch members, and their duties were specific and unique. Article IV of the Student Council Constitution stated:

> [Reinforcement Squad members] will serve as peer mediators and will advise the student council and its advisor on school policies and systems. In addition, this group shall oversee the conversation regarding any violation of the student conduct policy that impacts student council members.

They were tasked as circle keepers and problem-solvers, working to solve problems in the student community and interface directly with school policies. We partnered with a local restorative justice organization to train peer mediators and build staff capacity for restorative dialogue.

At the same time, the school's site council took on the task of redefining the school's core values. Rather than go the easy route with *Safe, Respectful, Responsible*, school leaders opened up the conversation to the community. What resulted were three core values rooted in the school's identity: *Community, Perseverance, Integrity*. The student council purpose and mission statement attempted to align to these values:

> [Our mission is] to improve school climate through promoting our
> core values: Community, Integrity and Perseverance.... We believe
> that a healthy school starts with students wanting to be there and
> be involved, and it is our mission to accomplish this. However, it
> is our ultimate goal that the improvement of school climate leads
> to more learning and higher achievement for all Student Council
> members.

Our students practiced and modeled democratic processes while taking themselves seriously as community leaders. As student advocacy grew, the narrative about who our students were and what they were capable of shifted.

Given the opportunity to speak about restorative justice and the importance of student voice to the Portland mayor and city council in December 2015, our student leaders put it like this:

> Personally, I believe that students need and should have a voice
> in schools to make schools and learning more enjoyable and more
> engaging. If we were able to have some say in how we are being
> taught and sometimes what we are being taught and what type of
> environment we are being taught in, it tends to make it a lot eas-
> ier for students to retain and actually remember what we are being
> taught. . . . When students feel safe, it is easier to learn, and peer
> mediation is helping create the sort of positive environment that
> makes our students feel safer.

Student Perception Is True North

"Do you have, like, a 'student climate' survey?" asked Mr. B. I didn't know exactly what he meant. He continued: "You know, we ask students to respond to the survey and set goals based on the results. So, you might see that 50% of students feel positively about something and you set the goal that you want 80% to feel that way."

I wanted to write a student growth goal related to our work in student leadership but didn't know how to collect data. The idea that we would simply ask students seemed novel in its simplicity. By centering student perspectives, we can better understand their experiences and identify potential shifts in our practice. My mind swam with possibilities.

How do we measure the impact of school systems on the perception of students? How do we use these measurements to focus our initiatives and articulate our visions? Are we adaptive and responsive? How easily and with how much disruption can we pivot our focus? How much room for innovation is there and who gets to innovate? How do we decentralize power and decision-making so that the voices of the largest school stakeholder (students) are represented in school systems? How do we deconstruct the systemic hierarchy of public schools to model democratic principles?

Cobbling together a number of statements, organized into specific categories, we began surveying our middle school students three times a year: fall, winter, and spring. Students responded to each statement on a Likert Scale (*Strongly Agree → Agree → Neutral /I Don't Know → Disagree → Strongly Disagree*; see Figure 14.3).

The resulting data provided context for our conversations as a school community. It gave teeth to our anecdotes, diffused our misconceptions, and provided feedback, focus, and direction for our initiatives. A complex ecosystem of student perception emerged and invited new questions, such as "Why do students feel the way they do?" and "How will students feel if we try x?" We looped students into these conversations, inviting our student council to use the data to set goals with us, and we reported outcomes to the teachers, school district, and community.

As we tracked data longitudinally and performed simple statistical analyses on quantitative responses to the survey, patterns emerged from year to year. Students were typically more negative in the winter and spring and were more hopeful in the fall. We took the first full year of data to represent out baseline and measured improvement from there. Each year provided an opportunity to try new things to interrupt established patterns. What will happen if we focus on community building in the spring, because we noticed a big dip in community statements last spring? What will happen if we put extra effort into integrating our core values into our content lesson planning?

Over time, this student-centered approach to data (putting the perception of our students at the core of our decision-making)

CORE VALUE STATEMENTS
Learning to work through problems is important to my success in life
It is important to do the right thing, even when no one is around to see it
It is important to learn how to work with others
School is important to my success in life
PERSEVERANCE STATEMENTS
Most students at my school do not give up when they cannot solve a problem easily
Most students at my school do all their homework
Most students at my school try to do a good job on their schoolwork even when it is not interesting
Most students at my school try their best on schoolwork even when it is difficult
INTEGRITY STATEMENTS
Most students at my school follow rules and expectations when adults are not around
Most students know it is not OK to cheat if other students are cheating
Most students at my school follow directions and instructions
Harassment, intimidation and bullying by other students are not a problem at my school
COMMUNITY STATEMENTS
Students in my school treat one another with respect
My teachers really care about me
There are opportunities for students to get involved in our school outside of regular classroom work
My classmates make me feel welcome, respected and listened to on a regular basis
COMMUNITY GROWTH STATEMENTS
Students are safer at our school this year than they were last year
Students are safer at our school this year than they were three years ago
Students learn more at our school this year than they did last year
Students learn more at our school this year than they did three years ago
STUDENT RELATIONSHIPS WITH TECHNOLOGY
There is not a lot of school drama on the internet
Students do not use cell phones to film drama at school
Students do not spread rumors and gossip on the internet or through text messages outside of school
Students don't use their cell phones in class on a regular basis
Students understand the school's cell phone policy
STUDENT VOICE STATEMENTS
Students have a voice at our school
Students have an opportunity to influence school rules and expectations
Students have an opportunity to plan school activities and events
Student Council and Leadership make the school a better place
Adults listen to students ideas about how to make the school a better place
School assemblies help me learn about important activities coming up
School assemblies are fun and interesting
I know how the money from fundraisers is spent
Students have a say over how money from fundraisers is spent
PBIS STATEMENTS
Getting your LIFE Band is hard but worth it
There are good prizes and privileges for LIFE Band wearers
I know what I have to do to earn my LIFE Band
Students have to earn B Bucks, they aren't given out for no reason
B Bucks are useful
I know what I have to do to earn a B Buck

Figure 14.3. School Climate Survey Statements

served to democratize our planning, improve student perception, and shift student narratives about their role as school leaders. Figure 14.4 shows school climate survey responses over a period of 3 years. The data report the average percentage of students who "strongly agreed," "agreed" or responded in the "neutral/I don't know" category per year over 3 years.

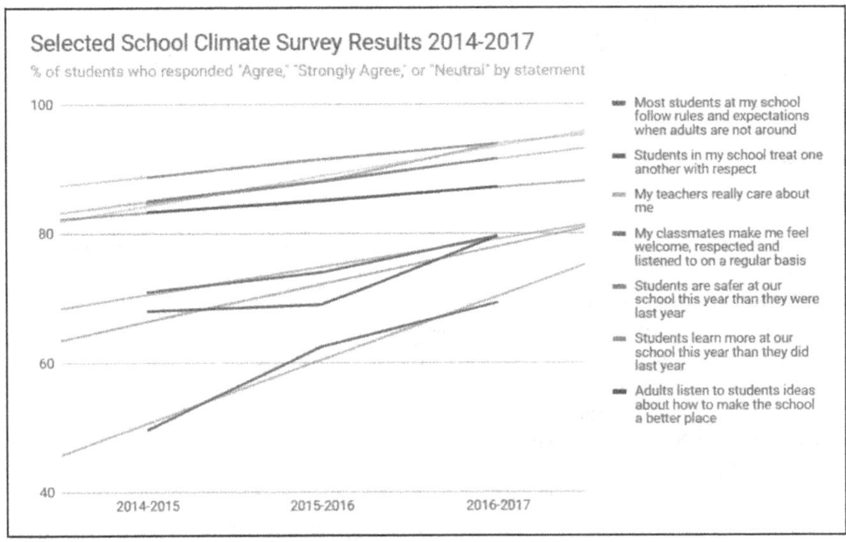

Figure 14.4. Selected School Climate Survey Results, Grades 6-8, 2014-2017

Centering student perception in reporting and decision-making processes, developing and integrating the school's core values, formalizing student representative structures, inviting students to the table as problem-solvers to seek redress, and contextualizing student learning within their community measurably improved student experience.

A New School: Shifting Contexts

In 2017, I left my teaching position to serve as an assistant principal in another school district. The school was coming out of a period of struggle, where negative narratives had rooted in the student community and disrupted the educational process over a period of years; the student community was culturally, racially, and politically distinct from my previous community. It was mostly White and working class, with pockets of low-income housing in a rural suburb of Oregon's largest city, Portland.

The national context and dialogue had also shifted. According to the Federal Bureau of Investigation (2017) online database, reported hate crimes increased by the largest percentage in at least a decade, elevated to highest number of hate crime incidents since 2008. Our students, especially our students of color, carried additional stress related to emerging national conversations about race, immigration, and school safety.

Trying to keep our sense of true north (Moore & Gino, 2013), we implemented the school climate survey in order to measure and monitor student perception over time. We also developed a theory of action to more specifically articulate the function of the school climate survey in our school community (see Figure 14.5).

Theory of Action, Collaborative Improvement

ADMINISTRATORS will....

Develop and maintain systems to measure and communicate school climate data to community stakeholders.

SO THAT

TEACHERS can....

1) *Identify areas of school climate growth and plan initiatives*
2) *Engage students in reflective conversations about areas of community growth*

SO THAT

STUDENTS can....

1) *Engage in a reflective cycle of inquiry and improvement*
2) *Identify and communicate areas of growth*

Figure 14.5. Theory of Action, Collaborative Improvement

We wondered if centering student perspectives in planning conversations would improve the perceptions and attitudes of students and staff related to school. Administrators would maintain data and reporting systems and bring data to the community (school board, families, teachers, and students). We would also provide professional development to teachers on restorative practices, improvement science, cycles of inquiry, and Plan–Do–Study–Act cycles and facilitate opportunities for teachers and students to collaborate.

We would utilize a school climate survey to monitor our progress. This survey was very much informed by previous work, although some questions had to be adjusted. For example, we didn't need to ask questions about the "LIFE Band Program" (a "high achiever" behavior program at my previous school site), but we did want to measure student perceptions related to hate speech in the school community, knowing that the national dialogue made monitoring essential. We also wanted to measure student perceptions related to the implementation of specific classroom practices. We wanted staff to use the CHAMPS Classroom Management system; thus, we surveyed students with two related statements: "Students know what a teacher's expectations for an activity are before the activity begins" and "My teacher uses CHAMPS."

As contexts change, so, too, must the questions we ask. If things have changed, why have they changed, and what questions can we ask and what data can we collect to probe whether to adopt, adapt, or abandon a practice?

Our problem of practice and assumed primary and secondary drivers remained consistent, and we took similar steps to address each. We continued to believe that centering student perspectives and inviting students to participate in decision-making on behalf of other students, and the institution as a whole, would increase engagement and improve outcomes.

Collaborative Action and Pattern Disruption: The Process Is the Point

The 2017–2018 school climate data presented similar patterns: Student perception declined over the course of the school year. This was especially true during the spring of 2017–2018 (see Figure 14.6).

As we moved through the 2018–2019 school year, positive growth began to emerge. When comparing year-over-year survey results, we found that statements showed improvement (71%) between the fall of

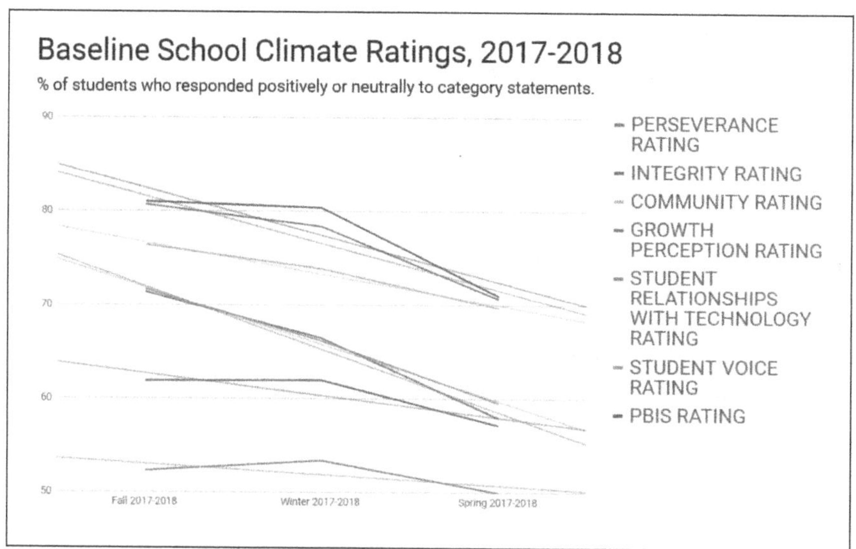

Figure 14.6. Middle School Baseline Data, 2017-2018

2017–2018 and the fall of 2018–2019. The process of measuring student perception and taking collective action toward systems improvement again appeared to improve student perception over time.

Our winter 2018–2019 results not only indicated the same year-over-year trend toward improvement but also presented a similar pattern as the prior school year: losing positive momentum going into the spring. When comparing year-over-year survey results, we found that fewer statements (66%) improved between the winter of 2017–2018 and the winter of 2018–2019. We wondered about how to interrupt this pattern and turned to teachers for solutions.

In February 2019, we presented the school climate survey data to staff and asked them to participate in a "Collaborative Action Research Project" in grade-level teams. Certified and classified staff were asked to (a) use school climate survey data to identify a problem of practice, (b) identify potential primary and secondary drivers, and (c) make a plan to address the problem of practice. We framed the spring survey as the "summative assessment," and dedicated staff and grade-level team time to working on the projects. Staff were provided a great deal of agency to identify problems and seek solutions.

Data suggest that going through this process together disrupted the established pattern of a decline in student perception between the winter and spring, stabilizing our school improvement efforts. When comparing year-over-year survey results, we found that more statements (88%) improved between the spring of 2017–2018 and the spring of 2018–2019. Many statements showed improvement of less than 10% year over year (see Figure 14.7).

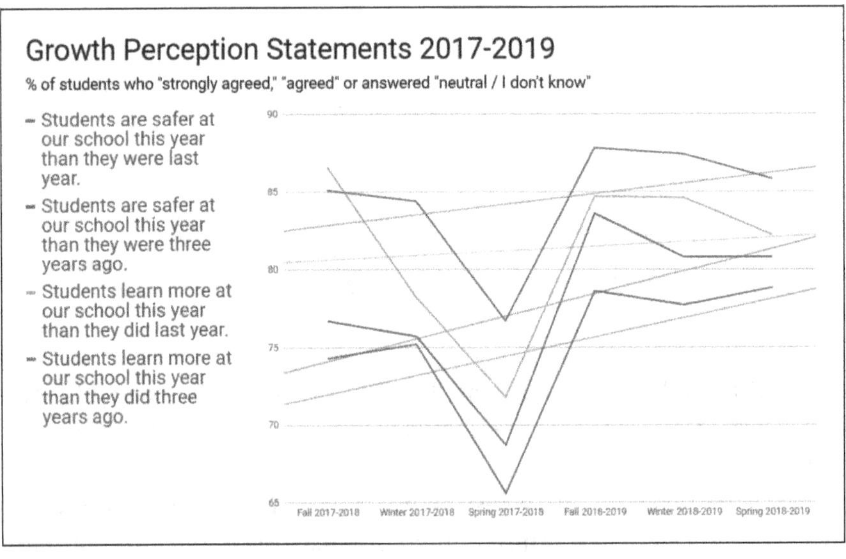

Figure 14.7. Growth Perception Over Time, 2017-2019

Continued Growth in a Third School Context

In 2021, the implementation of data-driven improvement science processes continues at a middle school in southwest Portland. Familiar needs present themselves in the data: Students report feeling disconnected from the institution of school. Similar measures are moving toward implementation: formalizing student representative systems, centering student perception in decision-making processes, and using student perception data to drive innovation and seek adaptive solutions.

We have leaned into racial equity work, understanding that the damage caused to our communities by racist rhetoric requires constant attention to address and repair. In partnership with the Anti-Defamation League's (n.d.) No Place for Hate initiative, we have developed a strategic plan to develop common vocabulary in our school community to participate in challenging conversations about race (see Figure 14.8).

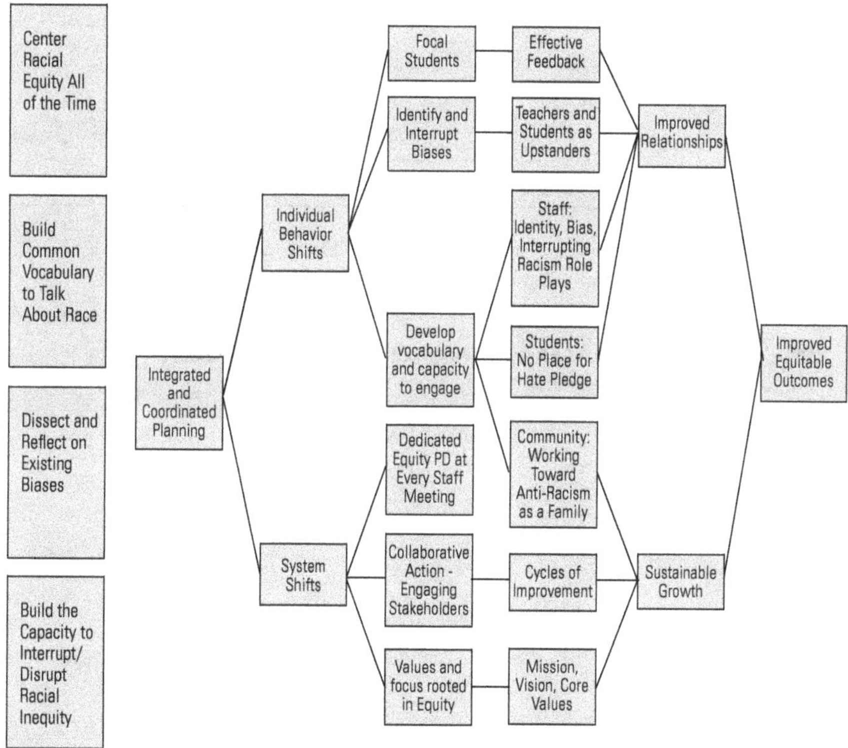

Figure 14.8. Racial Equity Strategic Plan

Early data indicated improvement in the area of student voice (see Figure 14.9).

Our data also showed improvement with climate, specifically related to racist and homophobic language (see Figure 14.10).

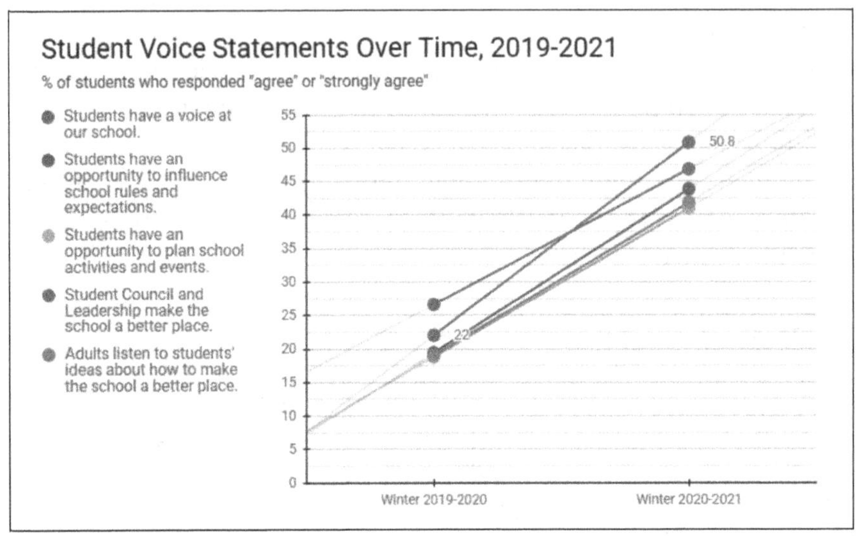

Figure 14.9. Student Voice Statements Over Time, 2019-2021

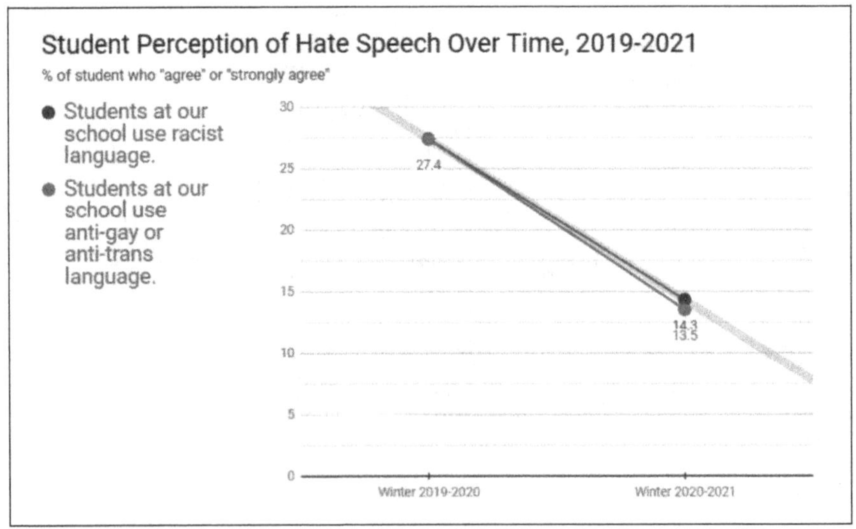

Figure 14.10. Student Voice: Racist and Homophobic Language

Additional monitoring and longitudinal data analysis will be needed to understand how distance learning during the pandemic impacted these improvements and how to sustain them once we return to in-person learning.

The pandemic has also presented the new challenge of adapting our processes to ask relevant questions to our specific pandemic environment. We have used these data to concentrate our professional development on meaningful improvements for the student experience. Specifically, we have centered on effective feedback in the distance learning environment and leaning into existing structures related to the school's implementation of AVID practices. We chose this focus by centering student responses to statements related to their experience during distance learning (see Figure 14.11).

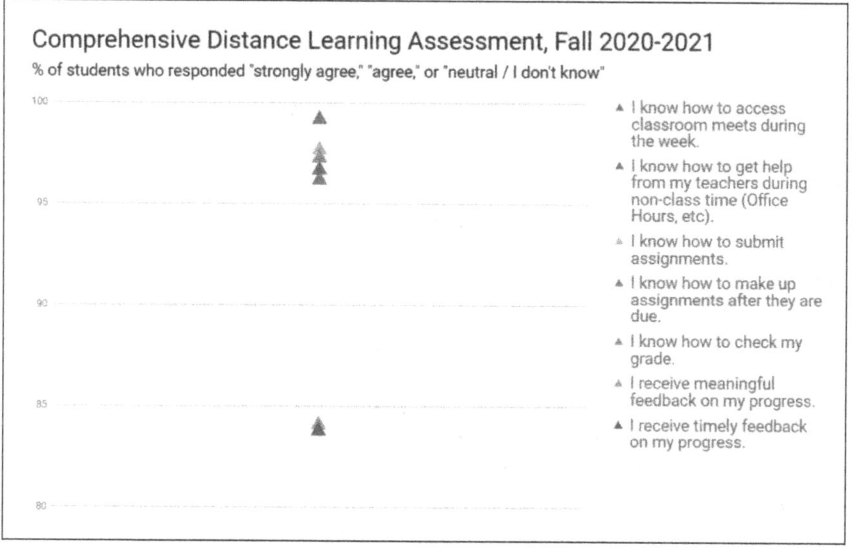

Figure 14.11. Comprehensive Distance Learning Assessment, Fall 2020-2021

Our students, teachers, and administrators continue to use student voice to plan initiatives, collect, and analyze data regarding the impact of our work and adapt, abandon, or adopt our improvement strategies. When student voice is placed at the center of school decision-making, when teachers and administrators plan improvement initiatives that respond to the specific concerns of students, and when students are invited to participate in the business of school through formal representative systems, our schools are successful.

Discussion Questions

1. Improvement science is a democratic school improvement method that can be used to increase student voice in schools. What are the challenges and opportunities for using improvement science to increase student voice?
2. Reflect on the statement: Including the voices of those who are most impacted by the change enhances the humanity of those in our schools (Peterson, 2014) and is also key to improvement science. What about the improvement science change methodology matches the strategy of seeking student voice?
3. What specific improvement science tools align with the goal of seeking student voice to increase connection and success in school? How have you used them or how could you use them?

References

Anti-Defamation League. (n.d.). *No place for hate: Join the movement.* https://www.adl.org/who-we-are/our-organization/signature-programs/no-place-for-hate

Federal Bureau of Investigation. (2017). *About hate crime statistics, 2017.* https://ucr.fbi.gov/hate-crime/2017

Moore, C., & Gino, F. (2013). Ethically adrift: How others pull our moral compass from true North, and how we can fix it. *Research in Organizational Behavior, 33,* 53–77. https://doi.org/10.1016/j.riob.2013.08.001

Peterson, D. S. (2014). A missing piece in the sustainability movement: The human spirit. *Sustainability: The Journal of Record, 7*(2), 74–77. https://doi.org/10.1089/SUS.2014.9810

CHAPTER FIFTEEN

Increasing Equity Through Family Engagement

GLORIA MCDANIEL-HALL, RYAN MCCARTY,
AND LANDON BROWN

What does it mean to increase equity through family engagement? This chapter shares an ongoing partnership between a trio of school leaders and researchers collaborating across organizational boundaries to address problems facing schools (Bryk et al., 2015). Specifically, we use tools from improvement science (IS) to advance equity through culturally responsive family engagement. Our partnership includes Dr. Landon Brown, a Black male principal in his third year at Emerson Academy (ECA), an urban K–8 charter school in a midsized midwestern city; Dr. Gloria McDaniel-Hall, a Black female assistant professor at a private midwestern university who is a former principal and Landon's former manager within the charter network; and Dr. Ryan McCarty, Gloria's White male colleague at the university and a former literacy coordinator, principal coach, and teacher in urban schools. Combined, they have more than 50 years of experience leading school reform efforts.

Like many educators, we feel a heightened sense of urgency to enact lasting change in response to the murders of George Floyd, Ahmaud Arbery, Breonna Taylor, and countless others, and we are energized by the Black Lives Matter movement and our organizations' growing commitment to diversity, equity, and inclusion. We witnessed firsthand the stark inequities that the COVID-19 pandemic exposed in Black and Brown communities. Family engagement has never been more important. Although we have much to learn, the children in our schools deserve an equitable education *now*. We feel compelled to use IS to accelerate meaningful change, refining processes and tools to advance equity. This chapter addresses the following goals:

1. Examine how IS methods, specifically Plan–Do–Study–Act (PDSA) cycles, root-cause analysis (RCA), and empathy interviews can accelerate efforts to advance equity through parent engagement at one urban school
2. Share the voices of actively engaged, culturally, and linguistically diverse parents as they advocate for their children's academic and social needs, including perceived barriers and recommended changes
3. Apply and refine an existing equity framework (Clark-Louque et al., 2019) to analyze parent perspectives, refine family engagement practices and policies, and inform future equity initiatives

The link between engaged families and enhanced student learning is clear (Global Family Research Foundation, 2018). Equity-focused family engagement means more than attracting parents to open house or parent–teacher conferences. Engaged families provide invaluable insight into the strengths, motivations, and needs of their children and the larger community. The National Association for Family, School and Community Engagement (2009) defines family engagement as (a) a "shared responsibility" in which schools and community groups meaningfully engage families, who, in turn, "commit to actively supporting their children's learning"; (b) an "enduring commitment" that evolves as parent roles adjust and children grow; and (c) a process that "cuts across and reinforces learning in multiple settings" (p. 1). Clark-Louque et al. (2019) assert that *equitable* family engagement includes families and community organizations providing "ongoing meaningful contributions to decisions, policies, and practices that *serve the diverse needs of the community*" (p. 17). Families and community partners also "advocate (for) closing achievement gaps, and develop and model *advocacy for social justice practices*" (Clark-Louque et al., 2019, p. 17), furthering the school's commitment to equity.

Families have long sought a "place at the table" when decisions are made (Parent Teacher Association, 2019, p. 1). Families not only deserve a place at the table; they should also help plan the whole "dining experience." Clark-Louque et al. (2019) distinguish between mere family involvement (defined as "doing *to*") and true engagement ("doing *with*"). Family engagement is an adaptive challenge (Heifez et al., 2009) that requires strategic planning, relationship building, open communication channels, and ongoing feedback.

Our Context

The school and community cannot live apart, and context matters deeply in equity work. ECA emphasizes college-readiness, provides a unique moral focus curriculum, and partners with a local school board. The student racial makeup is 57% Black, 30% white, 9% multiracial, and 4% Hispanic, and 100% of students are eligible for free breakfast and lunch (Ohio Department of Education [ODE], 2021). Emerson had recently undergone a dramatic turnaround under Landon's leadership, making the leap from a school rating of F to C in 1 year (ODE, 2021). While Landon has built accountability systems and earned buy-in from faculty, students, and families, many schools stall in the transition from good to great (Merseth, 2009), making this a pivotal period.

The ECA leadership team regularly analyzes attendance, formative and summative assessments, and parent survey data to measure progress. This chapter emphasizes data from a series of informal Zoom interviews with Landon and Gloria and a Zoom focus group (Vaughn et al., 1996) with seven parent advisory council members using empathy interview methods (Nelsestuen & Smith, 2020; Portigal, 2013). Our institutional review board approved our procedure, and all parent quotes are from these interviews.

Leaders often assume deficit views of minoritized families, ignoring how families might narrate their own experiences (Griffin & Cummins, 2012). In contrast, "educators who create culturally relevant learning contexts . . . see students' [and parents'] culture as an asset (and) not a detriment" (Milner, 2011, p. 69). Indeed, the voices of families of color and the recognition of their academic, social, and economic experiences are required for a complete analysis of any educational system (Ladson-Billings, 1997).

Emerson's school/district board policy on parental involvement (Student Intervention Services [SIS], 2021) emphasizes productive relationships with students and families to increase student achievement and family engagement. ECA holds quarterly meetings (Pastries with Parents), publishes weekly principal newsletters (*Word on the Street*), sends weekly teacher briefings, and regularly updates its Facebook page with calendars, announcements, and event pictures. Parents serve on school climate committees and the school improvement plan team. Communication occurs in multiple formats including social media, phone calls, and texts to elicit parent input on strategic plans. A partnership with Phi Beta Sigma fraternity provides tutoring, male mentorship, and school supply giveaways. Leaders survey families at the fall Title I parent meeting, the spring school improvement plan parent meeting, and other events (SIS, 2021), helping ensure school improvement work is done *with* and not *to* the school community.

Improvement Science at Emerson Academy

IS has the power to transform the ways we identify, process, and solve problems in schools. The first step is to clearly define what the team is trying to accomplish. Landon's broad goal was to increase family engagement to enhance educational equity. Our guiding definition of equity emphasized knowing students' unique strengths, challenges, and barriers to success and helping them build on strengths, overcome challenges, and remove obstacles. Emerson's leadership team wanted to promote equity by involving families in efforts to help their children meet their individual growth targets in reading and math on the Northwest Evaluation Assessment- Measures of Academic Progress (NWEA-MAP) exam (an online, adaptive standardized assessment). These efforts included individualized instructional interventions during and after school. However, a recent survey revealed that many parents did not feel these interventions met their children's learning needs. Reform-minded leaders often fall victim to a *solutionist fallacy*, identifying an answer before fully understanding the problem and its causes (Bryk et al., 2015). We used IS to step back and focus on the user experience (in our case, the families), rather than assuming their wants and needs (Crow et al., 2019). Such a process not only demonstrates respect; it also yields more effective solutions.

PDSA Cycle Overview

The PDSA cycle is a central inquiry process underlying IS that promotes continual improvement. Smaller scale interventions help minimize initial variation, allowing leaders to fine-tune the approach before scaling up (Bryk et al., 2015). A visual overview of our PDSA cycle is provided in Figure 15.1.

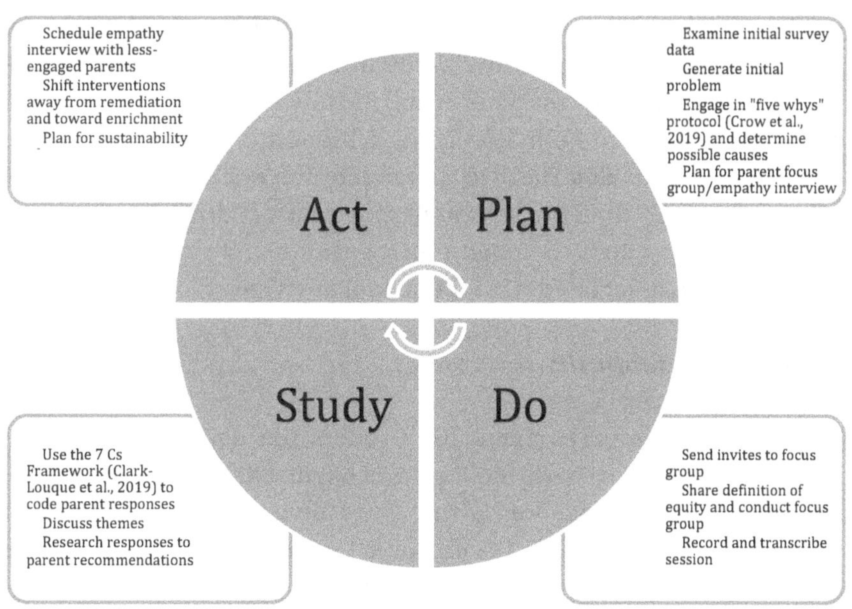

Figure 15.1. Plan-Do-Study-Act Overview

RCA

At the start of the "Plan" phase, Landon's leadership team engaged in an informal RCA, a deliberate method for deeply understanding a problem and its potential causes (Crow et al., 2019). The specific RCA chosen was the *five whys* technique: identifying an initial problem and asking, "Why?" five times in order to generate a deeper understanding of its intersecting causes (Langley et al., 2009).

The initial problem was "Parents feel interventions are not meeting their individual student's needs." The team asked, "Why is this?" and the response was "Parents must not fully understand all the interventions we have enacted." After asking "Why?" four additional times, the team examined several potential causes, from difficulty accessing digital apps used for interventions to confusion about individual NWEA-MAP growth targets to insufficient explanations at Open House. After unpacking these possibilities, the team realized that, in fact, parents understood the interventions and their purposes yet still did not feel they met their child's needs.

The voices of families from minoritized communities are rarely prioritized. Input is typically collected from decontextualized surveys or informal conversations at schoolwide events. In contrast, we wanted a method to help discern individual families' perspectives. Therefore, we decided the "Do" portion of the PDSA cycle would be a Zoom focus group with several parent advisory council members, who reflect the school's demographics, have students in Grades K to 8, and have been associated with the school anywhere from 1 to 8 years.

Focus Group Empathy Interviews

Empathy interviews (Portigal, 2013) emphasize deeply understanding and validating others' feelings and experiences, and, therefore, have clear implications for culturally responsive school leadership (Nelsestuen & Smith, 2020). Our hour-long empathy interview (see Figure 15.2) occurred in February 2021.

Landon welcomed parents and explained our purpose, and Gloria and Ryan introduced themselves and shared the informed consent

Selected Parent Semi-Structured Interview Questions:
1. What specific steps has the school taken to include your voice in decision-making?
2. What specific steps could the school take to determine the unique strengths of your child/children?
3. What is one aspect of your child's schooling that could be improved if their needs were considered?
4. How can we increase parents' and students' voices in planning?
5. What are some potential barriers we may face and how can we overcome them?
6. Besides your child's report card and test scores, how else can we measure success?
7. What are other schools doing that you would like us to try?

Optional Follow-Up Questions
(intended to examine parent feelings, express understanding and empathy, probe for further examples, and elicit new perspectives).

Make it feel informal
- Play music during transitions
- Incorporate humor
- Share best memories of the school

Pursue tangents
- Keep going...
- What makes you say that?
- I want to hear more about...

Share stories
- Tell us a story about your child's time at Emerson
- How does your own experience influence what you want for your children?

Pay attention to silences and body language
- If it's silent, and no one's talking, that's fine.
- Don't feel rushed or uncomfortable; take your time.

Avoid binary questions and focus on thoughts and feelings
- What did that make you think?
- How did that make you feel?

Figure 15.2. Parent Focus Group Empathy Interview Protocol (adapted from Nelsestuen & Smith, 2020)

process. Landon and Gloria then alternated asking questions to foster a dialogue while Ryan took notes. The Zoom recording was transcribed, and initial coding was done by Gloria and Ryan, who shared emergent themes with Landon for feedback.

To analyze the transcript, we applied the "7 Cs of Culturally Proficient Family, School and Community Engagement" (Clark-Louque et al., 2019), a research-based framework that includes guiding principles for teachers and families. Beginning with the descriptions of the 7 Cs (collaboration, communication, caring and compassion, culture, community, connectedness, collective responsibility) in the Clark-Louque et al. (2019) text, we determined key words and developed a consensus understanding of each concept as it applied to ECA. Simple descriptive statistics were used to determine the frequency and percentage of codes to illuminate potential patterns and themes. A description of each code and a representative focus group quote is included in Table 15.1

Results and Implications

Because two codes, *collective responsibility* and *communication*, accounted for 61.8% of all coded segments (35% and 26.8%, respectively), we share insights from these codes in particular and additional observations about the empathy interview process.

Collective Responsibility. There were a total of 34 codes of "collective responsibility" from six of the seven families. Gloria realized that the parents' vision of collective responsibility was similar to the Kwanzaa principle of Ujima, which emphasizes working together to strengthen our families, since the well-being of families is intimately connected to community well-being. One parent shared they "really appreciate (Principal Brown's) constant push and constant efforts in replacing the 'Is' with 'Wes'" (Speaker 6, Line 29). Another parent contrasted feeling heard at Emerson with negative experiences at other schools:

> You want to believe that your thoughts, your ideas, your opinions, and what you have to say, especially when it comes to your child's education, matters. And, you know, you can enroll a child in the school and sometimes feel like you're not made a part of it. (Speaker 4, Line 31)

These were clearly parents that craved agency and involvement in their child's education.

Parents were also willing to share responsibility for student learning. One participant noted that "as parents, we have to then challenge them at home, which is our job" (Speaker 4, Line 63). Another mother of a former Emerson valedictorian now attending an elite private high school wondered how other ECA students would fare there:

Table 15.1. Seven Cs Code Descriptions and Example Quotes From the Focus Group

Code	Description	Example Quote
Collabo-ration 3 total codes (3.1% of total)	• Families and school leaders work together as equals • Everyone can safely and fully participate in meetings, decision-making, and reform • Shared sense of trust, respect, and belonging • Commitment to continuous improvement of family engagement	"Everybody's situation is unique, but being able to relate to someone else that has remotely been there too, that really does help people open up" (Speaker 1, Line 130).
Commu-nication 26 total codes (26.8% of total)	• Mutual exchange of ideas and information • Action is taken by both parties in response to communication • Effective and active listening • Participants feel safe to share ideas • Communication is ongoing and employs a variety of methods based on family need	"Social media seems to be kind of a gateway to a lot of positive outcomes" (Speaker 6, Line 71).
Care & Compas-sion 11 total codes (11.3% of total)	• Schools demonstrate genuine caring for students, parents, and community • Parent and community values and resources are respected • Students are valued regardless of their social or academic history • Relationships are reciprocal and develop over time • Families and leaders believe school is, and should be, a supportive environment	"Whether it's COVID, whether it's work, whether it's lack of resources, as far as the internet or whatever, there's gotta be something that we can do to reach out" (Speaker 5, Line 100).
Culture 10 codes (10.3% of total)	• Shared core values, practices, and norms guide school culture • Culture includes both school culture and families' individual cultures (racial, ethnic, social, religious, etc.) • Culture is shaped through positive interactions with culturally and linguistically diverse families • Mission statements, slogans, and language contribute to a sense of culture • Culture should be collectively developed, not imposed upon a community	"That makes a big difference because (Principal Brown) has created a culture where, 'Hey, if you need, if you want to talk to me, if you have any questions, you can do that'" (Speaker 4, Line 33).
Commu-nity 5 codes (5.2% of total)	• Educators know the demographics and understand the culture of the community they serve • Educators know important community organizations, leaders, and community resources • Teachers and school leaders are visible and participate actively in the larger community • Community is viewed as an asset to student learning and knowledge of the community guides strategic planning	"Looking at the inclusion and the togetherness that (Principal Brown) has created and set forth, to me that's kind of a rarity in today's society" (Speaker 6, line 29).
Connect-edness 8 codes (8.2% of total)	• Students' sense of belonging and satisfaction contributes to a sense of connectedness with the school • Students believe adults and peers care about them and their learning as individuals • Adults support students' social, academic, and psychological well-being • Families and community members feel accepted, valued, supported, and involved in all aspects of education • Intentional actions are taken to build connections with school, adults, and peers	"All of us are connected to you all and invested in (the school) through our children" (Speaker 1, Line 95).

Code	Description	Example Quote
Collective Responsi-bility. 34 codes (35.1% of total)	• Families and school leaders work together as equals • School works to institutionalize working and learning together for student achievement • Shared sense of collective efficacy and collective accountability over the quality of student learning • Teachers engage in planning, instruction, assessment, and professional development out of a sense of responsibility to students and families • Initiatives are seen as a shared responsibility	"I really appreciate (Principal Brown's) constant push and constant efforts in replacing the 'Is' with 'Wes'" (Speaker 6, Line 29).

Source: Adapted from Clark-Louque et al. (2019).

"Are we preparing those kids for that level of work?" (Speaker 4, Line 48). Parents also suggested incentives or "school swag" for children of families participating in school improvement efforts. "Your kid gets to hold you accountable saying, 'Hey mom, I'm right there. I want to get those five extra points so please make sure you send Principal Brown that email!'" (Speaker 1, Line 95). Using students to encourage family engagement was an innovative idea.

Communication. Communication was the second-most widely applied code, with 26 total codes by six different speakers (26.8% of total). Connecting with families has become even more urgent amid the COVID-19 pandemic. However, assuming minoritized families are harder to reach is grounded in deficit thinking. Emerson averaged 60% family attendance at pre-pandemic report card pickup events. After switching to virtual Google Meets events, more than 90% of families participated. The pandemic *removed* barriers such as finding childcare, calling off from work, and securing transportation. Digital tools like *Smore* newsletters (which include interactive social media features), and group texting apps like Remind are now used to maximize parent contact. Parents appreciate these multiple forms of communication:

> They might not be into social media (so) just in case, you have the ability to either text (or) send an email . . . so at least we get that parent engagement somehow, some way, if you don't catch us on the video conference. (Speaker 1, Line 95)

ECA intends to continue virtual options for school events post-pandemic.

True communication must be bidirectional. If families or students are unresponsive, it is likely we are telling, not communicating. One parent shared, "As a parent . . . if there's something you don't like, you (should) feel comfortable to say, 'Hey, you know what, I don't appreciate this'" (Speaker 4, Line 31). Another father stated,

> With COVID being in play . . . how many kids are sitting on zoom or a classroom meeting at 8:00 AM or 9:00 AM, and they have no interaction. And they're just listening to the teacher and basically being a "yes girl" or "yes boy" saying, "Yep, I understand"—they get no extra input whatsoever. (Speaker 1, Line 115)

Schools must create an environment where both parents and students feel comfortable speaking up and advocating for their needs.

Families also valued one-on-one communication that fosters a multidimensional view of their children. When one mother's primary-aged child joined Emerson, she said,

> No one knew his deficiencies or maybe something that (he) would like to be challenged on. So (in addition to) that parent survey, a one-on-one interview might have been beneficial—so that he would have (been) placed in the appropriate level. (Speaker 7, Line 41)

This need to be challenged was a consistent refrain. Another parent suggested one-on-one student interviews to seek their ideas for school improvement. In response, an administrator proposed a 15-minute "virtual home visit" over Zoom to meet each family, learn student strengths and needs, seek input, and reiterate classroom expectations.

Another parent shared an idea for virtual school planning meetings (which he named "Live at Five") held over Facebook Live or a similar platform, as a way of getting just-in-time input. "When you go 'Live at Five' with the parents, you know, you can also have some honest-to-God feedback from their students" (Speaker 5, Line 75). His idea helped us realize that, as leaders, we often view communicating with parents and children as separate tasks and then feel surprised when they have different understandings of our message.

A final theme was the need to engage those parents *not* participating in school events:

> You need to get a group of those parents that don't show up to par-
> ent meetings, (whose) kids are struggling—and then you ask them,
> "Why are you . . . what's the hindrance? And what's keeping you
> from doing what you need to do?" (The parents of) the kids who
> haven't logged on yet, you need to meet them. (Speaker 4, Line 120)

Too often, leaders make decisions based on suggestions from only the most involved families, while families who need school support the most have the least input.

Use of Empathy Interviews. Landon encouraged parents to "be open, be honest, be authentic" in their responses in the empathy interviews (Line 35) and showed striking honesty in return. When one parent asked whether ECA's graduates were truly prepared for elite high schools, he responded,

> I'm going to be honest . . . as much as we want to say that we have a
> rigorous curriculum and our kids would be at that advanced level of
> preparation, nope, they would not be. And that's a problem. (Line 57)

Landon also affirmed another parent's impression that teachers became complacent when students reached grade-level norms. "We are so guilty of that, especially in kindergarten through third grade. 'He's proficient. He's good. Let's move on.' We do, guilty as charged" (Line 64). These interactions demonstrate empathetic listening and a level of candor that builds trust and mutual respect.

When the parents encouraged Landon to reach out to those fami-lies *not* attending events, he had an "aha" moment, realizing his lead-ership team had assumed the underlying causes of low parent involve-ment without the input of one key stakeholder—the actual parents not attending. The pandemic helped Landon realize that many seem-ingly disengaged families were actually eager to visit classrooms vir-tually as guest readers, to chaperone virtual field trips, and to attend virtual school events when the barrier of visiting school in person was removed. Those less involved parents were likely willing to connect; he just needed to learn what they needed.

Next Steps and Recommendations for Future Collaboration

Based on our IS work in general and the empathy interviews in particular, Emerson made three major commitments: (1) address individual learning from a paradigm not of remediation but of acceleration and enrichment (Rollins, 2014), including aligning expectations with high-performing area secondary schools; (2) revitalize relationships with less engaged families to tell a more inclusive "Emerson Academy story," identifying challenging dynamics and addressing oversights head-on; and (3) continue to use IS tools to systematize communication and accelerate inclusive and responsive practices.

Within weeks of this focus group, Landon was promoted from his principal role at Emerson to director of school quality (assistant superintendent) within the larger charter network. He is excited to share the IS methods he honed at ECA with the incoming leadership team and with principals across his new region. Emerson's new leaders will come to understand that attitudes don't change overnight and building relationships with families requires lasting commitment. By focusing on insights from improvement science, Emerson can continue to engage families as true partners in student learning and take advantage of the adage of using the wisdom of the village to raise up their students.

Discussion Questions

1. Reflect on the three actions that made the most difference to the engagement of families in this case study? What would you add?
2. How does IS contribute to the development of unique strengths and assets of each member of the school community?
3. What are the dispositions that enable collaborative, equity-centered continuous improvement work? Reflect on these dispositions in your school.

References

Bryk, A. S., Gomez, L. M., Grunow, A., & LeMahieu, P. G. (2015). *Learning to improve: How America's schools can get better at getting better.* Harvard Education Press.

Clark-Louque, A. R., Lindsey, R. B., Quezada, R. L., & Jew, C. L. (2019). *Equity partnerships: A culturally proficient guide to family, school, and community engagement.* Corwin.

Crow, R., Hinnant-Crawford, B. N., & Spaulding, D. T. (Eds.). (2019). *The educational leader's guide to improvement science: Data, design and cases for reflection.* Stylus.

Global Family Research Foundation. (2018). *Joining together to create a bold vision for next generation family engagement: Engaging families to transform education.* Carnegie Corporation of New York.

Griffin, R., & Cummins, M. (2012). "It's a struggle, it's a journey, it's a mountain that you gotta climb": Black misandry, education, and the strategic embrace of Black male counterstories. *Qualitative Communication Research, 1*(3), 257–289. https://doi.org/10.1525/qcr.2012.1.3.257

Heifetz, R. A., Heifetz, R., Grashow, A., & Linsky, M. (2009). *The practice of adaptive leadership: Tools and tactics for changing your organization and the world.* Harvard Business Press.

Hoffman, J. V., Hikida, M., & Sailors, M. (2020). Contesting science that silences: Amplifying equity, agency, and design research in literacy teacher preparation. *Reading Research Quarterly, 55*(Suppl. 1), S255–S266. https://doi.org/10.1002/rrq.353

Ladson-Billings, G. (1997). Toward a critical race theory of education. *Teachers College Record, 97*(1), 47–68. https://doi.org/10.4324/9781315709796-2

Langley, G. J., Moen, R. D., Nolan, K. M., Nolan, T. W., Norman, C. L., & Provost, L. P. (2009). *The improvement guide: A practical approach to enhancing organizational performance.* Wiley & Sons.

Merseth, K. (2009). *Inside urban charter schools: Promising practices and strategies in five high-performing schools.* Harvard Education Press.

Milner, H. (2011). Culturally relevant pedagogy in a diverse urban classroom. *Urban Review: Issues and Ideas in Public Education, 43*(1), 66–89. https://doi.org/10.1007/s11256-009-0143-0

National Association for Family, School, and Community Engagement. (2009). *Family engagement defined.* https://nafsce.org/page/definition

Nelsestuen, K., & Smith, J. (2020). Empathy interviews. *The Learning Professional, 41*(5), 59. https://learningforward.org/wp-content/uploads/2020/10/tool-empathy-interviews.pdf

Ohio Department of Education. (2021, February 28). *Ohio school report cards.* Ohio Department of Education. https://reportcard.education.ohio.gov/school/detail/000577

Parent Teacher Association. (2019). *Bringing parents and families to the table: Family engagement in education.* https://www.pta.org/docs/default-source/files/advocacy/public-policy-agenda/2019/issue-briefs/issue-brief_family-engagement.pdf

Portigal, S. (2013). *Interviewing users: How to uncover compelling insights.* Rosenfeld Media.

Rollins, S. P. (2014). *Learning in the fast lane: 8 ways to put ALL students on the road to academic success.* ASCD.

Student Intervention Services. (2021, February). *School improvement process workbook.* Personal Collection of National Heritage Academies, Grand Rapids, Michigan.

Vaughn, S., Schumm, J. S., & Sinagub, J. M. (1996). *Focus group interviews in education and psychology.* Sage Publications.

CHAPTER SIXTEEN

Family Engagement: Increasing Equity Through the Reading Club Project

FOLUSHO B. ABAYOMI

Culturally responsive family engagement is a key equity issue in schools. The voices of historically underserved families are often not included in school improvement conversations. This project focused on increasing equity in first-grade reading through family engagement (Parekh et al., 2011). We examined the root causes of underserving historically marginalized students in reading. Through a family-led reading project, we sought to engage family volunteers in improving the reading levels of students working below grade expectations. We identified the root causes of the equity issues in reading, connected teachers with family volunteers, trained volunteers, and provided rich texts and supplementary resources to support students on a daily basis.

School Context

This equity-based improvement science project was situated in a publicly funded elementary school in Ontario, Canada. Claxton Urban Academy (CUA; pseudonyms used throughout) serves students from ages 4 to 11 and enrolls approximately 600 students annually. Students come from diverse ethnic backgrounds, many of whom are new immigrants and/or from historically underserved backgrounds. According to the school district's data, more than 40% of students come from lower income families and are mostly children of families new to Canada (CUA School District, 2018c). CUA's mission is to promote student success by providing equitable access to programs and resources, as well as enhancing opportunities that will allow for improved student achievement and well-being (CUA, 2018b). This improvement project occurred between January and June 2018.

Team Members

The collaborative team members involved in this project are first-grade teachers, speech/language and special education specialists, administrators, school superintendent, and family members. The goal of the team was to pursue family engagement as part of a wider school vision of promoting social justice and equity for students who are historically underserved, specifically those who are not at grade level in reading.

Equity Focus

In education, equity means access to opportunities and equitable outcomes for all students. It means educators and educational systems are offering support to ensure every student has an equal chance to be successful. Family engagement is a powerful tool for making schools more equitable, culturally responsive, and collaborative (Auerbach, 2009; Fruchter, 2007; Olivos, 2006). The specific focus on family engagement to increase student success raises issues of equity as middle and upper class families are often significantly more involved in their children's education than low-income families, with children from low socioeconomic status more at risk for lower academic achievement (de Carvalho, 2001; McLoyd, 1990). Moreover, the Ontario Ministry of Education (MOE) asserts that ensuring equity is a necessary foundation for improving student achievement in all Ontario schools; schools must ensure that students of all backgrounds, identities, and personal circumstances are provided with opportunities and support to succeed (Ontario MOE, 2014).

Disparities continue to persist among students of historically undeserved racial, socio-economic, cultural, and home language backgrounds (CUA School District, 2018c). The Developmental Reading Assessment (DRA) data ranked CUA as one of the bottom five schools in its school learning network (CUA School District, 2018c). DRA is an individually administered assessment used to evaluate students' reading capabilities and is a tool used by teachers to identify reading levels, comprehension, fluency, and accuracy. Through collaboration with families and teachers, we intended to identify root causes and potential change ideas that would eliminate the reading disparities.

Problem of Practice

Although the school's improvement goal included promoting equity and inclusion, data continued to indicate we were not successfully teaching reading to low-income students who composed 50% of our students. In addition, families who are recent immigrants indicated they are consumed by their daily work schedule, some with multiple jobs or are working on swing, split, or night shifts. Additionally, families indicated they would like access to books to read at home.

As the improvement team began to understand the underlying equity issues in reading, especially the lived experiences of students and families, conversations shifted from blaming families to reflecting on how to promote partnerships and assist families in improving the reading skills of their children. It was obvious that to move forward, the existing support system must be reviewed and alternative ways to equitably support and meet the needs of our students must be considered as essential. Sticking to the status quo was no longer an option given the goal of improving the reading skills of CUA underserved students. As Boykin and Noguera (2011) point out, to address educational inequities, we must address the circumstance in which learning takes place for our students and create school environments where race or socio-economic status do not predict student success.

The Improvement Science Process:
Plan–Do–Study–Act Cycles

Plan

In planning for this project, we included components of improvement science: identify the need for change, identify the problem of practice, set clear and measurable goals; use disciplined inquiry to drive improvement; and employ evidence-based, data-driven, and action-oriented efforts to solve identified problems. We added that we wanted to use existing communication channels to communicate with staff and families. The focus was on continuous improvement, and data were continuously used to inform the process throughout.

Data Used to Inform PDSA Cycles. We used student learning data such as the DRA data, running records previous reading recovery data to identify students whom we were not successfully serving. Once students were identified, deeper conversations about equity and why students were falling behind were initiated. Next, we conducted family interviews to help us identify the root causes of the problem. We then conducted a family and student survey to identify reading interests, reading levels, access to books, how often students read, and how families can support reading.

The team next developed action plans based on information related to the root causes (Van Barneveld, 2008). The root cause analysis helped us define and describe a desired future state in contrast to the present reality. As Donohoo (2017) pointed out, understanding causes and effects will motivate educators to "examine what they think will work against the realities of what is actually happening given their existing culture, specific context, and unique population" (p. 60).

Drawing from existing data analysis, family interviews, and teachers' perspectives, the two action research questions below were created to help ascertain the root cause/s of the achievement gap and to determine possible solution(s):

1. What are the root causes of the achievement gap in reading for our Grade 1 students?

2. How can we equitably support first-grade students in reading through increased family engagement?

Our data analysis indicated that families wanted to be involved and that additional resources would increase the families' ability to be involved. Data indicated teachers needed a deeper understanding of students' lived experiences and how to effectively engage families. Consistent professional development, reevaluation of the resources used, and a whole-school understanding of the reading expectations/levels for all grades were also key.

Change Ideas. Our team identified the following potential change ideas: increase student access to rich texts and culturally relevant books; incorporate students' lived experiences into our teaching practices, develop a family-led reading club, and small-group and individual guided, shared, and independent reading support.

The families' engagement resulted in the creation of a family-led reading club that allowed family volunteers to physically come into the school building on a daily basis to support students in improving their reading skills. It is important to note that the six family-volunteers who started the project were required to complete school district and police screening/reference checks prior to working with students. Families and community volunteers were not related to the identified students.

Do

In this stage, we used improvement science tools to manage the change process while providing support, empowering staff, and building capacity. The focus was to act on the developed vision, document observations, identify challenges, and analyze collected data. Teachers and family volunteers were trained in culturally relevant pedagogy throughout this process. Administrators continued to work with the team and lead teachers to build capacity and mobilize change actions relating to teachers' perspectives on efficiency, underlying assumptions, about students we had historically not been successful teaching.

As teachers and family volunteers were working on the plan, they were also creating new action plans based on new knowledge and competencies acquired through debriefing, analyses of data, and reflection. The team members continuously implemented changes in practices, developed shared knowledge and understanding, and collected evidence. This collaborative process addressed the inquiry questions, created new knowledge, helped us refine our thinking and mindset, and increased our collective efficacy. As instructional practices and mindset shifted with a focus on improving both teaching and learning, teachers became more aware of their collective power to enhance students' performance. The team met on a weekly basis throughout the planning and implementation of this improvement project.

Study

In this stage, a variety of tools were used to measure and track the change actions implemented so far to determine progress and challenges. At this point, the focus was also on summarizing learning and making necessary modifications to attain the envisioned future state for CUA's first-grade students. The team continuously worked collaboratively on the analysis of student learning data and documented observations to ensure deeper reflections on learning and the project's outcome.

Using pre- and postassessment tools, the team examined achievement data (such as report cards, DRA levels, family/student informal interviews, observations) to determine if there was evidence of improvement in student performance and if further change actions were needed. In addition, school administrators engaged in classroom walk-throughs to observe how change actions were implemented. Walk-through observation charts and checklists were utilized. Findings from observations helped not only in formulating conclusions but also in planning for the next steps. At the end of this stage, changes in beliefs and mindset ensued as teachers reconciled discrepancies between their initial thinking and learning that emerged through reflection and critically considered instructional practices and student learning. Pre- and summative and formative assessments were utilized to gauge student progress. There was an ongoing utilization of student learning data by the improvement team to inform teaching practices and refine the teaching strategies and resources used with a focus on improving students' reading skills.

Act

At this final stage, the team focused on making modifications as needed and interpreting data to formulate the next steps through reflective practice. Apart from debriefing on future considerations, the team also focused on how to formulate new approaches to enhance family engagement based on the new knowledge acquired through this improvement project. Based on findings from data analysis, gains were made. To preserve the gains and accomplishments, the team purchased more books matching students' reading levels and more culturally relevant reading books that included teachers' guides and other relevant supplementary resources for the first-grade team. The team agreed to continue the home reading program in which students took leveled, culturally responsive books home on a daily basis; continued with daily guided reading program (in small groups); continued the family-led reading program; and shared learnings and gains with the school community through existing communication channels.

Taking Improvement Efforts to Scale

To ensure continuous improvement, the team also decided to start a new PDSA cycle with a focus on CUA kindergarten students. It is important to begin the improvement of early literacy at the foundation level as the initial findings in the planning stage indicated that students are coming to first grade with limited literacy skills. As Henderson and Berla (1994) point out, when schools partner with families to support student learning, children tend to succeed in school and throughout their lifetime. The hope is that an application of similar action plans at the kindergarten level will increase equity in reading for first-grade students (see Table 16.1)

Table 16.1. Plan–Do–Study–Act (PDSA) Functions Utilized

Model	Stage 1	Stage 2	Stage 3	Stage 4
PDSA Cycle	**Plan** Defined objectives, questions, and prediction Planned to carry out the change	**Do** Carried out the plan Documented observations and problems Analyzed collected data	**Study** Completed analysis of data Compared outcome to prediction Summarized learning	**Act** Made changes as needed Planned and intend to start next step/ cycle in the next school year

Managing the Improvement Plan Implementation and the PDSA Cycle

Managing change implementation plans according to Cawsey et al. (2016) means making sure the change actions and continuing operations of the organization are successful. Therefore, in facilitating this implementation plan, the team members ensured that the resources needed such as human, money, time, and valued expertise are managed effectively to ensure success. Part of the implementation goal was to ensure that CUA's school business continued to operate effectively while the change action plans were being implemented. This goal was achievable because most of the resources needed were already in place to support the implementation plan. For example, prior to this project, professional learning communities were already existing. First-grade teachers are already meeting weekly to engage in professional development and engage in school or district initiatives. Thus, there was minimal disruption to the day-to-day activities and routines of CUA students during the implementation process. Also, debriefings, reflections, and celebrations were occurring during weekly meetings. This allowed team members to share accomplishments, challenges, and next steps and provided multiple perspectives and opportunities to co-review the tools and strategies used for further improvement of the implementation project. A key concept of improvement science is to conduct PDSA cycles in short time frames.

Teachers were able to adjust their change ideas weekly to ensure each child was improving.

Improvement Project Outcomes and Learnings

Continuous utilization of student learning data and process by first-grade teachers and support staff informed practice and refined reading instructional strategies. With intensive reading support from teachers and family-volunteers through guided, shared, and independent reading at school and at home, coupled with the use of culturally relevant resources and professional development for teachers and training for volunteers, students' reading skills increased significantly. At the beginning of the project, 43 out of 73 students were identified as working below grade level (Levels 0–3). At the end of the project, 17 students (Group 3) moved to Levels 18 to 20, surpassing the overall school and board expectation; 16 students (Group 2) progressed to the targeted level (Levels 14–16); and 42 students (Group 1) moved up by at least four levels. By the end of June, many students increased their reading levels, with 33 students showing dramatic reading growth (see Figure 16.1).

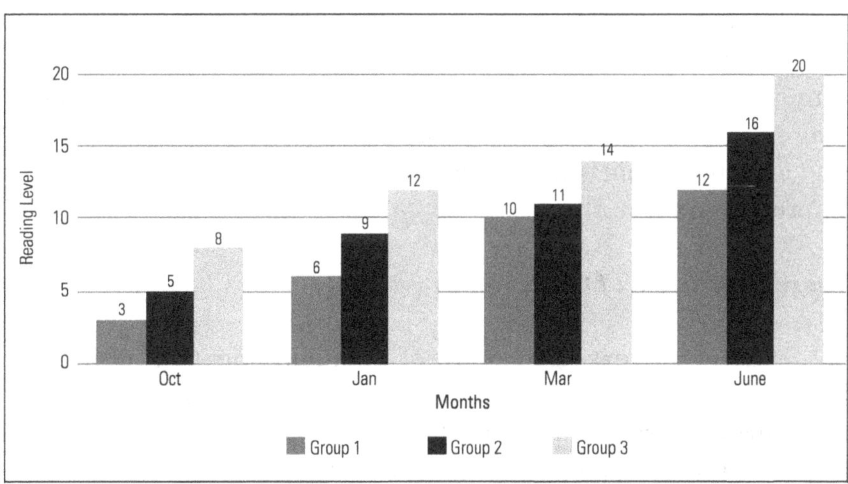

Figure 16.1. Grade One Reading Tracker Chart

It is important to note that although students did not meet the expected/mandated board reading level, many students made significant gains. The students in Group 1 will continue to receive intentional literacy intervention and support in Grade 2.

Lessons Learned for Increasing Equity in Schools

Family engagement increases equity and empowers families in ways that honor their strengths and value their voices. Reaching out to the community to seek family volunteers who are familiar with students' cultural backgrounds and lived experiences allowed for the inclusion of diverse family voices and perspectives that enriched and informed the planning and implementation of this project. Furthermore, allowing families autonomy and involving them in the school improvement plan decreased the "one-sided conversations" families often experience. In this equity-focused project, one key lesson learned is the importance of home–school collaboration in making a difference to students' learning and the demonstration of how both teachers and families can collaboratively develop knowledge and skills while working together to serve students of all racial, ethnic, socioeconomic, and linguistic backgrounds. In addition, the outcome of the project indicated that instruction can focus on improving early reading skills and family engagement in education simultaneously. In this project, families' engagement increased as the school and home connection was enhanced, teachers' knowledge and teaching skills improved, and most important, the reading skills of students of all backgrounds improved significantly.

Increased Sense of Community

In addition to increasing the sense of accomplishment for the families involved, there was also an increased sense of community and belonging. During debriefing and reflection discussions, families shared personal experiences, knowledge gained, and strategies that were beneficial to students and teachers. According to family volunteers, they were happy to be able to give back to the community. Most important, they were glad to be working collaboratively with teachers to support students' learning. They all noted that they now understood the challenges of a teacher's job and how they could engage in deeper conversations to support students. CUA witnessed a significant increase in family engagement through the reading program. The relationship between school and home was also improved as communication channels were enhanced through the communication log sent home on a daily basis.

Benefits for Staff and School

This improvement reading project increased the sense of accomplishment among teachers. The team members created positive relationships with families and increased their understanding of students' specific needs, interests, and lived experiences. In addition, teachers enhanced their knowledge of reading strategies and the resources available for supporting students' reading skills in the early years. With the continuous use of data and the exposure to evidence-based processes to solve the identified problem in this project, teachers thought about problems differently and learned how to use data for improvement instead of using it for accountability. Also, the bottom-up improvement science approach helped in empowering and motivating teachers to engage actively in the project. For example, at the initial stage teachers analyzed baseline data and collectively came up with ideas regarding the root causes of the problem and possible solutions. As asserted by Fink and Markhol (2011),

> the only way to improve reading achievement was to improve the quality of teaching, and that meant teachers had to be open and willing to examine their practice, learn new strategies, and incorporate those new strategies into their existing practice. (p. 324)

This is exactly what happened during this project as the teachers involved learned and incorporated new strategies into their literacy programs. Also, rich conversations and reflections around culturally responsive teaching and learning were developed during the process.

The involvement of family volunteers provided the opportunity to share and learn about the diverse families of CUA students and their lived experiences. Throughout this project, one consistent pattern was the increase in collaboration between grade one teachers and other support staff involved. Teachers planned together, shared ideas, teaching strategies, and experiences especially on what is working and what is not. As a result, teachers were using the same resources, incorporating new teaching styles, and differentiating instructions to meet specific student's needs. Furthermore, teachers invested in examining and learning from ministry documents and other related teaching materials which ultimately influenced teaching and learning in the classroom. Overall, the significant increase in reading levels shows the importance of engaging families and utilizing student learning data to identify, analyze, and establish explicit strategies that can be used to drive improvement.

Although there were many gains and benefits to students, families, and the school community, there were also a few challenges during the implementation of the project. For example, attaining teachers' buy-in was a challenge at the initial stage as teachers seemed to perceive this project as another district initiative requiring accountability. Conversely, we learned that using improvement science methods can empower teachers and families. We also learned that time constraints, conflict with schedules, and difficulties with getting appropriate culturally relevant resources for this grade level were some challenges that the team addressed during the implementation of the change actions.

Benefits for Students

Increased sense of accomplishment and love of reading was evident as interest and demand for more books to read or take home increased. Students enhanced their learning and through the guided reading and one-on-one support provided by teachers and family volunteers and improved motivation and self-confidence. Students whose families were not able to help at home benefited immensely when they read with an adult at school on a daily basis. Students' reading level/

grade increased and most of them developed the love of reading as they were exposed to a variety of books at their levels and interests.

Conclusion

In recognition of CUA's context, this data-driven, action-oriented project sought to close the achievement gap for underserved students by increasing and using family engagement as a tool for making school more equitable and collaborative. In collaboration with families and based on data analysis, the root causes of the achievement gap in reading were identified; using the PDSA framework as a guide, change actions were developed and adopted; family volunteers were trained; rich texts and supplementary resources were provided; and families and teachers engaged in teaching, co-learnings, and a journey to support underserved students in reading.

The success of this equity-focused project calls for continued attempts at developing and implementing similar projects through data-driven and evidence-based processes in order to effectively solve identified educational problems.

Undoubtedly, the development and implementation of intentional equity-focused family engagement positively influenced the involvement of families not only in improving students reading skills in this project but also in enhancing active participation in school events. However, CUA's contextual challenges and solutions should not be perceived as a classical representation of all low-income neighborhood schools with similar demographics. Nonetheless, the outcome of this project and the lessons learned can be utilized to inform equity-focused family engagement and improvement plans. When using improvement science tools and processes, educators must consider the specific needs and context of the school community. Given that context matters and "one hat may not fit all," schools should modify or adapt this project to fit their own specific context. As Martin (2007) indicated in explaining integrative thinking, what works in one context may not work in another.

Discussion Questions

1. In your school or district, what are common assumptions about why children are not reading at grade level?
2. If the background or home life of students or families is blamed for a lack of progress on literacy goals for children, how could you reframe your improvement work to ensure children of all backgrounds are successfully taught literacy skills?
3. What improvement science tools or empathy interview questions might help to contribute to a successful improvement project in which literacy skills are successfully taught to children of all backgrounds?
4. Many grade-level teams, schools, or districts enact the practice of teaching literacy using only one theoretical framework, resulting in educational disparities in literacy. What change process and improvement tools might be helpful to ensure that children of all backgrounds are successfully taught literacy skills in your context?

References

Auerbach, S. (2009). Walking the walk: Portraits in leadership for family engagement in urban schools. *School Community Journal, 19*(1), 9-32 https://files.eric.ed.gov/fulltext/EJ847415.pdf

Boykin, A., & Noguera, P. (2011). *Creating the opportunity to learn.* Association for Supervision and Curriculum Development.

Cawsey, T. F., Deszca, G., & Ingols, C. (2016). *Organizational change: An action-oriented toolkit* (3rd ed.). Sage Publications.

CUA School District. (2018a). *Reading assessment.* Internal document.

CUA School District. (2018b). *School improvement plan.* Internal document.

CUA School District. (2018c). *Demographics & achievement report.* Internal document.

de Carvalho, M. E. (2001). *Rethinking family school relations: A critique of parent involvement in schooling.* Teachers College Press.

Donohoo, J. (2017). *Collective efficacy: How educators' beliefs impact student learning.* Corwin.

Fink, S., & Markholt, A. (2011). The leader's role in developing teacher expertise (pp. 317-333). In M. Grogan (Ed.), *The Jossey-Bass reader on educational leadership* (3rd ed.). Jossey-Bass.

Fruchter, N. (2007). *Urban schools, public will: Making education work for all our children.* Teachers College Press.

Henderson, A., & Berla, N. (1994). *A new generation of evidence: The family is critical to student achievement.* Columbia, MD: Committee for Citizens in Education. https://files.eric.ed.gov/fulltext/ED375968.pdf

Martin, R. L. (2007). *The opposable mind: How successful leaders win through integrative thinking.* Harvard Business Press.

McLoyd, V. (1990). The impact of economic hardship on Black families and children: Psychological distress, parenting, and socioemotional development. *Child Development, 61*(2), 311–346. https://doi.org/10.2307/1131096

Olivos, E. M. (2006). *The power of parents: A critical perspective of bicultural family involvement in public school.* Peter Lang.

Ontario Ministry of Education. (2014). *Achieving excellence: A renewed vision for education in Ontario.* https://www.kcdsb.on.ca/UserFiles/Servers/Server_12116929/File/Programs/Safe%20Schools/Ontario%20Ministry%20of%20Education%20Documents/achieving%20excellence.pdf

Parekh, G., Killoran I., & Crawford, C. (2011). The Toronto connection: Poverty, perceived ability, and access to education equity. *Canadian Journal of Education, 34*(3), 249–279. https://journals.sfu.ca/cje/index.php/cje-rce/article/view/941/1072

Van Barneveld, C. (2008). *Using data to improve student achievement.* Faculty of Education, Lakehead University. https://thelearningexchange.ca/wp-content/uploads/2008/12/Dec5DataMonograph.pdf

CHAPTER SEVENTEEN

Centering Equity and Starting Small to Transform School Climate

MICHELLE LI AND KIRSTEN EBERSOLE LACROIX
(CO-FIRST AUTHORS) AND DONNA BRAUN

What does it take to transform educational systems so that each and every child has their unlimited, unknowable potential unleashed every day? In working toward this vision, the Center for Leadership and Educational Equity (CLEE) has affirmed that it minimally takes pervasive leadership of diverse stakeholders for whom the impact matters most: students, families, and educators. In continuously honing practices to develop and support such leadership, CLEE's work is guided by three key assumptions. First, leaders are not born but rather are developed through powerful learning. Furthermore, a leader is anyone who takes responsibility for something they care about. Finally, the complex learning and leading needed to transform schools are not possible by individuals alone, but rather by a critical mass that is developed through collaboration to enact improvements. This chapter illuminates how these assumptions guide an evidence-based continuous improvement method that CLEE uses across multiple K-12 contexts to impact educational equity. The story of one school's early efforts highlight how to use facilitative leadership (CLEE, 2020a) practices in leading improvements that address root causes of inequities and manifest both instructional and cultural shifts toward a vision of equitable outcomes.

CLEE integrates leadership development with a method of continuous improvement that builds the capacity of educators to facilitate collaborative cycles of improvement by implementing six Core Leadership Practices (Braun et al., 2017) described in Table 17.1. The improvements are aimed at strengthening educator practices in the instructional core and at reorganizing school systems to increase equitable outcomes between focal groups (i.e., students who have been historically underserved) and peer groups.

Edward R. Martin Middle School (MMS) in East Providence, Rhode Island, is one of nine schools participating in a multiyear statewide improvement network funded by a U.S. Department of Education

Table 17.1. Core Leadership Practices

Practices	Description
Setting Direction	Continuously engage self and others in developing a shared understanding of (a) the current reality and why inequities exist, (b) a vision of high and equitable outcomes for each and every student, (c) key goals to galvanize the community, and (d) evidence-based improvements in educator practices.
Monitoring Progress	Collaboratively collect, analyze, and use relevant data throughout improvement processes to (a) understand strengths and needs, (b) plan steps to adapt to meet needs, (c) monitor effort and growth toward the vision, and (d) connect effort to outcomes to build efficacy.
Building the Capacity to Teach	Facilitate learning experiences and structures that promote improvement of their craft aimed at meeting each and every student's needs, including building a culture where people are psychologically safe to take risks, take responsibility to improve, and see their impact.
Building the Capacity to Collaborate	Facilitate collaborative learning that (a) utilizes strengths of colleagues, (b) deepens craft by constructing understanding together, (c) creates a receptive space for challenging and expanding assumptions to align with vision, and (d) shifts culture from autonomy to coherence and collective commitment.
Building the Capacity to Lead	Create conditions to amplify the leadership of diverse stakeholders (students, families and educators) through (a) stepping up or down to make space for silenced voices, (b) take action outside own comfort zone, (c) proactively plan and facilitate protocols effectively collaborate, and (d) advocate for whatever it takes to achieve equity.
Reorganizing Systems	Build a shared commitment, not just compliance, to clear, evolving systems and structures that ensure high and equitable outcomes, including (a) time for adequate adult collaboration, (b) structures to support a positive learning culture for all, and (c) systems to ensure access to excellent teaching and learning for each and every student.

Note: The Core Leadership Practices are derived from primary research (Braun et al., 2017) and leadership development research (Leithwood et al., 2004, 2010), used to create the Center for Leadership in Education Equity Learning Community Survey (Braun et al., 2015), and found to be significantly and positively correlated with learning growth most significantly for the focal group, and also for the peer group (Braun et al., 2020).

grant awarded to the Rhode Island Department of Education (RIDE) focused on school climate transformation. The network is currently in Year 2 of 5. Although the practices that are described in this chapter are used throughout CLEE's leadership development programs, including the School Climate Transformation (SCT) network, this chapter reveals the depth of growth and manifestations of change that occur in school communities through the ways that MMS educators enact the practices of continuous improvement. Furthermore, the ways CLEE facilitated learning for MMS educators are described.

Context and Background

Located in an urban ring public school district in East Providence, Rhode Island, MMS serves approximately 670 students in Grades 6 through 8. Of the entire student body, 54% is characterized as economically disadvantaged and 16% receive special education services (MMS, 2019). The racial/ethnic percentages of the student body are as follows: 2% identifies as American Indian or Alaska Native,[1] 1% Asian, 15% Black or African American, 9% Hispanic, 9% two or more races, and 62% White. MMS currently has 60 certified teacher teachers and 27 certified staff (support personnel). In 2018–2019, 15.7% of MMS students were chronically absent, and several subgroups had disproportionate rates of chronic absenteeism: 35.5% of American Indian or Alaska Native, 21.9% economically disadvantaged, and 21.9% students with disabilities. MMS earned two stars in the state accountability system (in which one star is the lowest and five stars is the highest rating); its two-star rating was driven most by performance on the Achievement and Growth criteria of the state accountability system. Three groups of students were identified for targeted support and improvement: Black or African American students, Hispanic students, and students with disabilities (RIDE, 2019). Because the school had a lower performance in achievement and growth than the district's elementary and high schools and because other indicators of

---

1 Demographic and subgroup labels used in this paragraph mirror that of RIDE.

school climate pointed to the need for improvement, district leaders identified MMS for inclusion in the SCT network opportunity.

The composition of MMS's SCT network team reflects several design features that are pivotal to their promising results in early implementation. First, they created a diverse team composed of a district administrator, school principal, dean of students, and guidance counselor, as well as educators representing various disciplines in the school and students. Each team member brought a unique vantage point needed for the team to have a schoolwide impact on the mindsets and practices of the rest of the school community. Student team members shared an equal footing with the adults in leading the work, bringing their expertise as students and voicing their own perspectives while building the capacity of their facilitation and leadership skills.

Second, two key leaders on the team had a background in the CLEE improvement methodology prior to the initiation of the network. The principal of MMS, William (Bill) Black, and the multilingual director for East Providence Schools, Yanaiza Gallant, entered the work with previously built capacity in the CLEE improvement model. Bill Black served as a mentor in CLEE's principal preparation program, the Principal Residency Network, which utilizes the CLEE improvement model and tools described in this chapter. While a principal of Orlo Elementary School in East Providence, Yanaiza Gallant also served as a mentor in CLEE's Principal Residency Network and engaged in the CLEE improvement model to lead the school to transform its practices and student learning results. Both leaders joined the SCT network with an ongoing practice in CLEE's Core Leadership Practices (see Table 17.1). Given their background, these leaders made critical moves described in this chapter to organize the work for success.

Third, MMS designed their teams to allow for accelerated implementation. Given a history of initiatives that were perceived as top-down and ultimately led to inconsistent results, the principal of MMS knew it was essential to build widespread shared ownership in order for the work to have the desired impact. When asked to describe his role on the team, Bill Black responded that he "co-planned meetings, empowered staff to lead, carved out time during faculty meetings, organized common planning time, communicated to staff, students and families along the way." Notable in his response is the absence of designating himself the team lead. Rather than take a role as the driver of the work, he and other administrators fully participated in and ensured that team members had the authority and support to lead the work with the staff. This move represents a strong implementation of the practice of Building Capacity to Lead (Table 17.1). For example, a point person communicated with CLEE staff and organized the work at the school level. This shift from the principal to a staff member as the point person created an impactful team dynamic that rippled throughout the school. The principal's full participation communicated his commitment to the process while aligning his value of shared leadership with his actions to create space for others to take on significant leadership roles.

To build shared ownership for the improvement work, a two-tiered team structure was organized: a seven-member *away* team and a five-member *home* team. The away team participated in the SCT network learning days facilitated by CLEE that occurred outside of the school with the other school teams in the network. The away team then brought what they learned back to train the home team. Both the away and home teams participated in school-based team coaching sessions facilitated by CLEE. The two student team members, Justin and Rozaria, eighth graders at the time, were on the away team and attended network learning days and portions of team coaching sessions. The two-tiered structure allowed more staff members to have a clear role in leading the improvement work based on their time and capacity. The structure also enabled both teams to then fan out across the entire school to facilitate the improvement process, which, in turn, led to a faster ripple effect of the implementation and allowed for a high level of shared language and coherence across the school. As team member Colleen Murphy, school guidance counselor, shared in a focus group interview:

> We came up with the agenda [where] everyone had a different role
> of presenting and involving the entire faculty. . . . We really empow-
> ered the staff and people working on the [front] lines, which I think

was really powerful . . . the administration wasn't necessarily coming up with the agenda. It was the people actually working in the trenches, I think, which was helpful because they heard from their peers and everyone was involved in the process. And it was . . . well received and really positive.

CLEE facilitators implemented a number of practices to guide and support the essential moves that the principal made in forming the teams. Prior to the first full network learning day, CLEE hosted launch sessions for school and district administrators on how to organize their teams and data for successful first steps of the improvement process. Importantly, CLEE facilitators provided guidance in building a diverse team. The need for diversity is amplified in schools and districts with higher turnover rates in positional leadership. Having staff from a variety of roles, as well students on the team, builds the capacity of the team at an accelerated pace, helps the principal feel supported in leading complex change (increasing the likelihood that they will remain in their position because they are not the only driver of the efforts), and builds broader shared ownership of the work across educators in the school who feel that the improvements are being done *with* them instead of *to* them. Implementing the efforts to organize the work early are critical in order for shared leadership to manifest. Amanda Rapoza, an art teacher at MMS, described the impact of the team composition:

> We all have different strengths and it's great to be able to have that input and bring that strength to the team. . . . So having that diversity helps to lead our group to a better place because there's so many different perspectives that people bring.

An apocalyptical test of the MMS's teams' leadership arrived in March 2019, only seven months into the SCT network formation, when the COVID-19 pandemic caused schools across the state to shift to distance learning overnight. Instead of a global pandemic derailing their improvement efforts, the MMS teams leveraged their work to sustain momentum, create hope, nurture resiliency, and focus their efforts on student learning in concert with the circumstances the pandemic forces the school to face.

Equity Focus

CLEE facilitates school leaders and teams, including MMS and the other schools included in the SCT network, to implement the CLEE Core Leadership Practice, Setting Direction, by identifying and focusing on inequities *within* their schools, or where a school's disaggregated data reveal disproportionate student learning outcomes between groups of students and their peers. This first step in Setting Direction is a distinguishing practice of the CLEE methodology, designed through years of organizing continuous improvement efforts, to center a focus on equity from the onset, not as an afterthought. The theoretical rationale for having teams aim to reduce a specific inequity between a focal group of underserved students and their peers is as follows: By focusing on inequities within a school's student outcomes, teams increase their sense of efficacy that through collaboration, they can impact the students who are most underserved (Braun et al., 2017). Their assumptions of students' abilities are influenced in positive ways: educators begin to raise expectations for students and see that through their own and their students' efforts, each and every student can learn at high levels (CampbellJones et al., 2010; Hammond, 2014). When a school community believes in its ability to impact the learning of all students and has developed a culture of trust and risk-taking, it is more willing to take collective responsibility for all students. The resulting high level of internal accountability (Elmore, 2004) to increase equitable outcomes powers motivation to continuously improve.

Problem of Practice

The SCT network maintained a shared problem of practice: discovering and implementing practices that increase high and equitable academic and well-being outcomes for each and every student, especially for those in historically underserved groups. Often when schools focus on school climate, they inadvertently separate improvement in social-emotional learning (SEL) from those in the instructional core. Yet, CLEE has found that when efforts for improvement are not focused on the instructional core, efforts do not have the intended outcomes of improving student learning and increasing equity for students who are not currently being served well. To guide the SCT network, CLEE designed constructivist learning experiences to facilitate teams in exploring the interdependence of SEL and academic learning. MMS team member, Pamela Thacker, spoke to this when reflecting on her learning:

> We've had so many things throughout the years that have come down that don't make sense to me. But this makes sense how these two things [academic learning and SEL] fit together. This led to me being open to learning and being part of this and wanting to see my school do better, but also wanting myself to be better, improve myself.

To address the problem of practice, the driver diagram (Figure 17.1) articulates the network's theory of improvement: Using Core Leadership Practices to facilitate building educators' capacity to improve academic learning and SEL and to create a transformative culture increases academic and well-being outcomes for each and every student.

The primary drivers to reaching the network aim (i.e., increase high and equitable academic and well-being outcomes by developing a transformative culture) are the integration of SEL standards with instructional core improvements. In order to pull on these primary levers of change, leaders and teams use the Core Leadership Practices, which are the secondary drivers. This shared network theory of improvement provided a common language and vision for the many different teams joined together in solving a shared problem.

Tools Used in the Improvement Science Process

CLEE facilitates groups to learn and implement all the Core Leadership Practices (Table 17.1) as they implement the improvement method. In doing so, leaders and teams put the tools of improvement science into action to identify and understand the inequities in their school and then to address the inequities. The Core Leadership Practices are the *adaptive* vehicle that drives *technical* tools used in the improvement science process. Leading complex change with the goal of increasing equity in student learning outcomes requires meeting adaptive and

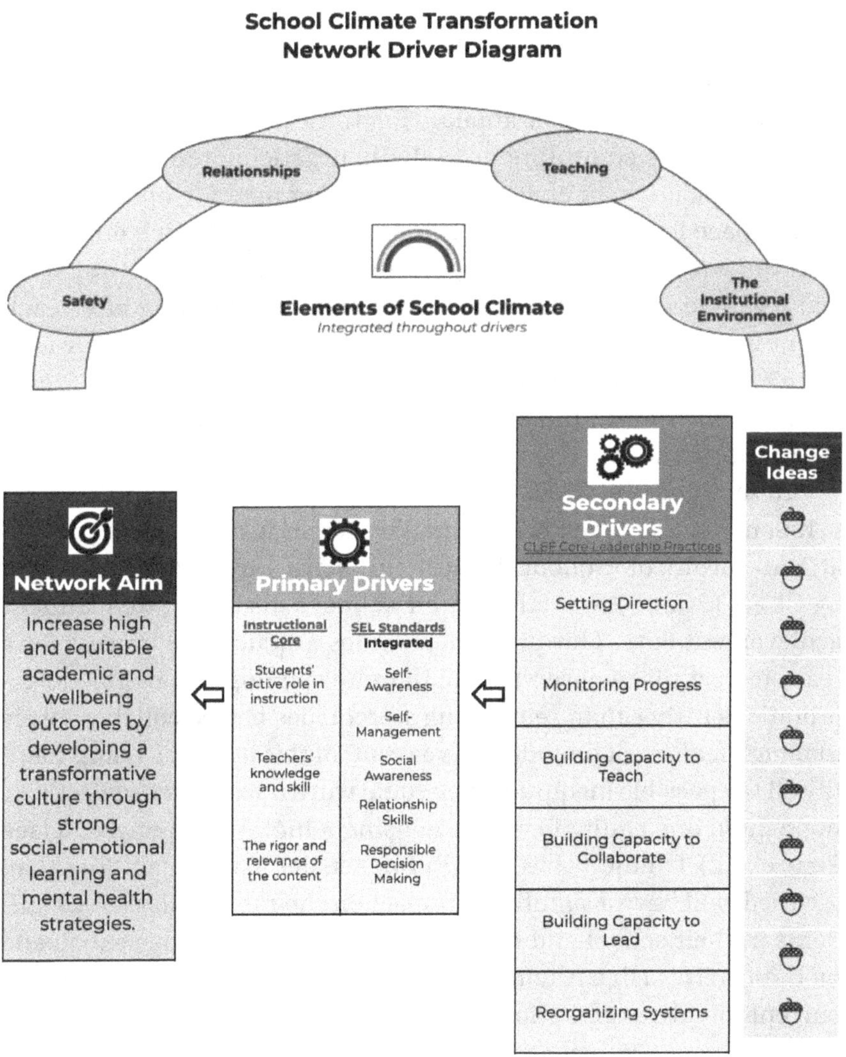

Figure 17.1. School Climate Transformation Network Driver Diagram

technical challenges. So much of reaching a network aim depends on teams' capacity to bring the work back to the school and lead their colleagues in changing mindsets, beliefs, and practices. CLEE facilitators intentionally build this capacity as they design learning for the network. Facilitators both model and gradually release facilitation to network participants to build their capacity to use these processes and tools for deep, transformative collaborative learning at their schools. For example, in developing a shared understanding of the network's aim, CLEE facilitators model practices such as creating learning agreements; operationalizing the agreements and developing each other's commitment to them; practicing top 10 facilitator moves (Breidentstein et al., 2012); designing meeting openings that create space for participants to connect inward, with each other, and with the work of the day; using protocols to ensure equity of voice and leverage the expertise of the group; and debriefing after each learning experience to reflect on how the process led to their own learning and how to use them in their own contexts. Table 17.2 provides an overview of the methodology with some key tools by Core Leadership Practice.

To set direction, CLEE facilitated MMS and the other SCT teams to first understand their current reality. Teams used the Atlas Looking at Data protocol (School Reform Initiative [SRI], 2020) adapted by CLEE (2020b) to analyze their school's disaggregated student achievement data. This protocol provides a structured process for a team to first make observations, thereby opening up possible interpretations rather than reinforcing stereotypes before collaboratively making meaning of their data. As a result of this protocol, teams identify all the possible inequities they could work on and then collectively hone in on one equity focal group using a high-leverage graph (see Figure 17.2). On the y-axis is High Impact, defined as inequities that, if closed, will have a significant impact on the most underserved students in their school and have a ripple effect across the school, and on the x-axis is High Alignment, defined as inequities that align with current initiatives and priorities and where resources are available to enact changes that will impact the inequity. Based on their analysis of data, the MMS team identified students receiving special education

Table 17.2. Center for Leadership and Educational Equity (CLEE) Improvement for Equity Method Steps by Core Leadership Practice

	Description of How Teams Implement the Steps	**Tools**
Setting Direction	**Understanding current reality, setting a vision:** (a) analyze disaggregated student achievement data to identify an inequity between a focal group of students (i.e. historically underserved) and their peers. (b) setting a vision and goals to increase equity (c) analyzing a variety of data to investigate the root causes of the inequity	Collaborative inquiry and data protocols Learning Community Survey Network driver diagram Root-cause analysis and empathy interviews
Building the Capacity to Teach	**Plan and Do:** (a) prioritize which root causes to address (b) determine which research evidence-based instructional practices will address root cause (c) make and enact a plan to facilitate the implementation of the instructional practices among colleagues using Core Leadership Practices	Prioritization and planning graphic organizers Evidence-based instructional practices
Monitoring Progress	**Study:** (a) identify a practical measure to determine the impact of the plan (b) collect data (c) analyze data to understand the impact of the steps taken and how they are addressing the root cause	Practical measures Data visualizations Data dialogue protocols
Reorganizing Systems	**Act:** (a) decide whether to adopt (continue), adapt (adjust), abort (stop) the practices identified to increase equity (b) decide what other restructuring may be needed (e.g., schedules, funds, personnel)	Data dialogue protocols
Building the Capacity to • Collaborate • Lead	Throughout the process, educators use facilitative leadership practices that empower shared leadership	Lead for equity dispositions

services in English language arts as their equity focal group. From there, they set a goal for the degree of student learning they aimed for the focal and peer groups to achieve.

Focusing first on a small, keystone (Duhigg, 2014) area of improvement is a hallmark of CLEE's improvement model. When teams focus their improvement efforts on a high leverage equity focal group, they can study a group of students for whom the system is not working. In doing so, the team surfaces educator beliefs and practices that

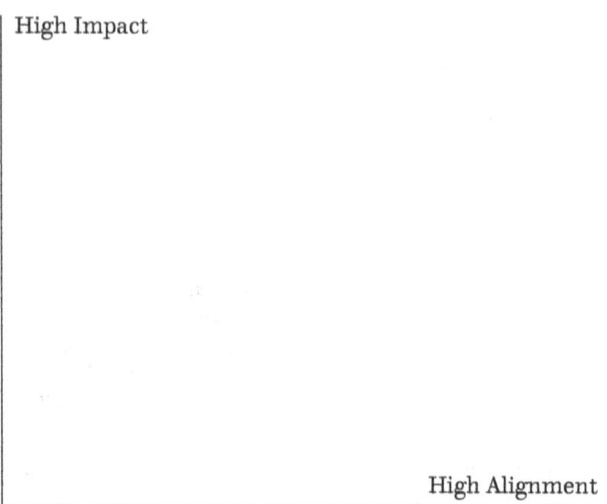

Figure 17.2. High Leverage Graph

contribute to the current results and can then determine change ideas that are needed to improve student outcomes. Studying the system through the lens of students for whom it is not working clarifies which decisions lead to patterns in curriculum and instruction that consistently fail to meet specific students' needs:

> The tight focus on a small group of students makes facing and addressing those conditions manageable; shifts the conversation from generalities and assumptions about why struggling students can't learn to specific information about what they don't know and how teachers can help them learn it; and illuminates places where a small, strategic system change can make a big difference. (Scharff et al., 2010, p. 58)

To gain a clearer picture of the practices (knowledge, skill, dispositions) of the adult professional learning community in the school, teams analyze the results of CLEE's Learning Community Survey (LCS; Braun et al., 2015). The LCS measures the perception of staff on the degree to which the Core Leadership Practices are pervasively implemented. A high degree of implementation of these practices is strongly correlated with an increase in student learning, especially for the focal group (Braun et al., 2020). MMS administered the LCS at the beginning of each school year to determine the key areas they needed to focus on to improve the adult learning community to impact the instructional core area for their focal group and peer group.

Along with empathy interviews that team members conducted with students in their equity focal group, the LCS results also informed the fishbone root cause analysis CLEE facilitated teams through to articulate possible reasons for the inequity. In conducting this analysis, CLEE protocols require teams to delimit root causes to those inside the instructional core. Doing so keeps teams focused on areas that are within their influence. For MMS, this process was key in helping them see the interconnectedness of SEL, academic learning, and the school climate. The MMS team identified the following root causes:

- students and teachers unintentionally have low expectations for the focal group because teachers prioritize SEL/supporting students emotionally over academic content;
- there are no consistent systems in place to review student IEP goals or to share and implement best practices among colleagues to align and stay on track with content;
- what students know and/or are able to do does not align with state standards, so grades/levels in school are not an accurate reflection of student current ability;
- teachers may not have the training on how to effectively use data to engage students with special needs and scaffolding to support the needs of all students; and
- students are not in environments where they have opportunities to lead or advocate for their learning and content is not scaffolded and differentiated to meet their needs.

Plan–Do–Study–Act (PDSA) Cycles

By setting direction collectively, the SCT network solidified its shared purpose, built a common vocabulary, and generated a camaraderie between cross-district teams to learn with and from each other as a networked improvement community. The MMS away-team members trained the home team members in using the processes and tools they learned during network days. Together, the two MMS teams engaged in drilling down to the specifics of their PDSA cycles during school-based coaching sessions supported by a CLEE coach. The MMS team used the Core Leadership Practices of Setting Direction, Building Capacity to Teach, and Monitoring Progress in their PDSA cycles. The team theorized that, in order to impact school climate for students, they needed to start with adult culture. They drew a connection between their first root cause (see the earlier discussion) and the adult culture in their school. Thus, the MMS team led a schoolwide PDSA cycle to develop a shared understanding of (a) why school climate is integral to student learning, (b) SEL standards, and (c) the integration of SEL and the instructional core. To accomplish this, the MMS SCT team used a faculty meeting to share the reasons for focusing on the equity focal group, including disaggregated student learning data, the big-picture context of the SCT grant focus, and their roles in the work. They then spotlighted Rhode Island's SEL Standard 1: Self-Awareness and engaged teams of teachers in collaboratively exploring "I Can" statements for the standard and then producing their own examples of what Self-Awareness I Can statements look like in their classrooms. Student team members Justin and Rozaria were each paired with a faculty member in leading table conversations. Having the authentic leadership of students in the work focused adult conversations on assets rather than deficits and brought a user's perspective that is often missing when designing improvements. To measure the impact of this first PDSA, the MMS team designed and administered a survey as their practical measure:

1. How well did we meet the goals of our meeting today? (scale 1–5)
2. What is one hope you have for this work (i.e., integrating SEL and academic standards)?
3. What is one area you would like further support in as you think about next steps?
4. Anything else you want to share with us?

The results of this survey informed their next PDSA cycle, which focused on using the Core Leadership Practices of Building Capacity to Teach and Building Capacity to Lead. Each team member facilitated colleagues to collaboratively plan lessons that integrated self-awareness into the instructional core during common planning time meetings. This was a further evolution of the change idea, or an adaptation, based on the results of practical measure. Student members Justin and Rozaria then each took a leadership role in rolling out the lessons during classes to their peers, helping students understand the importance of SEL as it connects to academic learning. Throughout the improvement process, the MMS team returned to update their root causes. As the teams lead the process, new insights were formed, and these key learnings were integrated into the team's evolving understanding of root causes.

Teams then shared their learning from PDSA cycles with the entire SCT network. The MMS team's learning became the SCT network's learning, and the network's learning became MMS's learning. Over time, with intentional design in tapping the expertise of the group, CLEE built the collective capacity of the group in leading complex change.

Lessons Learned for Increasing Equity in Schools

MMS is still in the early stages of leading this multiyear initiative. Yet, convening a network in which the expertise is constructed by and derived from the group, when done well, can yield positive results even in the early stages. Because of the abrupt shift to distance learning in the 2019–2020 school year, school teams were not able collect end-of-year student achievement data. However, in the fall of 2020, each team administered the LCS to its adult learning community. MMS's Year 2 LCS results (Table 17.3) showed growth across every single Core Leadership Practice amid a global pandemic.

Table 17.3. Edward R. Martin Middle School Learning Community Survey Means by Core Leadership Practice Over 1 Year

	Fall 2019 $N = 55$	**Fall 2020** $N = 45$	**Growth**
Setting Direction	2.92	3.15	.23
Monitoring Progress	2.87	2.97	.10
Building Capacity to Teach	3.34	3.39	.05
Building Capacity to Collaborate	3.11	3.24	.13
Building Capacity to Lead	2.72	2.89	.17
Reorganizing Systems	2.87	2.98	.11

Note: Scale is 1 = *Strongly Disagree*, 2 = *Disagree*, 3 = *Agree*, and 4 = *Strongly Agree.*

MMS team member Colleen Murphy reflected on how their work set them up for success in an especially trying time:

> And I can say that, you know, with a small period of time . . . the school totally evolved in and changed. And we wouldn't have gotten through the pandemic in the spring if it wasn't for the work that we did with CLEE. So . . . I'm excited about the future.

Key learnings are listed in Table 17.4 with their corresponding Core Leadership Practice. Although the learning was exemplified in the MMS experience, these lessons can be used to replicate a wide range of teams, schools, and networks in efforts to use improvement science to increase equity.

In holding students and equitable outcomes at the center of their work, and in implementing Core Leadership Practices to drive transformational change in the instructional core and school climate simultaneously, the MMS team advanced their learning and leading toward the network aim. In the words of student team member, Justin,

> When I went to CLEE, I regained a sense of confidence that I had lost with growing up and maturing and becoming a teenager and being exposed to the world. And so when I went to CLEE and I found out that people really care about things; they really care about my

opinions and they will listen . . . that gave me a sense of confidence. And so now that I'm in high school . . . that confidence has kind of transferred now. . . . I'm confident enough to take harder courses. I'm confident enough to expand my horizons within learning.

Table 17.4. Key Learning in Leading Improvement for Equity by Center for Leadership and Educational Equity (CLEE) Core Leadership Practice

Practice	Key Learning	Quotes from Edward R. Martin Middle School (MMS) Team Members
Setting Direction	(a) Compose teams with varied members and clear roles, including district and school leadership who participate and make room for others to lead (d) Create a clear aim to increase equity for a focal group of students who have been underserved to motivate urgency and purpose, even in a pandemic.	We (students and staff) came up with the agenda that everyone had a different role of presenting and involving the entire faculty. (MMS guidance counselor, Colleen Murphy) The principal wanted to make sure that all grades and all disciplines were heard from . . . all those voices heard. (MMS department coordinator, Pamela Thacker)
Building the Capacity to Teach	(a) Make deep connections between academic and social emotional learning (b) Use the expertise in the network and with network partners to build the instructional capacity of the team	I learned to acknowledge any biases that I have . . . and to try to understand that . . . and how my own self management skills affect what I look like as a teacher . . . incorporate those into my class. (MMS department coordinator, Pamela Thacker) . . . to have that input and bring that strength to the team (MMS educator, Amanda Rapoza)
Monitoring Progress	(a) Have a data point person to accelerate the communication between the school and facilitators, and create a stronger use of data (b) Focus efforts to build capacity around practical measurements to ensure team sees the impact of their change ideas, learn and keep the momentum	It is about school improvement, increasing equity, and the strong data use. Using this learning and this work to fuel our future here, because I think it's ever, it's always changing. (MMS Dean of Students, Mia Millea)
Reorganizing Systems	(a) Carve out and protect time for the team to collaborate and lead the work during staff meetings and Common Planning Times (b) Integrate improvement science methods into existing systems (e.g., multitiered system of supports, common planning) for sustainability	I think it was really powerful when the two teams came together and [the] administration gave us the go-ahead to plan the faculty meetings. (MMS guidance counselor, Colleen Murphy) We could also use those protocols and we were the role models for how to use them. . . . And then we can all go back and do that to the full faculty. (MMS educator, Pamela Thacker)

Practice	Key Learning	Quotes from Edward R. Martin Middle School (MMS) Team Members
Building the Capacity to Collaborate	(a) Create group norms for learning (b) Use Learning Community Survey to determine strengths and needs in the adult learning community (c) Adapt collaboration tools (e.g., moving to all virtual sessions) to maintain participant engagement in constructive and highly collaborative learning	Taking it slow, trusting the process and going through these protocols. (MMS department coordinator, Pamela Thacker) CLEE has strengthened our social skills as well. Those exercises that we would do, we would have to interact and engage and have conversations with people that we didn't know or never met before. So now I find myself talking to people that I've never met like we've been acquaintances for a long time. (MMS student, Justin)
Building the Capacity to Lead	(a) Develop leadership and facilitation skills with adults and students (b) Organize teams to share leadership and accelerate implementation (i.e., away and home teams)	We were like leading the group. As students, we have our own way of looking at things. So they would come to us and say, Hey, I have an idea [what] do you think as a student, if you saw this, how would it influence you? And me, I would give my honest opinion. (MMS student, Rozaria) This awesome team worked so very hard to be so inclusive and thoroughly think through the process and protocol of how they're going to . . . elevate student voice. You can see the end result, which is just students as leaders in this building (Director of Multilingual Learners, Yanaiza Gallant)

Leading for high and equitable outcomes in student learning involves meeting both adaptive and technical challenges. By starting with small changes focused on increasing equity, building shared leadership, and enacting Core Leadership Practices while using the tools of improvement science, the MMS team laid strong foundations for the ongoing complex work of leading school climate transformation.

Discussion Questions

1. Given your context, how could you create the conditions for centering voices that have historically been ignored or undervalued in improvement efforts?
2. Which students would you include in a focal group to improve your understanding of an equity issue in your setting? Who might you be missing?

3. What questions could you ask students to more deeply understand how the school's climate is not serving them well and what could be improved?
4. What data sources, in addition to focal group answers, could you use to more deeply understand the root causes of the problem of practice in your setting?

References

Braun, D., Gable, R., & Billups, F. D. (2015). *Learning community survey validity and reliability study*. https://docs.google.com/document/d/1dyr6_p6gNSNpDq3bAR EehBmqy_276EjLNpvl9WZe2qQ/edit

Braun, D., Gable, R., & Billups, F. D. (2017). Leadership practices to increase equity through closing intraschool achievement gaps. *Journal of Educational Leadership and Policy Studies, 1*(1), 44–63. https://files.eric.ed.gov/fulltext/EJ12 26950.pdf

Braun, D., Billups, F., Gable, R., LaCroix, K., & Mullen, B. (2021) Improving equitable student outcomes: A Transformational and collaborative leadership development approach. *Journal of Educational Leadership and Policy Studies, 5*(1/2). Retrieved from: https://go.southernct.edu/jelps/files/2021-spring-volume5-issue1/2-Improving-Equitable-Student-Outcomes-A-Transformational-and-Collaborative-Leadership-Development-Approach.pdf

Breidenstein, A., Fahey, K., Glickman, C., & Hensley, F. (2012). *Leading for powerful learning: A guide for instructional leaders*. Teachers College Press.

CampbellJones, F., CampbellJones, B., & Lindsey, R. B. (2010). *The cultural proficiency journey: Moving beyond ethical barriers toward profound school change*. Corwin.

Center for Leadership and Educational Equity. (2020a). *Equity statement*. https://docs.google.com/document/d/1eOWHnio4Hg8Q25DQkp99uxZtHElcLPFQW5 GpAqYqTpo/edit

Center for Leadership and Educational Equity. (2020b). *CLEE-Hub: Thirty minute ATLAS protocol*. https://docs.google.com/document/d/1d4rSMJCU973cY0J-DJXNx7iX3JVe7ppA5Vbk1YRdGYE/edit

Duhigg, C. (2014). *The power of habit: Why we do what we do in life and business*. Random House.

Edward R. Martin Middle School. (2019). *Application to Rhode Island Department of Education for the School Climate Transformation network* [Unpublished document]. Center for Leadership and Educational Equity; Providence, Rhode Island.

Elmore, R. (2004). *School reform from the inside out: Policy, practice, and performance*. Harvard Education Press.

Hammond, Z. L. (2014). *Culturally responsive teaching and the brain: Promoting authentic engagement and rigor among culturally and linguistically diverse students*. Corwin.

Leithwood, K., Seashore Louis, K., Anderson, S., & Wahlstrom, K. (2004). *How leadership influences student learning*. Wallace Foundation. http://www.wallacefoundation. org/.../0/ReviewofResearchLearningFromLeadership.pdf

Rhode Island Department of Education. (2019). *Edward R. Martin Middle School, 2018–19 report card*. https://reportcard.ride.ri.gov/201819/SchoolAccountability? SchCode=10109&DistCode=10

Scharff, H. A., DeAngelis, D. A., & Talbert, J. E. (2010, April). Starting small for big school improvement. *Principal Leadership, 10*(8), 58–61.

School Reform Initiative. (2020). *Atlas: Looking at Data protocol*. http://www.school reforminitiative.org/doc/atlas_looking_data.pdf

Sustaining One Another While Leading Equity-Focused Improvement Science Efforts

DEBORAH S. PETERSON

As we work to improve our nation's schools, we need to ensure that what we do in our classrooms and schools helps children of every racial, ethnic, linguistic, socioeconomic, gender, and ability background succeed. We need to ensure we are elevating and affirming our nation's children, their families, our schoolteachers, and our leaders as they have made it their life mission to create a better future for each child in our care.

For too long we have left too many behind, particularly our children who are Black, who are Brown, who are recent immigrants, who live in poverty, and whose manifestation of diversity is somehow deemed less worthy of an education. Our hope for each child in our communities is that the success we yearn to ensure for our own precious family members, we also commit to providing for the children in every family.

In this book, the authors have shared improvement science processes and tools that have increased systems that promote equity in their classrooms and schools. They have shared how a change idea might have worked in one context and yet not in another. They have shared their data and how the data informed their work. They have shared how they adapted, adopted, or abandoned change ideas. And they have shared how they worked together with students, families, and community partners to ensure their improvements helped children who had not yet been well served, despite their best intentions and efforts. Becoming skilled in leading such system changes is a critical characteristic of social justice school leaders; improvement science tools and processes provide the resources for leading these efforts while including the voices of teachers, leaders, and, in particular, historically underserved students, families, and the community.

I want to also emphasize the importance of sustaining the spirit of our courageous teachers and leaders as they lead equity-focused improvement science efforts. In Peterson (2014), I proposed a theory for sustaining the human spirit of social justice leaders. The theory complements key components of the sustainability movement. I expand on the theory here to fold in improvement science concepts, as well as concepts from several social justice heroes (Bell, 2016; Crenshaw, 1991; Darder, 2002; Frattura & Capper, 2007; Freire, 1997; Gay, 2010; Ladson-Billings, 1994; Nieto, 2006; Noguera, 2008; Tatum, 1997). I encourage equity-focused improvement science leaders to affirm the human dignity and human spirit of every child, family member, colleague, teacher, leader, and community member as they implement equity-focused improvement science efforts in their schools.

1. Create sustainable processes that honor the human dignity of those who are impacted by decisions, with an intentional focus on enhancing the spirit of those historically harmed or ignored by our schooling system.
2. Engage in culturally responsive care for ourselves, those whom we serve, and those with whom we work.
3. Ensure that we know how the intersectionality of our unique cultural background impacts our decisions and others.
4. Honor ourselves, and those around us, as precious humans with great potential, and when our improvement efforts succeed, honor the contributors and expand the effort. When we fail, let's learn from the failure without shame or blame and then adapt or abandon our effort.
5. Engage in work that builds on our strengths and ensure others' strengths are celebrated and utilized to the benefit of the orga-

nization and the individual, in particular those whom we have historically harmed, underserved, or ignored.

6. Solicit perspectives from those whose roles, expertise, experience, age, gender, race, ethnicity, religion, sexual identity, sexual orientation, or any manifestation of diversity that the dominant culture or our own cultural background has harmed or marginalized.

7. Strive to reach consensus using data, and when we can't, let's reexamine disaggregated data, and encourage those with the authority to make decisions to critically assess who has the power to make the decision, what the data reveal, how decisions advantage or disadvantage groups of individuals, and whether the group has been historically impacted negatively or positively by the dominant culture in our communities, organizations, and nation based on our data.

8. Express gratitude regularly for the people, processes, and systems that are working, even while recognizing that there is much more work to do.

9. Believe that conflict can result in deepened understandings of ourselves, our relationship with one another, and our aspirations—we affirm and enhance the dignity of every person while in conflict.

10. Sustain our own spirit and the spirit of others so that we each have the hope, clarity of vision, and courage to do challenging work, in complex organizations and in tumultuous times, to create a more just and equitable society.

The concepts, experiences, tools, and resources provided by our authors who have successfully used improvement science provide a pathway to improve the outcomes for every child, in every school, in every community. Let's start now! Our children are counting on us.

References

Bell, L. A. (2016). Theoretical foundations for social justice education. In M. Adams & L. A. Bell (Eds.), *Teaching for diversity and social justice* (pp. 3–26). Routledge.

Crenshaw, K. (1991). Mapping the margins: Intersectionality, identity politics, and violence against women of color. *Stanford Law Review, 43*(6), 1241–1299. https://doi.org/10.2307/1229039

Darder, A. (2002). *Reinventing Paulo Freire: A pedagogy of love.* Westview Press.

Frattura, E., & Capper, C. (2007). *Leadership for social justice: Transforming schools for all learners.* Corwin.

Freire, P. (1997). *Pedagogy of the oppressed.* Continuum Publishing.

Gay, G. (2010). *Culturally responsive teaching: Theory, research, and practice.* Teachers College Press.

Ladson-Billings, G. (1994). *The dreamkeepers: Successful teachers of African-American children.* Jossey-Bass.

Nieto, S. (2006). Solidarity, courage and heart: What teacher educators can learn from a new generation of teachers. *Intercultural Education, 17*(5), 457–473. https://doi.org/10.1080/14675980601060443

Noguera, P. (2008). *The trouble with Black boys and other reflections on race, equity and the future of public education.* Jossey-Bass.

Peterson, D. S. (2014). A missing piece in the sustainability movement: The human spirit. *Sustainability: The Journal of Record, 7*(2), 74–77. https://doi.org/10.1089/SUS.2014.9810

Tatum, B. (1997). *Why are all the Black kids sitting together in the cafeteria: And other conversations about race.* Basic Books.

ABOUT THE AUTHORS

Deborah S. Peterson, EdD is Associate Professor Emerita at Portland State University. With degrees from the University of Washington, University of Oregon, Portland State University, and Lewis and Clark College, Dr. Peterson has led numerous equity-focused school improvement efforts in school and district roles in the Pacific Northwest and has published in several journals and made numerous presentations throughout the United States and internationally on topics related to leadership, equity, and diversity. Receiving numerous grants and awards for her equity-focused scholarship, she, with research partner Susan Carlile, recently focused on the experiences of successful female leaders in law, medicine, government, business, technology, and engineering and the perceptions of men regarding the barriers and supports to their success.

Susan P. Carlile has over 50 years of experience in K–12 education as a teacher, a middle and high school principal, a director of curriculum, and instruction for a large, suburban school district near Portland, Oregon. As a professor of practice and program lead for the Educational Leadership and Policy Program, she has facilitated the leadership development of more than 600 school leaders, received 18 grants for her work, and presented and published in dozens of state, national, and international forums of leadership. Susan Carlile has a BA in English and fine arts from the University of California, Berkeley; an MA in curriculum and instruction, a leadership certification from the University of Oregon, and graduate work in education at the University of Washington and Harvard University.

Folusho B. Abayomi, EdD, is a school administrator based in Ontario, Canada. She received her EdD in educational leadership from the University of Western Ontario. Prior to becoming an administrator, she was a lead teacher in inner-city schools overseeing special education processes and fostering a culture of shared leadership and collaborative inquiry. Her research interests are effective parental engagement, educational leadership, and the utilization of collective teacher efficacy in closing achievement gaps for traditionally underserved students. She is passionate about school community engagement and challenging historical forms of oppression and marginalization in school systems. Folusho and her husband, Charles, have two children.

Emily Anderson has taught business, student leadership, and math at the high school level while also coaching several athletic teams, in addition to teaching math and serving as instructional coach at the middle school level. Currently serving as the dean of middle school students, Emily's passion for equity and instruction has provided opportunities for her to work closely with the district leadership team to create and implement a multitiered intervention program that focuses on the academic, social, and emotional needs of every student. In addition, she has used improvement science in her district to focus on family education and interventions around attendance. She lives in Portland, Oregon, with her wife and three children.

Bryce Bennett has more than 16 years of experience working in public education, including teaching at the high school and university level, coaching at the middle and high school level, serving as a high school counselor and assistant principal. He is passionate about improving the lives of our youth by building relationships, leading culturally responsive systems, and developing teams where the members feel valued, accepted, and encouraged.

Kileen Birmingham, MS, is a licensed school psychologist working as a teacher on special assignment, consulting and coaching special education teams, administration and building staff. She has worked in the field of education for 19 years in a variety of roles supporting youth and those who educate them. As a consultant, she is a passionate advocate for equitable education and sees her role and the role of her colleagues as pivotal in creating lasting change for this generation and generations to come. Improvement science has been key to that work and made evident through recent research considering psychoeducational evaluations during the COVID pandemic and the reduction of disproportionate eligibility decisions for students of color.

Landon Brown, a native of Atlanta, Georgia, currently serves as the director of school quality (DSQ) for National Heritage Academies. He has worked in public education for 23 years at the elementary, middle, and high school levels. Often viewed as an energetic servant leader, Dr. Brown has led school turnaround efforts and was named the Ohio Alliance of Public Charter Schools Leader of the Year. Dr. Brown received his BSEd in middle childhood education from Georgia State University, MEd in middle grades education from Mercer University, and his EdD in educational leadership from Youngstown State University. He enjoys working with school leaders to embrace the huge impact leadership has on creating successful schools. In his current DSQ role, he is leading school improvement efforts in urban Louisiana schools.

Victoria Brown earned a BA in Spanish from Portland State University, an MAT in teaching from George Fox University, and administrative licensure in Oregon. She has been a dual language educator for 7 years and has taught kindergarten, second, and third grades and is now serving as assistant principal. In addition, she has been the facilitator and coordinator for professional learning and behavior intervention in her building. Nominated for the All Means All award, she has rooted her work in ensuring equity for historically underserved students through addressing systems of oppression in public education.

Ryan Carpenter currently serves as the superintendent for the Estacada School District (Oregon). While he has served as superintendent, the Estacada School District has also received accolades for organizational excellence. In 2020, the Estacada School District was honored as one of only 19 school districts in the United States to be recognized as a Model PLC District by Solution Tree. Estacada Schools also achieved the highest honors from its employees and in 2020 was selected for *The Oregonian*'s Top Workplaces in the State of Oregon. For 6 consecutive years, Estacada High School has also been recognized as a "Top High School" by *US News and World Reports*. Carpenter is also a published author in several national journals and books.

Amie B. Cieminski, EdD, is an associate professor of educational leadership and policy studies at the University of Northern Colorado. Previously, she served as the director of professional learning and the director of secondary school leadership in a large public school district. Amie has worked in elementary and secondary schools as a teacher, assistant principal, and principal in diverse settings. She is involved in several organizations for professional learning and reviews school improvement plans for the Colorado Department of Education. Dr. Cieminski earned her BA in Spanish education and Hispanic studies at St. Olaf College; her MA from California State University, San Bernardino; and her EdD from the University of Northern Colorado. Her research interests include leadership development, equity, school improvement, and instructional practices for leader development.

Susan Connolly is a language development consultant supporting districts in Washington State with multilingual/English learners. Her major areas of focus are students experiencing long-term English learner status and designing and implementing multitiered system of support for multilingual/English learners. She has previously worked as a professional development specialist as well as in higher education in teacher preparation.

Bill Eagle has been a teacher, an instructional coach, a principal, and a federal programs director. He currently serves as the associate director of student success and learning for the North Central Educational Service District.

Benjamin Hargrave is the principal at Estacada Middle School in Estacada, Oregon. As an educational leader, Ben follows evidence-based leadership strategies to strengthen staff capacity when practicing DuFour Model PLCs, supporting the inclusion of all learners, implementing restorative discipline practices, and developing the school's intervention models. Ben's leadership actions are problem-specific, solution-oriented, and supported with evidence.

Teresa Kennedy, PhD, is a professor of bilingual science, technology, engineering, and mathematics (STEM) education. She focuses on equity, ESL, and bilingual education. She is a member of the UTeach STEM teacher preparation faculty and graduate faculty member for the ED in school improvement in the School of Education. She also serves as the executive secretary for the UNESCO nongovernmental organization Liaison Committee. Her research interests include bilingual education, early language acquisition, phenomenon-based learning, and equity in STEM education. Dr. Kennedy holds a PhD in education from the University of Idaho.

Toby King is the founder of Improving Outcomes for All, a consulting firm that supports districts and schools as they make systemic changes for improved results for all of the students they serve. As a teacher and a school leader, Toby ensured each of his students had access to the support they needed so that they could be independent and successful.

Ryan McCarty, PhD is an assistant professor in reading and language at National Louis University (NLU) in Chicago, Illinois, where he runs the North Shore Summer Reading Improvement Program. Prior to his time at NLU, he served as a literacy coordinator, a coach, and a teacher in Chicago Public Schools and the suburbs. He also coached principals with a national nonprofit in western Massachusetts. Dr. McCarty's recent research examines disciplinary literacy, argument writing, and helping multilingual students excel in advanced coursework. He also studies digital inquiry and is a faculty member of the Summer Institute in Digital Literacy, an award-winning professional development program. His work has been published in literacy journals and book chapters. An expert in design-based research, he is the chair-elect of the Formative Experiment and Design-Based Research Innovative Community Group of the Literacy Research Association. He regularly partners with area school districts to provide professional development and support.

Dr. Gloria McDaniel-Hall currently serves as an assistant professor in the Educational Leadership Department at National Louis University in Chicago. She is also a senior curriculum and instruction specialist with National Heritage Academies Schools, a national charter school company. She has been an elementary school teacher, principal, and director during her 35-year tenure as an educator. All her experiences have centered on urban education. She is passionate about the fact that education is the human rights issue of our time. She has devoted her life to equity for all members of the school community. She holds a BA from the University of Illinois in elementary education, an MBA from the University of Illinois with a focus on marketing and human resources, an MA from Concordia University in educational leadership, and an EdD in educational leadership from Concordia University.

Kristine J. Melloy, PhD, is an experienced classroom special education teacher, data and instructional coach, high school principal, teacher educator, and educational leader educator. Her research includes studies related to students with disabilities and preparation of educational leaders to provide effective educational services in inclusive school environments.

Thomas Lee Morgan, PhD, is the director of inclusive teaching and an assistant professor in educational leadership at Sacred Heart University. As a critical scholar, he enacts a P–20 focus on equitable education through the lens of diversity and inclusion. He has experience as a teacher, a school leader, and a district leader in various settings, including in private, charter, and public schools at the elementary, middle, and high school levels across the United States. He also has experience serving students and families from diverse socioeconomic and cultural backgrounds. Dr. Morgan specializes in social-emotional learning, social justice leadership, culturally responsive pedagogy, and school improvement.

Greg Nelson lives in Portland, Oregon, with his wife and three young children. Greg has served in many roles, including principal intern, special education teacher, emotional growth center teacher, behavioral coach, and student manager. He has an immense passion for serving students and their families and is a strong advocate for teaching and nurturing the whole child (social/emotional as well academically). Greg has contributed to his district's response to the 2020 COVID-19 pandemic, ensuring the needs of each student and their families are met.

Michael Odell, PhD, is a professor of science, technology, education, and mathematics (STEM) education and holds the Sam and Celia Roosth Chair in the College of Education and Psychology. He holds appointments in the School of Education and the College of Engineering. He is the cofounder of the University Academy Laboratory School District and serves on the school board. He is also a member of the Texas STEM Coalition. He provides technical assistance and coaching to turnaround schools. He is the codirector of the UTeach STEM Teacher Preparation program and the codirector of the EdD in School Improvement Program. His research interests are education policy, sustainable education, project-based learning, school improvement, and STEM education. Dr. Odell holds a PhD in curriculum and instruction from Indiana University.

Dr. Kathleen Oropallo's educational and leadership experience spans more than 35 years across K–12, higher education, and the state, where she has helped schools and organizations achieve results that last. Her unique work experience with improvement crosses public, private, and nonprofit educational sectors as she partners with organizations seeking to develop organizational excellence and systemic change. Currently, as a leader coach with Studer Education, she continues to collaborate with organizations throughout the country as a valuable thought partner and trusted advisor. Her work also includes leadership development, designing and facilitating webinars and roundtables on a variety of topics such as continuous improvement, the science of improvement, organizational excellence, evidence-based leadership, organizational resilience, and building a culture around improvement.

Dr. Brian Rahaman is an educational leader who has devoted his career to school improvement. He has worked in or supported urban schools in Baltimore, Chicago, Philadelphia, and Washington, D.C., among other places. Brian currently serves as head of school in an urban charter high school in Washington, DC. In addition to leading a high school, Brian is also a consultant who specializes in school improvement and developing better instructional programs.

Joanna Carrillo Rowley, M.Ed., has served in numerous administrative positions including principal, assistant principal, and executive director of bilingual/ESL and is engaged in evaluating school improvement based on improvement science principles to embed the work in her organization. She holds a masters degree from the University of Texas at the Permian Basin. She began her career as an elementary teacher and her experience has predominantly been at Title I schools..

James Sanders, PsyD, is the assistant director of student services, overseeing special education, mental health, and social-emotional learning, and behavior for the Lake Oswego School District. He has been actively supporting students with disabilities for more than 20 years as a licensed psychologist, holding a doctorate in clinical psychology, with specializations in educational, pediatric, and developmental psychology. James is inspired to help others view behavior in the same light as a learning disability, a skill deficit that can be remedied through thoughtful personal relationships and a sense of safety, furthering rapid neurodevelopment and skill acquisition. More recently, James has been utilizing improvement science to help resolve disparities in equity associated with psychoeducational evaluation of students for special services during the COVID pandemic.

Cassandra Thonstad began her teaching career in 2005, serving as a high school math teacher for over a decade and an instructional coach for 4 years in North Clackamas and Newberg School Districts. In addition, she has taught at Portland Community College, George Fox University, and Portland State University. She has led work for proficiency-based grading across the state of Oregon and has led improvement science work in her current district since 2015. Cassandra is driven by a passion for the PK–12 school system and uses improvement science with an equity focus that challenges staff and students to change the trajectory of learners to meet their maximum potential while honoring each student's experience in the classroom.

Jeffrey R. Waters is a community justice advocate, educator, and school administrator who lives and works in Portland, Oregon. He was named a 2019 Mental Health Hero for his work on the Keep Oregon Well campaign and has previously published works about teaching the history of race, racism, and gentrification to middle schoolers in North Portland. His work centers student perception and seeks to empower communities toward agency, collective efficacy, and continuous improvement.

INDEX

7 Cs, 245

A
absenteeism, chronic, 67–68, 91–92
    Also see attendance, Eventide School
        District
academic success, definition, 132, 137
Accountable Talk, 81
Achenbach System of Empirically Based
        Assessment (ASEBA), 208
adverse childhood experiences (ACE),
        47, 53
advisory programs, high school, 131, 132
    Also see South High School
affinity surveys, 214
Aguilar, E., 169, 172, 183
aim statements, 72–74, 161–62
Allen, R.A., 208
Allensworth, E.M., 151, 152
Alvarez, L., 135, 136
Anti-Defamation League, 235
Aspen Institute, 11
assessment website, 211
Atlas Looking at Data, 280
attendance, increasing student, 81–82,
        86–87
    Also see absenteeism, Staytonville
        Middle School
Attendance Matters, 93
August, D., 170
Austin Independent School District, 37
AVID Demonstration School, 131, 143,
        147
AVID practices, 237

B
Baker, T.L., 31
Baltimore Education Research
        Consortium, 92
Bandura, A., 51
Banerjee, M., 208
Bateman, D., 191, 195
Beeman, K., 182
behavior intervention plans (BIP), 124
Behavior Assessment Scale for Children
        2 (BASC-2), 208
Bell, L.A., 4, 292
Biag, M., 12
bilingualism, 173

biliteracy, 173
Black, W., 274
Blood, P., 30, 32
Boyes-Watson, C., 36
Bradley, B.A., 2
Braun, D., 277, 282
Breidenstein, A., 280
Brown, L., 239, 241, 244, 245, 246, 250
Bryk, A.S., 1, 2, 5, 6, 32, 50, 106, 116, 118,
        159, 167, 189, 191, 196, 239, 243
Building Capacity to Lead, 275, 285
Building Capacity to Teach, 284, 285

C
CampbellJones, F., 277
Capital High School, 151–52
    aim statement and, 161–62
    context of, 152–53
    data collection and, 157–59
    data interpretation, 159, 160–61
    diagnostic process, 157
    improvement science and, 153–63
    improvement team at, 153–55
    improvement team charter, 156–57
    increasing equity at, 165–68
    measuring improvement at, 163–65
    PDSA cycles and, 156
    problem of practice at, 153
    testing diagnosis at, 162–63
    Also see on-track rates
Capper, C., 69, 70, 83, 122, 205, 206, 292
care and connection, 56
Carlile, S.P., 2, 6, 7, 104
Carpenter, R., 48, 53
CASEL.org, 52, 197
CAST, 197
Center for Leadership and Educational
        Equity (CLEE), 271, 276, 280,
        286, 287
    Atlas Looking at Data, 280
    Core Leadership Practices and, 274,
        277, 278, 279, 280, 281, 282, 284,
        286, 287, 288
    improvement methodology and, 274
    keystone areas of improvement, 281
    Learning Community Survey and,
        282
    School Climate Transformation and,
        273, 274, 275, 278

Setting Directions, 277, 284
Also see Martin Middle School
Centers for Disease Control and
    Prevention, 53
Central High School, 189
Central Washington School District
    (CWSD), 172–73
    driver diagrams and, 176–77
    empathy interviews and, 174–75,
        175–76, 177–78
    five-whys and, 174
    ideas for change at, 177–78
    ongoing improvement at, 181–82
    problem of teaching long-term
        English learners, 174–81
    testing idea at, 178–79
    Also see long-term English learners
Chafouleas, S., 15
CHAMPS Classroom Management
    system, 232
change ideas, 106–8, 109–10
Character Strong curriculum, 143, 148,
    149
check-in, check-out (CICO) system, 124,
    125, 126, 128
Child Find, 215, 216, 217, 218
Cieminski, A.B., 11
Circle Forward, 36
Clark-Louque, A.R., 240, 241, 245, 246
Clawson, K., 33
Cline, J., 191, 195
clustering, 194, 195
collaboration, 1, 51
Collaborative for Academic, Social, and
    Emotional Learning (CASEL),
    36, 52
Collaborative Problem Solving (CPS)
    strategies, 110, 118
collective efficacy, 51
collective responsibility, 246–48
collective teacher efficacy, 51, 52
Collie, R.J., 13
Collier, V.P., 170
Common Core, 136
communication, 248–50
compassion calls, 58
comprehensive distance learning (CDL),
    204, 215, 218
Consortium on School Research, 151
    attendance rates at, 38, 39
    building relationships for
        improvement, 31–32

count of suspensions and expulsions
    at, 40
discipline counts at, 38, 39, 43
do phase at, 34–38
improvement team at, 24
literature review for improvement,
    30
networked improvement
    communities and, 24, 27–28
opportunity gaps and, 25–27, 40, 41
plan-do-study-act (PDSA) cycles and,
    28–42
plan phase and, 28–30
problem-/project-based (PrBL/PBL)
    model at, 24–25, 27
restorative practices at, 33–34
retention rates at, 38, 41, 43
social-emotional learning at, 32
student demographics at, 26–27
study phases at, 38–42
teacher demographics at, 25
continuous improvement, 192–98
Core Leadership Practices, 274, 277,
    278, 279, 280, 281, 282, 284,
    285, 286, 287, 288
Cornell, D., 32
Correnti, R., 16
Council of Chief State School Officers, 52
Crenshaw, K., 292
Crow, R., 2, 3, 6, 209, 243, 244
Crowder, M., 11
culturally responsive family
    engagement. *See* family
    engagement
culturally responsive practices, 113, 114,
    118
culturally responsive teaching practices,
    117, 136
Culture of Care, 68
Cummins, M., 241

D
Darder, A., 292
data-driven dialogue, 174
Deal, T.E., 12
DeHartchuck, L., 189
design-based research, 2
design team, 24
disabilities, students with, 185
    clustering and, 194, 195
    inclusive schools and, 190
    least restrictive environments (LRE)
        and, 188

do phases, 34–38
Domitrovich, C., 25
Donohoo, J., 51
Donahue, C., 2
driver diagrams, 34, 35, 72–74, 94, 139,
176–77, 209, 210, 211, 278, 279
DuFour model, 48
Duhigg, C., 281
Durlak, J.A., 10, 11, 14, 30, 31

E
Eagle Elementary School (EES), 121
empathy interviews at, 123
improvement implementation
challenges, 127–29
improvement science team at, 122
need for improvement at, 122–23
testing improvement changes at,
124–27
theory of improvement and, 123–24
Easton, J.Q., 151, 152
Edmonds, B.C., 135
efficacy, 51, 106
Eisner, E.W., 51
Elmore, R.F., 49, 166, 277
ELS Dashboard, 59
Emerson Academy (ECA), 239, 251
communication with parents, 242
empathy interviews and, 241, 244–46,
250
improvement science and, 240–41,
242–50
student demographics, 241–42
empathy interviews, 3, 71, 89–91, 101,
112–13, 114, 123, 125, 134–35,
140, 174–75, 175–76, 177–78,
207–8, 241, 244–46, 250, 283
engagement continuum, 55
English Language Development (ELD)
services, 175
English language learners (ELL), 102,
108, 115–16, 135, 136
Also see long-term English learners,
multilingual/English learners
English Language Proficiency
Assessment (ELPA21), 174
equity, 5, 239–41, 291–93
academic success and, 135
definition, 5
increasing in schools, 165–68, 198–99,
285–88
long-term English learners and,
170–71
transformation of school culture and,
271–73
transformative SEL and, 19, 51–53
Also see family engagement, Martin
Middle School
equity audit, 69–71, 83–87, 103, 205
Equity Check, 213, 214, 215, 216, 217
Equity Elaborations, 52
equity-focused leadership, 77
Estacada Middle School, 48
care connections and, 56–58, 61–62
chronic absenteeism and, 60
Plan-Do-Study-Act cycles and, 49,
50–51
problems of practice and, 49–50
Spirit Week at, 62
vulnerable students, virtual schooling
and, 54–56
Estacada School District, 48–49
managing change at, 53–54
PDSA cycles at, 58–60
student demographics, 48
Eventide School District (ESD), 67–68
Evergreen Elementary School (EES),
67–68
improvement team at, 68–69
lessons learned from improvement,
77–78
need for improvement at, 69–72
student demographics, 70–71
testing improvement efforts at, 74–76
theory of improvement and, 72–74
Every Child Succeeds Act, 32
evidence-based leadership framework,
49, 53, 63

F
facilitative leadership, 271
family engagement, 239–41
definition of, 240
Federal Bureau of Investigation, 231
Fergus, E., 32
fishbone diagrams, 34, 35, 72, 92–94,
138, 159, 209, 210, 225
Fisher, D., 194
Five Whys, 3, 174, 244
Fixsen, D., 19
FLIGHT, 133, 134, 137, 140, 142, 143
Foote, J., 132
formative data, 1
Frattura, E.M., 69, 70, 83, 122, 205, 206,
292

free and appropriate public education
        (FAPE), 188, 190, 195
Freire, P., 292
functional behavior assessments (FBA),
        124, 126

G
Gallant, Y., 274
Gay, G., 118, 292
Gino, F., 231
Global Family Research Foundation, 240
Goldring, R., 9
Goodman, S., 190
Gregory, A., 32
Griffin, R., 241
Gwande, A., 3

H
Hahn, M., 34
Hall, G., 19
Hanchon, T.A., 208
Hammond, Z.L., 277
Hargrave, B., 48, 56–57, 59
hate crimes, 231
Hattie, J., 51
Heifez, R.A., 241
Hewitt, D.T., 30, 31
Hinnant-Crawford, B.N., 176
historically underserved students,
        serving during disasters, 47–48
Hobbs, M., 192
Hoffman, J.V., 2
Hord, S., 19
Hudson, E., 187, 192, 193, 196

I
Improvement Guide, The, 5, 167
improvement science (IS)
    aim statements and, 72–74, 161–62
    change ideas and, 106–8, 109–10
    collaboration and, 51
    driver diagrams and, 34, 35, 72–74, 139,
        176–77, 209, 210, 211, 278, 279
    efficacy and, 51
    empathy interviews and, 71, 89–91,
        101, 112–13, 114, 123, 125, 134,
        140, 174–75, 175–76, 177–78,
        207–8, 241, 244–46, 250, 283
    equity and, 2, 5, 292
    equity audits and, 69–71, 83–87, 103,
        205
fishbone diagrams and, 34, 35, 72,
        92–94, 138, 159, 209, 210, 225
    five whys and, 174, 244
    goals of, 50–51, 105–6, 155
    managing change and, 53–54
    networked improvement
        communities (NIC) and, 24,
        27–28
    plan-do-study-act (PDSA) cycles,
        28–42, 50–51, 58–60, 74–75,
        94–96, 108–9, 110–12, 112–13,
        113–15, 115–16, 124–25, 125–26,
        127–29, 133–39, 139–45, 178–79,
        192–98, 211–14, 232, 243,
        283–85
    problems of practice and, 49–50, 86,
        153, 189–92
    professional learning communities
        and, 48, 182
    six principles of, 50, 185–87
    social-emotional development and,
        15–16
    social justice orientation and, 2
    survey data and, 87–89
    tools used in, 13–16
    top down reform and, 50
inclusive schools, 190
individualized education plans (IEP),
        125, 189
Individuals with Disabilities
        Educational Improvement Act
        (IDEIA), 185, 188, 193
inquiry cycles, 1
internal accountability, 277
intervention programs, 121
    Also see Eagle Elementary School

J
Jagers, R.J., 11, 19, 51, 52, 61
Jung, L.A., 188, 190

K
Kindness Clubs, 17
Kindness in the Classroom Curriculum,
        14
Kindness Weeks, 17
Kozleski, E., 188
L
Ladson-Billings, G., 242, 292
Langley, G.J., 2, 5, 167, 244
leadership development, 271–72

Leading for Social Justice, 69
Learning Community Survey (LCS), 282, 283
Learning to Improve, 5, 167
least restrictive environments (LRE), 188, 190, 195
legacy, concept of, 226
LeMahieu, P.G., 10
Likert Scale, 228
Lipton, L., 174
long-term multilingual learners, 169–70
  equitable practices for, 170–71
  improvement science and, 171–72, 180–81
  understanding, 174–75
  Also see Central Washington School District, English language learners, multilingual/English learners
loose-tight model, 20

M
Malone, T., 136
March for Kindness, 15
Martin Middle School (MMS), 272–73
  Atlas Looking at Data and, 280
  climate and context of, 273–76
  COVID-19 pandemic and, 276
  demographics, 273
  driver diagrams and, 278, 279
  empathy interviews at, 283
  equity focus at, 277
  facilitative leadership and, 271
  improvement science tools and, 278–83
  increasing equity in, 285–88
  Learning Community Survey and, 282–83
  PDSA cycles at, 283–85
  problem of practice at, 277–78
  School Climate Transformation and, 273, 274, 275
McCarty, R., 239, 244, 245
McDaniel-Hall, G., 239, 241, 244, 245, 246
McFillen, J.M., 157, 160
McIntosh, K., 190
McLeskey, J., 189, 196
Mee, M., 34
Melloy, K.J., 188
Mendelson, T., 47

Merseth, K., 241
Milner, H.R., 26, 242
mindfulness suite, 36
Monitoring Progress, 284
Moore, C., 231
Morgan, T.L., 11
multilingual/English learners (m/EL), 169, 179, 182–83
multitiered instruction (MTI), 82
multitiered systems of support (MTSS), 190, 204
Murphy, C., 275, 286
Murry, F.R., 188

N
National Association for Family, School and Community Engagement, 240
Nauer, K., 72
Nelsestuen, K., 244
networked improvement communities (NIC), 24, 27–28
Nieto, S., 292
Nine Principles for Organizational Excellence, 53
No Child Left Behind, 136
No Place for Hate, 235
Noguera, P., 292
Nordstrum, L.E., 16
Northwest Evaluation Assessment-Measures of Academic Progress (NWEA-MAP), 242, 244

O
Ohio Department of Education, 241
Olsen, L., 170, 171
online assessments, 212–13
on-track rates, 151–52, 153–57, 157–63, 163–67, 167–68
  Also see Capitol High School
Oregon Department of Education, 132, 207
Orlo Elementary School, 274
Overstreet, C., 15

P
Parent Teacher Association, 241
Park, S., 196
Pastries with Parents, 242
Payton, J., 11, 14
perception checks, 210

Perry, J.A., 114
Peterson, D.S., 2, 6, 7, 12, 48, 104, 292
Pilcher, J., 53, 54
plan-do-study cycles, 14–16, 28–42, 49,
        50–51, 58–60, 74–76, 94–96,
        108–9, 110–12, 112–13, 115–16,
        124–25, 125–26, 127–29, 133–39,
        139–45, 178–79, 192–98, 211–14,
        232, 243, 283–85
Pogrow, S., 2
Portigal, S., 244
positive deviants, 3
power, student engagement and,
        221–23
    collaborative improvement, 231,
        232–33
    in a pandemic environment, 237
    pattern disruptions and, 232–34
    problem of engagement, 223–27
    racial equity strategic plan and, 235
    student advocacy and, 227
    student climate surveys and, 227–30,
        231, 233
    Student Leadership classes and,
        224–27
    student perception and, 227–30
    student voice statements, 235–36
    theory of action and, 231
Principal Residency Network, 274
problem-project-based models (PrBL/
        PBL), 24–25, 27, 41
problems of practice, 49–50, 86, 153,
        209
professional development, 147, 232
professional learning communities
        (PLC), 34, 58, 59, 60, 182
    DuFour model, 48
program review, 13–14
public schools
    as police states, 224
    systemic hierarchies and, 223
    turnaround models for, 23

Q
Quality Teaching for English Learners,
        136

R
racial equity strategic plan, 235
Random Act of Kindness (RAK), 15, 17,
        18, 19

Random Act of Kindness (RAK)
        Foundation, 14
Reinking, D., 2
relationship-focused tactics, 118
reliability, 207
resistance, 224
response-to-intervention (RTI), 82, 122,
        123, 124, 127, 190
Restart and Turnaround models, 24
restorative circles, 33
restorative practices (RPs), 29, 31,
        33–34, 41, 43, 51–53, 232
    campus-based, 36–37
    coaches, 37
Rhode Island Department of Education
        (RIDE), 273
Riddle, T., 30
RISE, 133
Rogers, T., 92
Rollins, S.P., 251
Romero, V., 122
root-cause analysis, 13, 209, 243, 284
Rother, M., 3
rounding, 54
Rowan, B., 16
Rural Middle School (RMS), 101
    change ideas at, 106–8, 109–10
    description of, 102
    empathy interviews and, 101, 112–13,
        114
    improvement team at, 105–6
    need for improvement at, 103–16
    problem of practice at, 101
    results of improvement, 116–17
    Also see student disciplinary referrals

S
Scharff, H.A., 282
School Climate Transformation (SCT),
        273, 274, 275, 278
School Culture Design Team, 34
School District of Philadelphia, 151
School District of Sunshine River
        (SDSR), 185–87
    improvement team at, 188–89
    improving equity in, 198–99
    PDSA cycles and, 192–98
    problem of practice at, 189–92
    Also see disabilities, students with
school exclusion, 31
school-to-prison pipeline, 4, 32

"self" concerns, 19
semi-structured interview format, 158
Sequoia Creek School District (SCSD),
    203–5, 215–18
  comprehensive distance learning
    and, 204
  demographics about, 203–4, 206
  empathy interviews at, 207–8
  equity audit at, 205–6
  implementation and challenges of IS
    at, 214–15
  improvement science team at, 205
  literature review for improvement,
    208–9
  multitiered system of supports
    (MTSS), 204
  need for improvement at, 205
  problem of practice at, 209
  testing change at, 211–14
  theory of improvement at, 209–11
  Also see special education
Setting Directions, 277, 284
Shanahan, T., 170
Shulkind, S.B., 132
Silverman, J., 34
Sinclair, S., 30
Skoog-Hoffman, A., 11
Smith, D., 205
Smith, J., 244
Smith, D , 52
social-emotional competencies, 31
social-emotional learning (SEL), 9–10,
    10–11, 23–25, 29, 31, 32, 36, 37,
    41, 42, 68, 135–36, 197, 277–78,
    284
  campus-based, 36–37
  coaches, 37
  equity focus of, 11–12
  lessons learned about, 16–19
  problem of practice, 12–13
  professional learning communities
    (PLC) and, 34
  transformative, 51–53
social justice, 4
solutionist fallacy, 6, 243
South High School, 131
  advisory programs at, 132
  barriers to student academic success
    at, 138
  change ideas for, 139
  Character Strong curriculum and,
    143, 148, 149

  empathy interviews and, 134–35
  FLIGHT and, 133, 134, 137, 140, 142,
    143
  improvement implementation and
    challenges, 145–48
  improvement science team at, 133
  need for improvement at, 133–39
  results of improvement, 148–49
  RISE and, 133
  testing improvement change, 137–38
  theory of improvement at, 137–38
speakers of other languages (SOL), 121
special education (SPED), 101, 102, 109,
    110, 115–16, 123, 124, 135
  equitable evaluation, COVID and,
    203–5
Spillane, J.P., 20
Spradlin, T., 135
Staytonville Middle School (SMS), 81–82
  attendance data, 86–87
  discipline incidents among male
    students, 84
  improvement outcomes, 96–98
  improvement team at, 82
  need for improvement at, 83–92
  review of improvement literature,
    91–92
  testing improvement change at, 94
  theory of improvement at, 92–94
STEM Academy Model, 25
student-centered learning, 32
student disciplinary referrals, 101–2,
    103, 111
  Also see Rural Middle School, special
    education
Student Information System
    scheduling, 195
Student Intervention Services (SIS), 242
Student Success Act, 69
Studer Education, 49, 53
Studer, Q., 53, 54
study phases, 38–42
Sullivan, A.L., 208
support days, 17
Surgrue, E.P., 72
suspension, 31

T
Taei, S., 9
task concerns, 19
Tatum, B., 292

Taylor, R.D., 136
teacher interviews, 158
Teacher Toolkit, 81
teaching with cultural relevance, 136
Terra Vista Independent School District.
　　　See social-emotional learning
Thacker, P., 278
theory of improvement, 14
Thomas, W.P., 170
Thonstad, C., 103
Thorsborne, M., 30, 32
toxic stress, 53
Transformative SEL Report, 52
transitional bilingual instructional
　　　programs (TBIP), 169, 181
trauma, 122
trauma-informed care, 114
trauma-informed practices, 112, 118
true north, 227, 231

U
Universal Design for Learning, 197
University of Chicago, 151, 152
University of Michigan, 156
Upward Bound strategies, 147
Urow, C., 182
U.S. Department of Education, 24, 32,
　　　68, 272
UTeach Institute, 24, 28, 42

V
Vaandeering, D., 33
Valdebenito, S., 31
validity, 207
Vaughn, S., 241
Volk, D.T., 10

W
Washington Association of Bilingual
　　　Educators, 180
Wedell-Wedellsborg, T., 61
Wellman, B., 174
wellness rooms, 128
Wellness Space, 115
Whiteside-Mansell, L., 47
whole-child curriculum, 10
Wills, T., 152
Woods, S., 47
Word on the Street, 242
working theory of practice
　　　improvement, 159, 160, 161

Wyatt, T.R., 136

Z
Zaff, J.F., 136